International
Security

International
SECURITY

An Analytical Survey

Michael Sheehan

LYNNE
RIENNER
PUBLISHERS

BOULDER
LONDON

Published in the United States of America by
Lynne Rienner Publishers, Inc.
1800 30th Street, Boulder, Colorado 80301
www.rienner.com

and in the United Kingdom by
Lynne Rienner Publishers, Inc.
3 Henrietta Street, Covent Garden, London WC2E 8LU

Library of Congress Cataloging-in-Publication Data
Sheehan, Michael (Michael J.)
  International security : an analytical survey / by Michael Sheehan.
      p. cm.
  Includes bibliographical references and index.
  ISBN 978-1-58826-273-8 (hardcover : alk. paper)
  ISBN 978-1-58826-298-1 (pbk. : alk. paper)
  1. Security, International. I. Title.
  JZ5588.S46 2004
  355'.033—dc22
                                        2004020539

British Cataloguing in Publication Data
A Cataloguing in Publication record for this book
is available from the British Library.

Printed and bound in the United States of America

 The paper used in this publication meets the requirements
of the American National Standard for Permanence of
Paper for Printed Library Materials Z39.48-1992.

10 9 8 7 6

For John and Maureen Madigan

Contents

Acknowledgments

This book took rather longer to bring to fruition than originally intended, which inevitably put even greater stress than usual on all those who are affected by such enterprises. I am pleased therefore to take the opportunity to thank those whose support and encouragement made it possible to complete the project. All the staff at Lynne Rienner were continuously patient and helpful. Richard Purslow, my original editor at Lynne Rienner, was encouraging in the face of what must have seemed interminable delays and has my deepest gratitude, while Elisabetta Linton encouraged me to bring the book to a successful conclusion. Jouko Huru read and made helpful suggestions on a number of chapters. Hugh Stuart was a great help with the bibliography. My wife, Donna, typed much of the manuscript, and a special thank-you goes to her and our children, Jordan and Ashton, who patiently awaited "their turn" on the computer.

International
Security

ONE

Introduction

The subject of security has been at the heart of the study of international relations for the past fifty years. Its political significance has been enormous during this period. It helped shape the way in which the Cold War was contested by the two superpowers and their allies, and in the post–Cold War era it has remained central to the debates over government policy agendas and the priorities they should reflect. At the same time it has been pivotal to the way the scholars of international relations have thought about the core purpose of the discipline and the location of its boundaries. For many students of international relations, it is the security aspect that makes the study worthwhile, for in the final analysis, the study of international relations is "the art and science of the survival of mankind" (Deutsch, 1968: ix).

"Security" is a term widely used in both the analysis and the practice of international relations. Issues such as war and peace, the balance of power, arms races, arms control, and disarmament have been at the heart of the university discipline of international relations since its inception at Aberystwyth in 1919. Indeed, it can be argued that the central concern with these issues, and particularly with the origins and conduct of war, was both the cause of the creation of the field and the defining core that subsequently enabled international relations to continue to distinguish itself from related disciplines such as history, economics, geography, and international law. Moreover, the concept of security has proven to be an extraordinarily powerful one: "no other concept in international relations packs the metaphysical punch, nor commands the disciplinary power of 'security'" (Der Derian, 1995: 24–25).

It might be expected therefore that, given the traditional academic obsessions with precision and definition, the core concept of "security" would have been analyzed and defined *ad nauseam* over the decades since 1919. Curiously, this has not been the case. Barry Buzan has argued that "security" falls within the category of an "essentially contested concept" characterized by "unsolvable debates about [its] meaning and application" (1991a: 7). Yet it would be more accurate to argue that, historically, security has patently failed to be subjected to such debate. When thinking about the meaning of security, it is necessary to be very aware of "the conspicuous silences of what is not being said, but is being taken for granted as part of the discourse" (Klein, 1988: 295). The beginning of a genuine debate about security and perhaps its emergence as an essentially contested concept are developments that have only occurred since the early 1980s, to a significant extent as a result of the writings of Buzan himself.

As late as 1975, Richard Smoke could argue that the field had "paid quite inadequate attention to the range of meanings of security" (Smoke, 1975: 259). This was the key point. Despite its willingness to agonize over the possible definitions of other concepts such as sovereignty, limited war, and nationalism, and to explore alternative interpretations, the meaning of "security" was treated as a given. Security theory became based on an unacknowledged consensus about what constituted legitimate knowledge about the social world. This had implications both for the way the subject was thought about, and for the policy prescriptions that could flow from it, and these in turn had fundamental consequences for people in the real world.

During the Cold War period the prevailing Western conception gradually shifted from "national security" to "international security." The former was oriented around the development of policies designed to allow states to increase their military security, either through unilateral force improvements or through membership of alliances. As the Cold War evolved toward the superpower détente of the 1970s, the prevailing terminology was increasingly that of international security. This reflected the belief that in the context of the mutual nuclear hostage relationship between the United States and the Soviet Union, and the massive military capabilities of both the North Atlantic Treaty Organization (NATO) and the Warsaw Pact, it was necessary to seek ways of enhancing one's own security without necessarily threatening to reduce that of the potential adversary, and to seek also to maintain the overall stability of the international system. For most of this period however, the *content* of security was seen as being fixed—military security against the military power of other states.

Since 1991, security has become a contested concept in international relations in a way that was not the case during the Cold War period of realist hegemony in security discourse. The traditional realist conceptualization has come under sustained attack from a number of directions, both because it was increasingly seen as unsatisfactory in its own terms, and because it was ignoring important aspects of an emerging international policy agenda.

During this period there has gradually emerged a consensus that the classical approach to security is inadequate and that a broader, multisectoral approach to security is preferable to the traditional understanding of seeing security concerns as relating only to issues of militarized relations between competing states. This is reflected at both the academic and the policy levels. A survey of contemporary international relations literature reveals that it is now conventional for international relations books on development, the environment, gender, and so on, to routinely include a chapter on security, and for books on security to include at least a genuflection in the direction of gender analysis, environmental security, and other features of a wider approach.

International organizations such as the United Nations and NATO now also operate with a definition of security that is multisectoral and embraces the broader agenda, and not just the military dimension. This represents a major change from earlier decades where the emphasis was on force projection, deterrence, and the maintenance of the balance of power. This reflects an increasing recognition by bodies such as the UN that, while the focus on military power during the Cold War was understandable, by defining security in purely military terms and giving it privileged status as "high politics," there was a massive failure to address human suffering in other areas, such as poverty, and a failure to counter environmental degradation.

The debate during the 1980s and 1990s opened up the concept of security to processes of widening and deepening, including exploration of its meaning and application to a broader range of areas. Barry Buzan and the Copenhagen school pioneered the widening aspect, in terms of identifying a number of new domains that it is appropriate to think of in terms of security, such as the economic and environmental realms. Ken Booth, Richard Wyn Jones, and others in turn explored the deepening aspect—that is, the epistemological and ontological implications of an extended security concept.

Critics of the traditional approach were keen not only to see a wider range of issues addressed as part of the security agenda, but also to see them prioritized by governments with the same sense of urgency and the same commitment of national resources that had previously been reserved for the military security sector. This inevitably triggered a profound debate over whether such an expansion of the concept was needed, and in what directions and to what extent it should be taken. The debate was centered on the question of what links certain threats, so as to make it reasonable to assume that they could all be discussed under the common rubric of security. What kinds of threats are simply "problems" deserving government attention and what are specifically "security issues"? Why are some issues "securitized" in this way, while others are not? For the advocates of a much broader approach to security, such as Barry Buzan and Ole Waever, this process of securitization has a "metatheoretical" function, because it makes clear that what counts as a security issue is always a result of political and social discourse (2003: 86).

There are now a wide variety of ways of thinking about and implementing security in international relations. The purpose of this book is to survey and critique these approaches and to analyze their similarities, differences, and relative utility. The objective is not to produce a final synthesis from the different approaches. This is ultimately not possible, because many of them are underpinned by epistemological and ontological differences so fundamental that they cannot be reconciled. Rather, the purpose is, first, to bring together for analysis the various traditional and postpositivist approaches, as well as the sectoral studies of security, in order to make possible a deeper understanding of the meaning and political purpose of the concept of security itself.

A second objective is to contribute to the debate about where the boundaries of an understanding of security might lie. Other than realism, all the approaches studied in this book are "critical" in the sense that they critique the traditional approach to security and put forward alternative ways of thinking about and operationalizing the concept. However, by no means all of them represent a fundamental break with traditional realist ways of interpreting the subject. Several embody an approach that engages with a sector in such a way that, while it is capable of being developed in novel and even postpositivist ways, it is equally capable of being discussed in a framework that is little, if any, different from a neorealist approach. This vulnerability to colonization by neorealist analysis and policy recommendation means that the multisectoral approach need not necessarily represent a decisive break with traditional security thinking, so that certain sectoral areas, such as the economic and environmental domains, remain battlegrounds between those with very different ways of thinking about security.

The book therefore looks at what meanings have traditionally been attached to security and the implications of various alternatives. Realism and realist-derived approaches are explored both because realism remains a powerful construction for thinking about security and because the various alternative understandings continue to define themselves to a large extent in contradiction to the traditional realist interpretation.

The "broader" agenda is then analyzed, both in terms of its own theoretical origins in the Copenhagen school and by way of the various sectoral approaches to security that have reflected this approach in the economic, societal, and environmental domains. The strengths and weaknesses of the postpositivist approaches to security are then examined in terms of their ability to constitute a genuinely alternative form of security analysis. The final chapter draws conclusions about which approach has the most to offer for the study of international security.

TWO

Realism and Security

For much of the twentieth century, realism exercised a hegemonic position in the study of international relations, dominating the analysis and teaching of security at universities, to the virtual exclusion of alternative perspectives. Indeed, the field of security studies has been described as "a child of Machiavellian and Hobbesian realism" (Crawford, 1991: 292). Outlining the key elements of the realist approach is necessary both to contrast it with the postpositivist approaches examined in later chapters, and also in order to identify the degree to which realist thinking can be, and often is, present in the approach represented by the "broadened" security agenda.

During the long domination of academic international relations by realism (approximately from the late 1930s to the late 1970s), the working definition of security was a strictly limited one, which saw its nature as being concerned with military power, and the subject of these concerns as being the state, so that the concept was routinely referred to as "national security."

These are rather large assumptions. Like all other concepts used in human thought, "security" is a social construction. The term has no meaning in itself (Krause and Williams, 1997: ix); it is given a particular meaning by people through the emergence of an intersubjective consensus. Over time the term becomes understood to have a particular meaning, though that meaning may continue to be questioned by some, and may evolve over time, rather than remaining static. A term such as *slavery* for example means the same thing in practice now as it did 200 or 2,000 years ago. But the way we understand it now and the moral standing we give to the institution of slavery are quite different. It is socially unacceptable now in a way that was not true 2,000 years ago.

It is therefore striking and important that the term *security* received so little serious scrutiny in the middle decades of the twentieth century. While its meaning was being treated as obvious and commonsensical, it was in fact the result of specific choices from a range of possible alternative conceptions.

5

In the immediate aftermath of World War II, the expression "national security" was coined to describe the area of public policy concerned with the preservation of state independence and autonomy. National security, deemed synonymous with security as such, was seen as being related to the need for states to maintain their political independence and freedom of national decisionmaking. The instruments for pursuing this objective included the armed forces, the diplomatic service, and the intelligence services. In addition, other levers of influence could be brought to bear, such as a state's economic strength or the symbolic strength represented by cultural influence. However, diplomacy and conventional warfare were seen as the primary means by which states sought to protect themselves from the threat represented by the armed forces of other states. During the Cold War, "deterrence" of nuclear and conventional attack through contingent threats of nuclear retaliation was added to the repertoire of the nuclear weapon states and their alliance systems. This was a clear, straightforward, and limited approach to security. That which needed to be secured (the object of security) was the state, and the mechanism by which security would be achieved was the manipulation of military capability in relation to actual or potential adversaries. David Baldwin argues that security was not what Cold War security specialists were actually interested in. Their focus was on military statecraft and they saw as security issues only those for which military statecraft was relevant (1997: 9).

This was a very narrow and limited way of thinking about security. It underpinned decades of military confrontation between the North Atlantic Treaty Organization (NATO) and the Warsaw Pact, in which governments based their policies of deterrence upon contingent threats to incinerate the civilian populations of the opposing alliance. It was an interpretation that denied to the vast majority of the world's population the resources and attention from governments that might have dramatically improved their quality of life.

While it is true that for most of the Cold War period this conception of security was not successfully challenged from within the mainstream academic and policy communities, it is not true that there were no such challenges at all. Attempts to explicitly or implicitly broaden the approach to security were made during this period, and significantly these included efforts made by scholars working within an essentially realist approach to the study of international relations.

An early treatment of the subject was made by the realist Arnold Wolfers in 1952. Wolfers made a crucial distinction between objective and subjective security, the absence of threats to acquired values as against the absence of fear that such values will be attacked. Wolfers also made the point that the realist conception of security was no less idealistic than conceptions proposed by its critics, since "the demand for a policy of national security is primarily normative in character" (1952: 483). Demands for a policy of strength based on armaments are no less normative than calls for disarmament or world government. They reflect value judgments and an ordered set of priorities about which social objectives should be pursued, and which should be prioritized in terms of government attention and spending. Realist treatments of security and defense policy tend to contrast it with normative claims for value-driven policies or changes in the nature of international relations. Yet traditional security concepts are themselves value-driven, although the values are largely unstated.

This is true for all approaches to security and to policies derived from them. It is never possible for a state or an individual to attain absolute security; there are always threats that may or may not materialize. It is a question of which security threats should be given most attention, and to what degree. States and other actors have choices regarding the kind of security they wish to achieve, and how much they want, in relation to the resources they have available to pursue it.

During the Cold War the dominant Western paradigm of security within strategic studies was open to the criticism of being ethnocentric and based on a narrow, conservative self-interest. But as the realist strategic analyst John Garnett noted in 1975, "for millions of underprivileged in Africa and Asia, to support the status quo is to prop up an unjust system. Those who are desperately poor naturally accuse Western states of caring everything for peace and nothing for justice" (cited in J. Baylis et al., 1975: 14–15). This is an important point. The conceptualizations of security prevalent among the key actors of the international system arise from a "specific cultural context: the highly industrialised democracies of the West" (Haftendorn, 1991: 5). Not only are they the result of a highly specific process of social construction during the middle decades of the twentieth century, but they are also deeply embedded in Western metaphysics.

Indeed, the construction of security generally is crucially influenced by national and regional culture, because these help shape the way actors understand security and the threats they believe exist, and also shape their particular responses to these understandings (Katzenstein, 1996: 1–2). Western metaphysics has constructed a state-based meaning of security that is based upon a particular understanding of the meaning of power and violence. "It is a form of alienated power, power by someone over something or someone else. Security is something imposed by the power of the state and its military organisations" (Dalby, 1992: 105).

Contemporary realism is not a monolithic approach. There are a number of different schools of thought within realism, and these differences can have important consequences in terms of shaping approaches to security. However, there are certain operational assumptions that are common to all the variants of realism.

The realist understanding of international security is structured by specific ideas about the nature of politics at the international level. For realists, the central reality of international relations is that the system is anarchic. That is to say, there is no world government analogous to the national government of states, which can maintain the law, administer justice, and prevent large-scale outbreaks of violence. In a state, the government and legislature define policy, draft and implement laws, establish a system of courts, prisons, and police, and thereby create and maintain a relatively secure framework within which citizens can go about their daily lives. There is a body both responsible for and capable of maintaining a reasonable degree of security within the boundaries of the state. In the international system, however, there is nothing analogous to this body and therefore states are compelled to rely on their own efforts and capabilities to generate national security.

As Alasdair Murray (1997: 184–185) has noted, in classical realism, the existence of anarchy is not part of a materialist explanation of reality, but is an intersubjective construction, the path-dependent result of choices made throughout the historical past. It is therefore, at least in principle, a situation, or an interpretation of that situation, that can be altered by human agency in the future. Hans Morgenthau himself, along with other classical realists such as Herbert Butterfield, believed in the virtue of humanity, eventually widening its conception of community beyond the nation-state.

In the anarchic international environment all states maintain military capabilities for their own defense. In wartime there is a clear military advantage gained from having larger armed forces and superior weapons systems or military doctrine. Other states can use methods such as spying to try to uncover the secrets of potential enemies, but failing that they are forced to estimate as best they can what the true military capabilities of these potential enemies are. When they are not sure just how great the threat or capabilities are, they assume the worst, believing that it is safer to overestimate a threat and plan for it, than to underestimate it and be overwhelmed if it materializes.

This situation gives rise to a fundamental element of realist security thinking, the security dilemma. In the international anarchy, "the self-help attempts of states to look after their security needs, tend, regardless of intention to lead to rising insecurity for others as each interprets its own measures as defensive and the measures of others as potentially threatening" (Herz, 1950: 157). States cannot escape the security dilemma; because military power is not inherently defensive, it will always appear offensive to others, regardless of whether or not it is being acquired for offensive purposes.

Nicholas J. Wheeler and Ken Booth define the dilemma in terms of the unresolvable uncertainty "that exists in the minds of one set of decision-makers as to whether the intentions of another set are benign or malign" (Wheeler and Booth, 1996: 4). The armed forces of other states in the system always appear to be threatening, and any change in their size or capability triggers a rise in feelings of insecurity. States cannot be certain about the intentions of other countries and therefore they err on the side of pessimistic caution and shape their policies in relation to the capabilities possessed by other states, rather than in relation to possible intentions. Bradley Klein has called this the grand master narrative of Western strategic discourse, "the Gothic Hobbesianism of a tightly structured, statist 'state of war' in which all states find themselves confronting an ineluctable security dilemma" (Klein, 1988: 297).

Robert Jervis also addresses the security dilemma issue, arguing that the "worst-case assumptions" noted above tend to produce self-defeating efforts to achieve national security. This is because, by triggering responses in other states, such efforts tend to produce a rise in subjective and even objective insecurities. The problem is made worse because of the inflexible images that the security dilemma creates. Even a state that wishes to achieve no more than the continuation of the existence of the prevailing status quo "will desire a military posture that resembles that of an aggressor. For this reason others cannot infer from its military forces and preparations whether that state is aggressive. States therefore tend to assume the worst" (1976: 64).

The realist approach tends to take for granted the answer to the question of whether or not such threats arise in an objective reality, rather than being social constructions, "the worst case result of a dialectic between what is observed and what is imagined" (Lipschutz, 1995: 2). Threats are real because realists believe the pursuit of power by states to be "ubiquitous and inescapable" (Smith, 1986: 220), and this generates between states inevitable conflicts of interests that can be mitigated, but that cannot be avoided.

The security dilemma is seen by realists as an "absolute predicament," and Jervis argues that seen in this light "the central theme of international relations is not evil, but tragedy. States often share a common interest, but the structure of the situation prevents them from bringing about the mutually desired situation" (1976: 93). This theme of tragedy runs through the work of many of the classical realist writers. George Kennan described statesmen as "actors in a tragedy beyond their making or repair" (1951: 78). The tragedy motif is particularly prominent in the writings of Raymond Aron, because he saw war as a human institution that could not be eliminated and that was in fact legitimate in particular circumstances, notably for the defense of the state. International relations was simultaneously a social and an antisocial environment, and this formulation in turn led him to advocate for statesmen an "ethics of responsibility" characterized by prudence rather than the "ethics of conviction" (Thompson, 1980: 175).

An obvious problem with this logic is that it clearly does not influence all states at all times. The relationships between the United States and Canada, or Norway and Sweden, are not characterized by this kind of paranoid insecurity about the purpose of each other's armed forces. Stephen Walt (1987), has attempted to refine realism in this regard with "balance of threat" theory. This approach seeks to modify balance of power theory to explain why states do not always align against the most powerful state in the system. This is because material power balances are not the only consideration; subjective judgments about postures and intentions also come into play. The same is clearly true about security relationships generally, but for the most part the basic assumptions of realism do not allow it to deal easily with these kinds of exceptions to what is considered a general rule.

For many realists, an inevitable effect of the operation of the security dilemma is that there is a clear limit to the degree of interstate cooperation possible in an anarchic international system. Cooperation is limited because of the "dominating logic of security competition, which no amount of cooperation can eliminate" (Mearsheimer, 1990). Because states exist in an environment of intense security competition, they are not generally inclined to cooperate with other states unless there are compelling reasons to do so.

Realism operates with a number of key assumptions. The universe is seen as a collection of facts out there waiting to be discovered. The role of the analyst is to uncover and describe the workings of this reality, not to pass judgment on it, for its central features are seen as timeless and immutable. This is not to argue that realism is therefore unable or unwilling to engage with abstract moral principles or normative issues. On the contrary, much of classical realism has been concerned with precisely this and demonstrates a concern to make clear the conflict between the pursuit of the abstract ideal and an environment characterized by cruel realities (Murray, 1997: 2).

The most important actor in the realist system is the sovereign state, which is governed by rational decisionmakers and institutions. The decisionmakers are obliged to accept the environmental constraints within which the state must attempt to achieve its objectives; "the task of the statesman is to work with such forces, rather than against them" (Thompson, 1996: 144). States are seen as unitary rational actors skilled at calculating the risks and advantages of different policies aimed at amassing power in a dangerous environment.

More generally, it can be argued that many realists operate with a conceptual apparatus put forward in Kenneth Waltz's 1959 book *Man, the State, and War,* in which the key dynamics of international relations are seen in terms of three levels, the individual, the national (or state), and the international. While this was a reasonable way of structuring his study of the origins of war in order to group similar explanations together, as a general explanation of the operation of international relations it is far too limited. Yet many realists have adopted this typology to the exclusion of alternative models of ordering and explanation. Critics see this limitation as having the effect of excluding other possible nonstate forms of security provision, and thereby making it almost impossible to discuss security without taking the state for granted (Dalby, 1992: 106).

Realists share the political perspective that the central purpose of the state is to protect the citizen against internal and external danger. The requirement to defend national interests results in the conception of national security being tied to military strength. The need to ensure state survival is seen as overriding all other policy considerations. Realists see governments and states as operating in terms of a clear hierarchy of issues when it comes to determining and implementing government policy. There are any number of issues to which a government might choose to pay attention and for which it will wish to develop policies—healthcare, agricultural production, reduction of unemployment, construction of transport networks, environmental protection, education, and so on. Defense and national security compose one of these categories. But realists argue that in the hierarchy of issues competing for the attention of government, national security always comes first; it always wins out in the competition for limited governmental resources. This is because it is seen as determining a country's ability to have such a hierarchy in the first place. National security determines whether a state or people are free from foreign domination or occupation. Only if they are free can they take decisions about what their social or political priorities should be. National security therefore has to take precedence over all other issues in order to maintain national independence. Security is a value that states pursue, but the question of how important security is for any collectivity is, and should be, open-ended. Realists, in contrast, foreclose such discussion by allowing the pursuit of security to take precedence over all other possible objectives, and by then defining security in a very specific way.

Realism takes a number of forms, and during the 1990s a version was elaborated that approximated more closely the actual experience of states within the international system. "Offensive" versions of structural realism see security as a scarce resource, which states pursue in a threat-filled environment. So-called defensive realism, however, acknowledges that for many states the external environment may not be necessarily threatening in terms of the traditional state-to-state military agenda. The need to respond to military security threats in the external environment is an unusual occurrence to which states only rarely have to respond. The security dilemma in the international anarchy is therefore not something that all states face at all times, but is rather a contingent and comparatively rare reality (Rose, 1998: 149). Defensive realism does not see security as being in chronically short supply, and therefore neither intense international competition nor war are inevitable features of international relations.

The Struggle for Power

Realists tend to see power politics and international relations as being synonymous. Influence is not power. For realists, it is concrete power that determines the outcome of international politics, and therefore states seek to maximize the power available to them. While accepting that the urge for power is not the only significant feature of international politics (Spykman, 1942: 7), it is nevertheless seen as the primary motivation of governments. Martin Wight (1979: 29) also noted that the term "power politics" had sinister overtones. It is a translation of the German word *machtpolitik,* meaning "the politics of force." It superseded the older phrase "raison d'état," which implied that statesmen cannot be bound by private morality, that there was a "reason of state" justifying unscrupulous action in defense of the national interest.

When realists use the term "power," they are invariably thinking of military power. Other forms of power (in the sense of mechanisms to produce influence over outcomes) are recognized, but the military is seen as the most important by far, though in the "defensive" realist version it is comparatively less important and forms of "soft" power have correspondingly greater utility and importance. For classical realists and neorealists, however, there is a difference between the perception of domestic and international politics. In domestic politics a wide variety of forms of influence are seen as being effectively at work, but in the international environment the use of force is the crucial weapon of last resort. The possibility of war is seen as a brooding presence in international relations, which no government can afford to discount. Realist calculations about a state's true power, even when they discuss other features such as economic strength, are essentially assessments of a state's capacity to fight wars effectively, or to prevent them from occurring through the deterrent power of its armed forces.

The realist conception of power and its relation to security are located in the idea of the "international anarchy." The latter simply means a world without central government and in principle the implications of this can be theorized in many ways. There is no inevitable logic that decrees that in the absence of world government the operation of a security dilemma is inevitable, and that this will give rise to the frequent use of military force. The absence of a world government has not prevented the development of an international order in which states are able to pursue their objectives peacefully most of the time. For realists, however, international anarchy means a fundamental contrast between a settled and peaceful domestic order and a violent and dangerous international order. Crucially, in this violent, unstructured external anarchy, it is impossible to construct political community. "As a result, security is ultimately about force and violence, matters over which the state has control, the state being defined in terms of the sole possessor of the right to use violence" (Dalby, 1992: 105).

The traditional realist conception of power is far too broad and undifferentiated, particularly in the writings of early realists such as E. H. Carr and Hans Morgenthau. Power is treated as an end, both ultimate and immediate, and also as a means. But little attention is paid to the question of how a state chooses which ends to pursue. Classical realists like Raymond Aron argue that states as actors define their goals, which in turn affect the system. Neorealists like Kenneth Waltz believe that the international system structurally imposes goals on states.

In addition, in terms of general theory, realists tend to ignore or at least pay insufficient attention to the circumstances under which particular forms of power might, or might not, be appropriate. Often, "power" is simply said to be what decides the outcome of a particular issue, and the varieties of power and the importance of context are not explored. However, when applying their general theory to particular policy debates, realists have often operated with a more differentiated conception of power. Kennan, for example, advocated a political, not a military containment of the Soviet Union, while Carr noted the importance of economic strength in determining outcomes in certain situations. Nevertheless, it has been military power that realists have normally emphasized.

As an instrument of policy, military power is seen as having a wide variety of uses, including demonstrating strength, breaking up threats, instigating or intervening in civil wars, deterring attack, supporting allies, acquiring territory and resources, subjugating foreign populations, acquiring prestige, and peacekeeping and peace enforcement, among others. Military power is also seen as the shield behind which all the other tools of influence can be wielded, such as diplomacy, economic instruments, propaganda, and so on. The effectiveness of military power is always relative to the situation in which a state is contemplating using it, but nevertheless war and military violence are seen as being rational tools of foreign and security policy. There is a clear recognition of its ultimate reality as the power to control through destruction and killing.

The very range of uses of military power contribute to the operation of the security dilemma. States maintain armed forces for a wide variety of reasons and may select appropriate forces to deal with particular problems. Yet to nervous neighbors it is the overall dimensions of another state's military capability that raise concern, and states are seen as invariably assuming that force buildups are directed against them. During the Cold War, NATO tended to be fixated by the overall size of the Soviet armed forces and their potential offensive capability against Western Europe. What was not always remembered was that a third of the USSR's forces were stationed facing the unstable border with China, while many other divisions were garrisoned in Eastern Europe, rather than threatening the West.

In their conception of the place of war in the international system, realists owe an intellectual debt to Carl von Clausewitz (1780–1831). In his classic work *On War* (1968), Clausewitz argued that war is part of the social and political totality, differing only in its means from peace. He began by defining war as "an act of violence intended to compel our opponent to fulfil our will." For Clausewitz, all wars were the product of the societies that fought them and therefore each age had its own kind of war, its own limiting conditions, and its own peculiar preconceptions. War was an act of policy. Policy was the guiding intelligence, war only the instrument. It was subordinate to policy, "a continuation of political intercourse with the admixture of other means." War *was* politics, and could not be divorced from political life. This was a quite different perspective from that which sees war as the breakdown of order. Realism is deeply rooted in Western metaphysics and modernity. Its approach to the instrumentality of war reflects this, with a Clausewitzian attitude that military violence is simply a tool of state policy, very different from premodern understandings of war as a breakdown of order in the *Res Publica Christiana*. For realists, therefore, security "means a somewhat less dangerous and less violent world, rather than a safe, just or peaceful one. Statesmanship involves mitigating and managing, not eliminating, conflict" (Donnelly, 2000: 10). Absolute security is unattainable, because the operation of international anarchy does not permit it.

Historical Antecedents

One of the features of realism that distinguishes it from poststructuralist approaches to security is an assumption that the nature of international relations has changed little, if at all, over the millennia. The foreign policy of states is seen as being "characterised by continuity, regularity, and repetition because states are constrained by the international system's unchanging (and probably unchangeable) structure" (Layne, 1994: 10–11). Realists therefore like to lay claim to a distinguished historical pedigree that can be traced back at least as far as the ancient Greek historian Thucydides. Thucydides (471–400 B.C.) was the author of *The Peloponnesian War,* a classic account of the great war between Athens and Sparta. Realists such as Wight and Morgenthau saw the writings of Thucydides as crucial in indicating that recurring patterns of human behavior are identifiable in all historical eras. According to Thucydides, what made war inevitable was the growth of Athenian power and the fear this caused in Sparta (Wight, 1979: 138). He is seen as the founding father of the realist perspective because the cause of the fear he identifies comes not from humanity's innate nature, but from the nature of interstate politics. To that extent he might be considered more of a neorealist than a realist.

Thucydides himself was not a proponent of naked realpolitik. He rejected the arguments of those who claimed that "might makes right," while recognizing that weaker states will invariably have to concede to the wishes of the more powerful. Instead he argued that those who deserve the most praise are the people who, while human enough to enjoy power, nevertheless pay more attention to justice than they are required to by the situation. Great statesmanship, he felt, consisted in finding ways to reduce the conflict between the good and the prudent. Thucydides is in another sense more a precursor of classical realism than of neorealism, in that he believed that there was a certain continuity in political behavior and that this was explained by a similar continuity in human nature, which "being what it is" makes it possible to understand clearly the past and the future (Thucydides, 1972: 48). According to neorealists, international structure determines decisions, but Thucydides held that neither a state's ends nor its means, nor therefore its choices, could be adequately determined solely through an analysis of international structure. Rational strategic action relied on both domestically and structurally determined attributes.

Classical realism sees behavior as being significantly shaped by "human nature" (Donnelly, 2000: 43–50). There are features of the characters of all human beings that are unlikely to change because they have proven to be so long-lasting. They reflect basic human needs. Thompson argues that these are the result of a basic human need for power and security that exists at all levels, down to the parents who assert themselves over their child in defense of an authoritative value system (Thompson, 1996: 89). Neorealism posits different but equally effective constraints through the structures that compose the international system, compelling states to pursue balance of power policies in order to survive (Waltz, 1979: 113).

The realist approach sees the world as anarchical and as dominated by a struggle for power and security against the military capabilities of other states in the system. This approach is sometimes described as Hobbesian, incorporating the ideas of Thomas Hobbes, the seventeenth-century philosopher and scientist, as another key figure in the realist historical pantheon. Hobbes described the state as essential, because without it there are "no arts, no letters, no society, and which is worst of all, continual fear and danger of violent death, and the life of man, solitary, poor, nasty, brutish and short" (Hobbes, 1946: i, xiii). For Hobbes, the citizen looks to the state to provide protection against domestic and foreign threats. Hobbes himself emphasized the dangers arising from domestic turmoil within a country, but modern realists, while embracing Hobbes within their pantheon, have emphasized external military threats from other states, which seems to suggest an assumption "that threats arising from outside a state are somehow more dangerous than threats arising within it" (Ullman, 1983: 133).

Classical realism is rooted in a particular conception of human nature, seeing it as destructive, selfish, competitive, and aggressive. Thus for John Garnett, "the realists take exception to those who put too much faith in human reason, to those idealists who refuse to recognise the world as it as, and who talk in pious platitudes about the world as it ought to be." Although Garnett stresses that this acceptance does not necessarily imply approval of such a world, he notes that "a student may be forgiven for seeing pessimism, even cynicism, in realist writing, and perhaps even a detached observer would detect in it a note of quiet satisfaction at the predicament of mankind" (1975: 11). In this respect, one influential realist described realists as "the children of darkness" (Herz, 1950: 159).

Certainly, realists tend to be conservative in outlook, to see the sovereign state as the norm in international relations, to see realpolitik as inevitable, and to be dubious about the possibility of overcoming the security dilemma (Garnett, 1975: 9–10). John Herz, for example, declared that "realist thought is determined by an insight into the overpowering impact of the security factor and the ensuing power-political, oligarchic, authoritarian, and similar trends and tendencies in society and politics, whatever its ultimate conclusion and advocacy" (1950: 158).

The worldview of this perspective is based on a rigid distinction between inside and outside. Outside, the environment beyond the state's boundaries is marked by a variety of dangers, and violence is unsanctioned. Inside the state, the government provides the necessary degree of security, and is the sole legitimate wielder of force. Therefore, except in the unusual circumstances of rebellion or civil war, the main threats to security come from beyond the state's borders. Since conflict is seen as a natural and inevitable feature of international relations, the assumption is that states will always seek to increase their power and capabilities if the opportunity to do so presents itself. Power vacuums need to be immediately filled, otherwise other states in the system will take advantage of the opportunities and thereby reduce the security of one's own country. Security inside, within the territorially bounded community, means guarding against dangers outside. State sovereignty is based on Weberian claims of the state's monopoly of the legitimate use of force and this has the effect of marginalizing other expressions of political identity (Peterson, 1992: 31).

Bradley Klein has called this realist tendency, to project contemporary conceptual models back in time, "chrono-centrism" (1988: 296). Contemporary categories are seen not as contingent perceptions molded by the myriad factors that shape thought in a particular era, but as transcendental principles, which can be identified throughout human history in all times and all places.

Neorealism

In discussing the "realist" approach to security it is necessary to note the distinction between classical realism and neorealism (also known as "structural" realism). The worldviews of both forms have much in common, but there are also significant differences.

One fundamental difference lies in the determining factors of the security dilemma. Classical realists such as Morgenthau saw this as originating in a flawed human nature, which was power-seeking and prone to violence. For

Morgenthau there were biological and psychological compulsions, "to live, to propagate and to dominate [that] are common to all men" (1948: 16–17), a view shared by Reinhold Niebuhr (1932: 18–19, 23).

One obvious philosophical problem with this assumption is that, if human nature is a constant, then how does one explain variations in international political behavior? The same unchanging human nature is presumably responsible not only for the international reality marked by competition, arms races, and war, but also for those areas of the world and periods of history characterized by cooperation and peace. The same human nature held responsible for the outbreak of world wars in 1914 and 1939 was operating in peaceful years such as 1924 and 1989. The classical realist view as an explanation of human political behavior is patently flawed, leading a later generation of realists to seek an alternative grounding for their explanations of international behavior.

Dissatisfied with the flaws in the "human nature" explanation, structural realists, beginning with Kenneth Waltz in 1979, argued that the explanation for the security dilemma lay instead with the structure of the international system and the patterns of behavior it compelled states to fall into. This explained the striking similarities in defense and foreign policy behavior displayed by states with very different political systems and ideologies, such as the United States and the Soviet Union during the Cold War.

Waltz, in surveying the long history of international relations, felt that it was characterized by recurring patterns and repetitive events. He explained this in terms of the systemic constraints operating on all states. These constraints were seen as being so powerful that they overrode the intentions of individual state actors. Structural realists believe that states and statesmen are virtually powerless to alter the system in which they find themselves.

Like classical realists, structural realists believe that the fundamental feature of the system is anarchy, the absence of any central control. They also believe that the primary objective of states is survival. Because the system is an anarchy, it does not provide individual states with protection or help. This, together with the belief that there is no international harmony of interests and that there is a capacity for evil and desire for power present in at least some human beings, "reinforces the system argument: not only do states not have protection, they are also in danger and so need it" (Taylor, 1978: 130).

Waltz argues that in this kind of system, governed by the principle of self-help, the units are compelled to be functionally alike—that is, alike in terms of the tasks they pursue, rather than in terms of their size or capabilities. States are forced by the realities of the system to acquire security through their own efforts. They can do this either by building up their own military strength or by developing clever strategies that will give them advantages over the other states in the system. They can join alliances and work to strengthen them, and they can act to weaken opposing alliances. This necessity to conform to the realities of the international system structure justifies the particular ordering of state priorities in the security field. For realists, it makes possible a better understanding of *why* rational policymakers "may make seemingly irrational commitments of scarce resources to armies and weaponry at the same time that manifest human needs go unmet" (Lieber, 1991: 6).

Not all structural realists believe that the existence of the international anarchy inevitably drives states toward competition and war, and ensures that any international cooperation will be "tenuous, unstable and limited to issues of peripheral importance" (Weber, 1990: 58–59). Charles Glaser, for example, argues that competition is not an inevitable consequence of realism's assumptions, but rather that structural realism predicts that there will be circumstances where a state's best security strategy will be cooperation rather than competition (1994–1995). For Glaser, cooperative policies can be seen as an effective example of a self-help strategy under certain conditions.

There is an important sense in which the terms "neorealism" and "structural realism" are seriously misleading; in fact, the post-1979 approach is different from classical realism in so many ways that it is not truly realism at all, but a different approach entirely, albeit sharing certain features. This is significant in terms of the relationship between realism and other approaches to the subject of security, where classical realism, while very different in outlook from the nonrealist approaches, nevertheless shares some crucial features.

Murray (1997), for example, has made a powerful case for the argument that classical realism represents a strongly normative approach to international relations in which the current international structures and processes are seen as being contingent and, to an important extent, path-dependent. Morgenthau, while stressing the idea of the national interest in his work, argued that "in the absence of an integrated international society, the attainment of a modicum of order and the realisation of a minimum of moral values are predicated upon the existence of national communities capable of preserving order and realising moral values within the limits of their power" (1952: 38). In other words the state serves as the receptacle for these values only in the absence of a higher order based on universally accepted moral principles.

The key feature for neorealists is that states must adopt the prevailing "best practice" or fail. As states adopt successful strategies "others will emulate them or fall by the wayside" (Waltz, 1979: 178). As states copy each other's successful practices, a balance of power emerges. Thus the international order is governed by balance of power politics. Waltz argues that the two basic elements of the system, international anarchy and states that wish to survive, are all that is required to generate balance of power politics. Whether actual balances will appear will depend on a number of different factors. What neorealism predicts is not so much finished balances of power, which are inherently difficult to sustain over very long periods, but rather the process of balancing.

Balance of Power

The balance of power is central to realist conceptions of international security. According to Morgenthau, "the aspiration for power on the part of several nations, each trying either to maintain or overthrow the status-quo, leads of necessity to a configuration that is called the balance of power, and to policies that aim at preserving it" (1978: 173). For Morgenthau, the balance of power system was not only inevitable, but also an essential stabilizing factor in international relations.

Realism sees states as existing in a highly competitive and dangerous environment in which they must do whatever is necessary to survive. States are therefore forced to play the balance of power game. This systemic pressure is fundamental to the neorealist account of balance of power put forward by Waltz (1979: 118).

However, although fundamental to both classical realism and neorealism, balance of power is seen quite differently in the two approaches. In the classical account, balances occur because of the consciously directed policies of the governments of the states that make up the system, which do not wish the system to be dominated by a single state or alliance that would be in a position to dictate to them. For Waltz, however, it is an error to suppose that if a balance of power is to come into existence, the states must act so as to create one. In the neorealist conception, balances of power form *despite* the efforts of the component states, which are in fact seeking to maximize their power and even achieve hegemony over the system, but their simultaneous efforts to do so effectively cancel each other out. In the neorealist logic, "if a state is to succeed, it has little choice but to make the acquisition of power its central, immediate aim" (Taylor, 1978: 122). Even Morgenthau believed that, in reality, what states were seeking was not "a balance or equality of power, but a superiority of power on their own behalf" (1978: 227).

In this calculation of power, it is military power that is being envisaged by realists. The early realist E. H. Carr argued that the military instrument is fundamentally important, that "the ultima ratio of power in International Relations is war. Every act of the state in its power aspect, is directed to war, not as a desirable weapon, but as a weapon which it may require in the last resort to use" (1946: 109).

Moreover, war is seen by virtually all writers on the balance of power as a fundamental instrument for achieving and defending such a balance. The prevention of war has not generally been seen as a purpose of the balance of power. The goal has been to prevent the domination of the system by one state or alliance, using war as the mechanism to achieve that end whenever necessary (Gulick, 1955: 89; Liska, 1957: 38; Wight, 1979: 184). Even preventative war can be justified using balance of power logic (Liska, 1957: 34). That logic can also provide a rationale for frequent resort to war. A "balance" of power is an objective, but for a wide variety of reasons a permanent balance is an impossibility. International relations is characterized by change. Power is therefore never permanently balanced and the states in the system must be continuously engaged in the balancing process in order to prevent the emergence of an irresistible hegemonic power. It is a system that, critics argued, led to "innumerable and fruitless wars, a cause of infinite contention and bloodshed" (Luard, 1992: 16). In many ways, balance of power theory is central to the realist explanation of international security, and the explanation of international relations generally. Waltz insisted that, "if there is any distinctively political theory of international politics, balance of power theory is it" (1979: 117).

Balance of power is not synonymous with realism. It is a modernist and rationalist theory, but it can be explained within a liberal or neo-Grotian framework as well as within the realist perspective. In the Grotian perspective, the international equilibrium was not a crude military balance, but rather represented an approximate equality of capabilities between the leading states such that none could dominate the others, thereby enabling the "social" aspects of the international system to operate, such as international law, mediation, a balance of threats and dignities, and the pursuit of limited foreign policy objectives. During the eighteenth and nineteenth centuries in Europe, the balance of power concept always involved more than just the minimalist commitment to oppose hegemony. It had a positive, normative connotation as well, standing for the commitment to the idea of the states of Europe forming a society, however rudimentary. Nevertheless, in its more conservative conceptualization, balance of power is at the heart of realist understandings of international relations.

The realist approach to the instrumentality of war has also been fundamental since the emergence of the approach in the 1930s. Carr, for example, strongly criticized the idea that states share a common interest in peace, so that any state that disturbs the peace is both irrational and immoral (1946: 51). Carr identified another realist precursor in Machiavelli. In *The Prince,* Machiavelli argued that the "main foundations of all states . . . are good laws and good arms" (Williams, 1992: 48) and that a prince should have no other aim or thought except the prosecution of war, its organization and discipline. Machiavelli viewed conflict and preparations for conflict as the norm, rather than as being exceptional. History was the repetition of cause and effect and conflict was the motive force. The security of the state was seen as justifying any means to achieve that end. Machiavelli's "realism" reflected a belief in the immutability of the security dilemma.

In the era of Western thought dominated by realist thinking on international relations, there also emerged a dominant technocratic discourse of strategic policy study. The purpose of this body of thought was the maintenance of the power structures and social order of the West. Strategic deterrence, counterinsurgency, military intervention, terrorism, crisis management, and so on, fitted into a worldview that believed that "a prevailing international structure of tightly bonded sovereign states is the preferred norm for world order. Challenges to that structure, whether by way of popular social resistance or revolutionary violence, are thereby relegated to the status of aggressive acts against a rational world order" (Klein, 1988: 300).

Realism focuses on state-to-state violence. It is "the occurrence of war, the use of mass, organized violence as a method for resolving conflict among states, that concerns us here" (Lieber, 1991: 248). However, in the 1990s, major armed conflicts tended to be intrastate rather than interstate. Of fifty-seven major armed conflicts from 1990 to 2001, only three were interstate (SIPRI, 2002: 63). Some authors went further to suggest that recent wars were non-Clausewitzian, that they lacked political objectives (Snow, 1996: 26).

Geopolitics

Neorealism operates at a high level of abstraction. In pursuing the goal of parsimony, Waltz ignored or underplayed any features that were problematic for the theory. This was achieved by simply relegating inconvenient aspects to the unit level of analysis and explaining everything in terms of the operation of the structural level. The unit level is made "the dumping ground" for anything that cannot be otherwise explained in the theory (Keohane and Nye, 1987: 746). The theory does not allow for structural change, and even the fall of communism in Europe and the end of the Cold War are not seen as representing change in terms of the "deep structure" of the theory. In the sense that realism prides itself on a workable engagement between theory and practice, neorealism is barely "realist." Nevertheless, it lends itself to broad generalizations about international security.

A politically influential security perspective reflecting the abstract structural realist worldview is geopolitics. Geopolitics as an approach is inextricably linked to Halford Mackinder, who outlined it in "The Geographical Pivot of History," published in 1904. The geopolitical approach stresses that "political predominance is a question not just for having power in the sense of human or material resources, but also of the geographical context within which that power is exercised" (Sloan and Gray, 1999: 2).

Geopolitics attempts to dramatically simplify international politics by reducing it to the struggle for control of a limited number of key areas. Although the geopolitical approach enjoyed a measure of popularity in the three decades after Mackinder's publication, the limitations of his ahistorical generalizations meant that it remained a minority perspective and was brought into disrepute from the mid-1930s to the mid-1940s through its close association with the Haushofer school and the Nazi Party in Germany.

During the Cold War period, balance of power and geostrategic reasoning were dominant approaches and there were clear geopolitical overtones in the reasoning behind the construction of the NATO alliance in the 1940s. From the early 1980s onward, however, a number of influential scholars in the United States could be identified with a reemerging geopolitical approach. Notable among them were Zbigniew Brezezinski and Henry Kissinger, who served as the national security advisers to Presidents Jimmy Carter and Richard Nixon, and Colin Gray. The end of the Cold War and the disappearance of the Soviet Union encouraged an effort to define the new geopolitical realities by this emerging school. For Sloan and Gray, geopolitics attempts to draw attention to the way in which location, space, and distance influence the projection of political power and to restore geography to a central place in the study of strategy and security.

Geopolitics attempts to link historical causation with spatial relationships. However, geopolitics is not just about the relationship between geographical space and international politics. In an important sense it is also about the creation and consolidation of the domestic political identity of the key units in international relations. Geopolitical discourse operates by envisaging a dangerous external reality that can be contrasted with the internal stability and absence of threat associated with the Hobbesian realist worldview. In this sense it is also about "creating the political identity of the domestic community" (Dalby, 1992: 107), and is a natural extension of the realist conceptualization of international relations and security.

Mackinder believed that while the geographical environment does not define the choices of decisionmakers, it nonetheless provides an important, if not conditioning, influence. However, Mackinder himself warned against the temptation of geographical determinism, arguing that the balance of power at any particular moment was "the product on the one hand of geographical conditions, both economic and strategic, on the other hand of the relative numbers, virility, equipment and organisation of the competing peoples" (1904: 437).

Geopolitics as an approach has always been controversial, attracting fierce critics, even from within the realm of realism itself. Morgenthau argued that geopolitics was an example of the "fallacy of the single factor," attributing overriding importance to a single variable, to the detriment of all others. For Morgenthau, geopolitics was "a pseudo-science, erecting the factor of geography into an absolute that is supposed to determine the power and hence the fate of nations" (1978: 164). However, Barry Buzan argued that in the 1980s the study of international relations had lost sight of the importance of geography in its search for abstract generalizations, and that this was something that clearly needed to be remedied. In classical geopolitics and in security complex theory the geographical element is crucial, because the sense of "threat" is crucially shaped by geographical distance and terrain.

Despite the criticisms, the geopolitical approach has been extremely influential for half a century. As the Cold War began, Mackinder's concepts played a vital part in the Western conceptualization of the communist military threat and the geostrategic policy of "containment." All the post-1945 presidents had an overarching vision of U.S. national security that was explicitly geopolitical and directly traceable to Mackinder's heartland thesis, that the great power that dominated Eurasia would effectively dominate the world. The approach remained influential through the administrations of Bill Clinton and George W. Bush at the beginning of the twenty-first century. The popularity of the approach lies in its promise of simplifying the complexities of the world down to certain transcendent truths about strategy and this makes it particularly congenial to a neorealist approach to international security.

Conclusion

Realism operates on the basis of a limited number of key assumptions, about the nature of the international anarchy, the central role of the state as international actor, and the primacy of military power as an instrument of state policy in the international context.

The end of the Cold War accelerated a number of changes in the structure of international relations. The membership of the state system altered, but in addition the role of the global market economy became more significant. The process of globalization and the effects of the information revolution meant that states found it increasingly difficult to deal with the new nonterritorial security problems through traditional state-centered responses.

During World War II and the Cold War, the evident militarization of international politics and the domestic disciplining of the frontiers of debate that accompanied it ensured that realist security discourse exercised a hegemonic role in the practice and analysis of international relations. However, from the early 1970s onward the evolution of international politics increasingly exposed the limitations of the realist approach in understanding, explaining, and generating effective solutions to an increasing range of problems emerging onto the international agenda. Despite the renewed Cold War in the early 1980s, these dissatisfactions with existing concepts triggered a radical reevaluation of the concept of security. But even prior to this reevaluation, contributions to the study of international security had generated substantial research arguing that security and insecurity were to a very large extent socially constructed. Particularly influential in this regard were theories on security communities and democratic peace.

THREE

Security Communities and Democratic Peace

R ealism operates within a clear paradigm. Nevertheless, it is an extremely broad church. Indeed, in many ways realism is not really a theory at all, but rather an ideology or worldview based upon a set of interlocking assumptions about the nature of social reality. Both prior to and subsequent to the emergence of the broader approach in the 1980s, some realist authors attempted to significantly challenge or suggest amendments to key features of the realist security canon. In the 1990s, for example, William Wohlforth (1993) and Fareed Zakaria (1998), published books that placed far more emphasis on the importance of the unit (state) level than had the neorealist works that followed Waltz after 1979. Their accounts of security significantly emphasize the importance of national perceptions of a state's power, rather than simply assuming an objective reality. Gideon Rose has referred to this approach as "neoclassical realism" (1998) in the sense that while maintaining key realist features such as the centrality of the state and of military power, there is nevertheless an attempt to treat security as a socially constructed feature, rather than simply as a "given."

In the late 1950s, Karl Deutsch and his colleagues also implicitly challenged the governing approach to security by exploring the concept of "security communities." Deutsch identified a nascent security community in the North Atlantic area. Such a community was one where the component states had come to reject the use or threat of force as a mechanism for resolving disputes. This was a clear break with traditional approaches to security, which emphasized the utility of military power and the inevitable nature of military threats. Moreover, Deutsch argued that economic and cultural cooperation was a far better route toward the formation of such a security community than was common membership in a traditional military alliance, such as the North Atlantic Treaty Organization (NATO).

This contribution was a smoking grenade for traditional interpretations of security, for it suggested that ideas and realities of security and insecurity were social constructions, the result of an intersubjective consensus that was capable of being altered by the actions of governments over time. They were not timeless realities, but contingent constructions, and human agency was restored to center stage, since the actions of states and societies could potentially transform relationships between particular states, changing them from enemies into friends.

In the development of the security community concept, the pathbreaking study was the book *Political Community and the North Atlantic Area,* published in 1957. This represented the findings of a large-scale interdisciplinary study designed, in Deutsch's words, to "throw light on an old problem. The old problem is the elimination of war" (Deutsch et al., 1957: vii).

The Puzzle of Security

Deutsch and his colleagues, writing at the peak of the Cold War in the late 1950s, believed that the acquisition of weapons of mass destruction by a number of states meant that war had become such a threat to humanity that it needed to be eliminated, before it eliminated the human race (1957: 3). He was well aware of the difficulties of achieving such an ambitious goal, but believed that if human civilization was to survive, humanity would have to eliminate war as a social institution. This in itself was a fundamental challenge to realist thinking, since realism assumes that war is a permanent feature of international politics. It is a result of the basic drives of human nature and the structural determinants of the international anarchy and security dilemma, and while to some extent it *might* be limited and its frequency reduced, a feature highlighted by "defensive" realists, it could never be eliminated. This was the great tragedy of international relations.

The dangers represented by the existence of war, and concern about how to control or even eliminate it, had been a central concern for the academic discipline of international relations since it had been established just after World War I. Deutsch believed that most people who had previously looked at the problem could be located in one of two camps. The realists believed that the historical record showed a continuous narrative of warfare and that therefore war was clearly inevitable, a feature of the human condition that could not be eliminated. The idealists in contrast saw history as a process in which there was a steady increase in the size of the political communities into which human beings organized themselves. This trend was likely to continue until its final stage was reached: a world community living together in peace.

Deutsch was not convinced by either of these positions, which he felt were crude simplifications. He and his colleagues approached the problem of war from a strikingly novel perspective. All previous studies of why wars occur had focused on war itself—what makes humans violent, what national and international factors explain why particular wars break out, and so on. For

Deutsch, the interesting questions were not, why do wars sometimes occur, but rather, why is it that most of the time they do not? Not, why is it that some states have frequently gone to war with each other, but rather, why is it that for some groups of states, the idea of war seems to have become inconceivable, even when their previous historical experience has included war between them? What was it about the relationship between states like Norway and Sweden, or Canada and the United States, that had allowed them to escape from a reality that appeared to be inevitable for the rest of humanity?

The problem was therefore to understand how it was that some states appeared to have permanently eliminated war in their relationships with each other. If it could be discovered why these particular states had ceased fighting against each other, it might be possible to expand this pacific behavior to other parts of the world. What was at issue in this investigation was the question of how it was possible to build political communities wider than those previously existing. Political communities were defined as "social groups with a process of political communication, some machinery for enforcement, and some popular habits of compliance" (Deutsch et al., 1957). It was obvious that not all political communities were able to prevent wars from breaking out within their boundaries, since revolutions and civil wars occurred, but some were clearly able to do so and it was this achievement that needed explaining. The focus was therefore on what came to be called security communities.

The linking of the concepts of security and community in this way was an important development. The broader security approaches that emerged in the 1980s are notable in that they are open to the possibility of the "referent object" of security going down as far as the level of the individual in some circumstances. Nevertheless, for the most part, security is something that is acquired or achieved in the social and political context of a community. A distinguishing feature of realism is its reluctance to embrace the idea of community at the international level, and this limits possibilities for building long-term stable peace and security regimes. Security and community are two sides of the same coin: neither is truly possible without the other, they are synergistically interdependent.

A security community was defined as a group of people who had become integrated—that is, a group who had achieved a sense of community, and of institutions and practices strong enough and sufficiently widespread to convince people that necessary social, economic, and political changes could be brought about peacefully. A security community is therefore one in which "there is real reassurance that the members of the community will not fight each other physically, but will settle their disputes in some other way" (Deutsch et al., 1957: 5). Clearly, if the entire planet were covered with such security communities, war as currently understood would be effectively eliminated.

For analytical purposes it is possible to identify two kinds of security community. The first is the "amalgamated" security community, where a previously warring group of societies merge formally into a single, larger political unit with a common government. Usually this occurs as a result of imperialism, with a powerful, expansionist state absorbing weaker states.

Since this involves the ending of international conflict by the method of eliminating most of the competing sovereignties, it is hardly likely to commend itself to most existing states and in any case runs counter to the political pluralism that has characterized the international system in the past two centuries, and would also represent a break with Western political theory. For this reason the second type of security community is more promising in terms of its potential capacity to reduce the amount of large-scale conflict in the international system.

The second type is the "pluralistic" security community. Here, the various states or sovereignties retain their independence and political autonomy, as with Australia and New Zealand, or Denmark and Sweden. They voluntarily cooperate and behave toward each other in a manner that precludes the resort to war as a means of resolving their disputes, but maintain their independence and autonomy. Deutsch believed that only three major conditions needed to be satisfied in order for a pluralistic security community to be brought into existence. The first was that the primary political values of the component states needed to be compatible. While two similar regimes such as Britain and the Netherlands might be able to form such a community, a democracy and a fascist dictatorship would not be able to do so.

This appears to be a relatively unproblematic point. However, it is not necessarily an obvious one. It has been historically quite common for new regime types to emerge with a belief that war with their ideological brothers would be impossible. Yet Christian states, Islamic states, and communist states, for example, all found this to be a false assumption. Ideological compatibility may be a necessary condition for a security community, but it is clearly not a sufficient one. Similarly during the 1950s and 1960s, Portugal existed in a condition of reciprocal nonthreatening attitude vis-à-vis its NATO allies, despite the fact that they were liberal democracies while it was a fascist dictatorship. The failure of Greece and Turkey to form permanently stable democratic regimes during the Cold War meant that their relations remained characterized by tension and the risk of war, and they did not become members of the security community that was characteristic of the other NATO states (Sheehan and Moustakis, 2002). Later generations of security community theorists have attempted to move beyond this limitation and explore the possibility of such communities emerging between states that are not necessarily democracies.

The second condition was that there needed to be established networks of political and other communication, so that governments and other politically active sections of society could respond to each other's messages, needs, and actions quickly and adequately and without resorting to violence. Thus, for example, France and Germany transformed their relationship after 1945 from habitual conflict to close alliance. One way they did this was to establish networks of regular communication at all levels, both governmental and nongovernmental, between the populations and officials of the two countries.

The third necessary element would be provided to a large extent by the dynamic interaction of the first two. It was argued that there needed to be a mutual predictability regarding the relevant aspects of each partner's political, economic, and social behavior. Such knowledge would emerge from similar political cultures in the sense that since each state resembled the other, they would be able to recognize this and know the other by knowing themselves. Similarly, the networks of communication would provide the information from which to build a predictable picture of the other.

The key feature is the idea of a transnational community. The existence of such a community is seen in the fact that its members share key values and understandings of reality and because of this feel a sense of shared identity. The border of a security community effectively exists at the point where cultural divisions are clear enough that intersubjective meanings are not shared between the populations on either side of the border, because "only with common meanings does this common reference world contain significant common actions, celebrations and feelings" (Adler and Barnett, 1998: 31).

By the late 1950s the North Atlantic area, although far from being integrated, had moved a long way toward being so. Only Spain and Portugal, which at that time were fascist dictatorships, were clearly incapable of achieving full integration with the other regional states; the relationship between Greece and Turkey remained problematic; and within the region as a whole, a number of countries had already achieved pluralistic integration with each other.

Factors Promoting Integration

Deutsch sought to identify the factors that had helped particular groups of countries to move toward the status of pluralistic security communities. The first of these was pluralism itself, which he saw as a policy that "concentrates upon increasing the machinery and traditions of mutual consultation, communication and co-operation" (Deutsch et al., 1957: 200). In the context of the North Atlantic countries, it sought to eliminate all expectations of warfare among the countries, together with all specific preparations for it. Pluralistic integration is historically more difficult to achieve than amalgamated integration, but it has been just as effective in terms of eliminating war from the area integrated.

In promoting integration it was seen as essential that there be a stress on pluralism and the preservation of national sovereignty, and an emphasis upon domestic issues in each country, because the ordinary citizens would measure the success of integration in relation to achieving domestic objectives. In contrast to what some proponents of European integration in the 1960s and 1970s would argue, Deutsch found that apart from the desire to remove the danger of war, what the citizens within the security community sought were political institutions, whether separate or common, that would provide them with a better quality of life in peacetime. They were not impressed by political arguments suggesting that integration would only provide each state with greater power than it would otherwise have.

In the long term, security would need to be more than just the absence of war—the delegitimization of war needed to be underpinned by domestic political changes leading to greater cooperation and integration of all aspects of social life. Values reflecting criteria of legitimacy would be crucial in the evolution and development of communitywide behavior.

Another finding that was important in relation to subsequent European history was that military alliances appeared to be poor vehicles for promoting the development of either amalgamated or pluralistic security communities. In themselves, they made little contribution. They provided an effective shield behind which positive community-building processes could occur, but they were not in themselves the fundamental institutional requirement. To be effective they needed to be associated with nonmilitary steps, which would provide the main dynamic in the security- and community-building process. Similarly, while the existence of external military threats could be helpful to the process of integration, it was not essential.

Integration is a process and not necessarily a unidirectional one. There can be setbacks as well as advances. The possibility of war might continue to exist for a considerable period after an integration process has begun. Political communities might in fact continually cross and recross the threshold that made war a possibility. Integration is not a simple matter of fact. It is highly dependent upon the long-term stability of the participating states and their ability to gradually embed common values and a depth of attachment to the process and the shared norms of the community. As a process, therefore, pluralistic security integration is lengthier and more uncertain than is sometimes assumed.

Communication was seen as the crucial mechanism through which political communities were built, a set of transaction flows that cumulatively built a social fabric. Communication allowed individuals and groups within society to develop shared identification and the "we" feeling that was the bedrock of a security community. Again, this was an interesting break with realism. Realism is an overwhelmingly materialist ontology, which evaluates and explains the working of the international system in terms of material forces. Deutsch's approach, in contrast, was social constructivist, seeing community as being built through intersubjective understanding and shared knowledge.

The idea of the necessary "bases of community" is a demanding one. It includes a sense of community arising from a mutual "we" feeling, trust, and mutual consideration of partial identification in terms of self-images and interests, of mutually successful predictions of behavior, and of cooperative action in accordance with it. This sense of community might be uniformly common to all the participating states, but significant differences in perception could occur. A key role in "social learning" would be the ability of the political elites to keep the integration process moving forward.

The key factors identified in successful integration were, first, a high correlation of values, which for the North Atlantic states were democracy, the rule of law, and social market economics; second, a slowly growing level of mutual responsiveness among political communities; and finally, a distinctive way of life characterized by growth of welfare and technological states, marked by governmental rejection of war as an instrument of policy and commitment to an economic "good life."

Fundamentally it was the increasing unattractiveness and improbability of war that was seen as being essential to the development of pluralistic security communities. The delegitimization of war was underpinned by domestic political changes leading to greater cooperation and integration of all aspects of life. Values reflecting criteria of legitimacy were critical in the evolution and development of communitywide behavior, helping to determine what was deemed acceptable behavior. Security, which Deutsch and his colleagues generally interpreted in a minimalist way as primarily the removal of war from domestic sociopolitical cultures, was essentially a value-driven process embedded in integrated communities and nations and states.

Subsequent research in this area has supported these insights. Emanuel Adler and Michael Barnett (1998: 39–48) have argued that since identities and interests are largely shaped by their transactional environment, sociopolitical practices hold the key to expansion of membership of the security community. This aspect is crucial if the extension of the definition of security is seen in the context of an intersubjective definition of "politics" and "political" (Drysek, 1990)

The boundaries of the community need not arise solely from geographical, geopolitical, or cultural factors (though these help), but can also arise from the spread of shared values and ideas. For Adler and Barnett, as individual and group (national, state) identities are increasingly shaped by membership of and participation in the community, state officials will increasingly refer to the boundaries of an expanded definition of the community. The purpose and identity of states will be increasingly derived from participation in the community. This has certainly become true of the states of Western Europe and to an extent has been seen in the interaction of Association of Southeast Asian Nations (ASEAN) member states.

Building on Deutsch's notion of an integration "threshold," Adler and Barnett suggest that security communities develop through "nascent," "ascendant," and "mature" phases, characterized by increasing types and depth of transactions, development of shared traits and expectations, and increased trust and self-knowledge (Adler and Barnett, 1998: 49–59). In particular, tightly coupled security communities demonstrate a widespread commitment to cooperative security measures, a high level of military integration, internal security coordination, free movement of persons, and shared forms of governance and rule-making.

The security community theorists conclude that the development of loosely and tightly coupled security communities across the world, essentially based upon mutual identification, may well represent the most promising route toward peaceful, stable security.

While Deutsch's state-centric realist approach places him in a different ontological and epistemological framework than that of the postpositivists, a nevertheless striking feature of his analysis is the emphasis placed upon the social construction of both identity and beliefs about security. Deutsch's realism is unconventional in this regard and in a number of ways represents a clear break with traditional realist approaches to security.

Whereas mainstream realism sees the insecurity generated by international anarchy as inevitable, Deutsch's approach sees it as contingent and is an early example of a social constructivist approach to security. Central to this is not just the idea that notions of security and insecurity are intersubjectively constructed, but also the idea that the building of community is an effective route to security.

Democratic Peace Theory

Security community theory challenges the fundamental assumptions of much of realism regarding the inevitability of conflict between sovereign states operating in an international anarchy. It does this because it focuses on the structural implications at the state level, the unit level of analysis in Kenneth Waltz's 1979 schema. In the neorealist perspective, the unit level plays a minimal role in explaining processes and outcomes in international politics. A similar challenge to realist explanations emerges from democratic peace theory, which exerted important influences at the state policy level in the closing years of the twentieth century.

In his 1994 State of the Union address, U.S. president Bill Clinton declared, "Ultimately, the best strategy to ensure our security and to build a durable peace is to support the advance of democracy elsewhere. Democracies don't attack each other." His comments echoed those of British prime minister Margaret Thatcher, who said during a visit to Czechoslovakia in 1990, "If we can create a great area of democracy stretching from the west coast of the United States to the Far East, that would give us the best guarantee of all for security—because democracies don't go to war with one another." Throughout the 1990s this belief that democracies are an exception to the realist belief in an inevitable security dilemma underpinned arguments in favor of efforts to promote democratization and to expand the memberships of NATO and the European Union. The argument itself long predated the 1990s, however.

As early as 1795 in his essay "Perpetual Peace," Immanuel Kant described a "pacific union" established by liberal republics and argued that democracies were less warlike than other forms of government. For two centuries afterward, however, Kant's arguments were largely ignored. For Kant, there were three main pillars underpinning the reluctance of democracies to go to war. These were the constitutional, the moral/cultural, and the economic. Democracies were representative governments. The government was put into power by the voters and could be dismissed from office if it was seen to have failed to deliver what the voters wanted. Wars were expensive undertakings, and in wartime taxation is inevitably increased to pay for the costs of the war. The electorate are never enthusiastic about higher taxes, and governments, recognizing this, would wish to avoid the expense of war (Friedrich, 1948: 251).

War also interferes with commerce and, for the most part, the "democracies" of Kant's era were also the leading trading states, and by interfering with trade, wars put profits at risk and undermined the stability of the international trading regime. Wars are also expensive in terms of human lives. Loss of life, mutilation, and serious injury may be heavy among the armed forces engaged, and possibly also among the civilian population. In any case, the electorate will include the soldiers' parents and other relatives and loved ones, who will resent their loss in battle. Again, foreknowledge of these realities will turn the electorate against war and this will be reflected in the policies of a representative government. In a monarchy or other authoritarian government, the citizenry must accept the consequences of government decisions, and have little or no influence in shaping them. This is not the case in a democracy, which is based upon certain values such as liberty and individual rights. These values, it was suggested, also extend to foreign policy and make a democracy reluctant to engage in war, since this would infringe fundamental democratic norms (Sorensen, 1992: 399).

For more than a century after he wrote, Kant's arguments received little attention. There were few democracies in the world and therefore not much chance to check the accuracy of his prediction. The argument was revived in 1964 by a U.S. academic criminologist, Dean Babst. He examined data on 116 major wars from 1789 to 1941 and found that "no wars have been fought between independent nations with elective governments" (1964: 10). Once again, little was made of these results, even though by then the discipline of international relations had come into existence, with a central interest in explaining the nature and incidence of war in the international system.

Not until the 1980s did a major debate begin to unfold on the subject. A number of international relations specialists debated the issue, with propo-

nents such as Michael Doyle (1983, 1986) and Bruce Russett (1993) supporting the thesis, and Steven Chan (1984) and Erich Weede (1992) opposing it.
The debate eventually produced a consensus on two points. First, that there is
little or no difference between democracies and nondemocracies in terms of
their proneness to war. Second, and crucially, that wars *between* democracies
are rare or possibly even nonexistent. Many scholars would agree with Jack
Levy that this "absence of war between democratic states comes as close as
anything we have to an empirical law in international relations" (1989: 270).

An important point to notice here is that the consensus is not fully in support of Kant's proposition. The historical record does not support Kant's argument that democracies do not want to go to war. Democracies have been just
as prone to go to war as have other forms of government. During the twentieth century, for example, Britain used military force against a great number of
states, including Germany, North Korea, Argentina, Iraq, Japan, and Egypt.
The same was true of France and the United States. There was no reluctance
to use war as an instrument of policy by these states or by other democracies.

Where there was a significant difference was in the willingness to use
such force against other democracies. Kant did not make this specific argument. He wrote about a general reluctance to go to war for republican
regimes. But the key fact is an apparent willingness to discriminate in terms
of regime. Democracies appear to be unwilling to go to war with those states
they deem to be fellow democracies.

The Importance of Definitions

In making this argument it obviously becomes crucially important to be very
specific about how "democracy" and "war" are defined. Otherwise, any state
that claimed to be a democracy might invalidate the argument and so might
any clash of any kind between two democracies (Ray, 1993). Historical examples like the war between Britain and the United States (1812–1815), or even
the U.S. Civil War (1861–1865), might be seen as cases of two democracies
at war, and certainly these and other cases are problematic for the argument.

In defining what constitutes a democracy, most scholars follow a vari-
ation of the general criteria laid down by Melvin Small and David Singer
(1976), who call for a number of elements to be present. These include the
existence of free elections with opposition parties, in which a minimum suffrage exists, with at least 10 percent of the adult population being able to
vote. In addition, the country should possess a parliament that has control
over the executive branch of government or at the very least enjoys parity
with it.

Other analysts have accepted these kinds of criteria, but felt that the specific requirements were not sufficiently demanding. Randall Schweller
(1992), for example, adds a number of other requirements. The necessary suffrage level is raised to 30 percent and in addition it is stipulated that female

suffrage should be granted within a generation of its initial demand in the country. In addition, the government should be internally sovereign over military and foreign affairs; it should not be effectively a satellite of another state. For a country to be accepted as being a genuine democracy, it must have had this system of government in place for a reasonable length of time, at least three years, and the democratic system must be seen as stable. Finally, the political rights of the citizens must be underpinned by individual civil rights. Schweller also argues that a democratic political system should be accompanied by an economic system characterized by the existence of private property and a free-enterprise economy. Freedom House in New York, a research institute, has divided states into those that are "free," "partially free," and "nonfree," based on a seven-point scale for political rights and civil liberties. However, essentially these variations in definitional criteria only change the number of democracies at the margins.

In the same way, there needs to be a reasonably clear definition of what constitutes a "war." The threshold of war is usually set at the 1,000 battle deaths used in the Correlates of War data set. A confrontation such as the so-called Cod War between Britain and Iceland, in which naval craft threatened each other but no lives were lost, would not count. Nor would small-scale clashes, even if fatalities resulted.

This issue is important, because Edward Mansfield (1988) has suggested that the particular data set chosen by investigators of this issue can have a huge impact on the conclusions reached. This includes issues such as whether or not civil wars should be included and specifically how civil wars themselves are to be defined. There are a large number of conflicts that are possible exceptions to the rule, including the U.S. Civil War, the War of 1812, the Peru-Ecuador war and the Finnish participation in World War II on the side of the Axis powers (Spiro, 1994: 59–62).

A number of early contributions to this debate confused two basic propositions. First, the argument that democracies are more peaceful or less warlike than other states. Second, the argument that democracies do not fight each other. These are quite different arguments. Babst argued strictly in terms of the latter. Small and Singer, and many of those who followed their arguments in the 1980s, criticized the idea of "the innate peacefulness of Liberal democracies." A further reason that the democratic peace thesis may have been ignored is that it seems too simple to be true (Gleditsch, 1992: 371).

In practice, in the decades following Small and Singer's criticisms, no international relations scholar has identified another relationship anywhere near as strong as that between democracy and the absence of war against other democracies. Nils Gleditsch argues on the basis of this that most research on the causes of war can now be thrown on the scrap-heap, and that the link between democracy and peace can be used as the source of its elimination. However, it is one thing to confirm the statistical reality of a correlation and another to explain why it exists.

▨ The Problem of Explaining the Correlation

Some critics in the 1980s argued that the theory was nothing more than raw empiricism (in the case of Babst) or philosophical speculation (the arguments of Kant and Doyle), because it didn't explain *why* the correlation existed. David Lake (1992), for example, argued that no current theory explains this striking empirical regularity.

However, if there has been no definitive explanation, there have certainly been a large number of explanations put forward to explain the apparent link. Typically, theories of democratic peace are divided into structural theories that emphasize institutional constraints within democracies, and normative theories that emphasize the ideas and values held in democracies.

The first argument is the one already noted, that leaders in democracies are subject to constitutional limitations and constraints arising from their perceived responsibilities to the electorate that placed them in power. For the constraints to hold, not all citizens have to be politically active. As long as the government believes a sufficiently high number will oppose a war as to make it politically infeasible, it will be deterred from going to war.

A second explanation focuses on democracies' self-perceptions. A functioning democracy is not simply a country where there are regular, contested elections. Rather it is a place where the democratic way of life is practiced. Democracy is a pervasive norm at many levels of the society and is used to regulate that society in many ways. Elections and referenda are used to select regional and local governments, to choose trade union officials and to determine when official strike action is permitted, to elect representatives to school boards and other representative bodies, and for many other purposes. These arrangements reflect an underlying belief that in any society there will be differences of opinion on important policy issues at every level, but that it is vital that these differences be resolved through dialogue, accommodation, and compromise, rather than by dictated outcomes and the use of force to impose one side's preference.

In such a society there is an assumption that disputes will be resolved peaceably, that it is likely that each side will settle for something less than their preferred perfect outcome and that the result will be accepted and adhered to by all sides. The structural features and institutional arrangements are powerfully underpinned by a civil society accustomed to operating within a democratic system and whose activities crucially support the successful operation of that society at all levels. Democracies are an exercise in nonviolent conflict resolution. They require an intelligent and informed citizenry determined to oppose the weakening of their country's democratic structures and to extend them whenever possible, and whose day-to-day social, economic, and political interaction in an open, tolerant, and nondeferential society ensures that its democracy remains effective and vigorous.

The significance of this for international relations is that when a democracy is involved in a dispute with another democracy, its own value system is fully operational. It treats the other democracy as an extension of itself, instinctively assuming that the same logic will apply that operates when conflicts are being resolved in its own domestic context—that is, through dialogue and compromise, leading to a mutually acceptable outcome. When a democracy is dealing with an authoritarian regime, however, it does not make this assumption, and the use of force remains a possibility. In this way, democracy works to prevent war with other democracies, but not necessarily with other forms of government.

It can also be argued that the habitual conflict resolution approaches practiced by democracies in the domestic context means that democracies invariably see mutual relationships as positive rather than zero-sum. They expect interactions with other countries to normally be characterized by outcomes such as trade that benefit both parties, even if one gains more than the other. They do not assume that any gain by another country must represent a loss to themselves.

John Owen (1994: 87–125) argues that the democratic peace hypothesis also incorporates a number of assumptions about the way liberalism works, and that contemporary democracies are liberal democracies. For example, liberal democrats believe that all people are fundamentally the same: they have the same general goals in their lives and hopes for themselves and their loved ones. Their overall well-being is best preserved by pursuing self-preservation and material well-being as their primary and overriding goals. In order for these goals to be successfully achieved, freedom is required, because it makes choice possible in a number of crucial areas, notably the economic and political, and this freedom of choice produces a more responsive and efficient set of institutions. The state itself operates on the basis of the same set of assumptions to a greater or lesser extent. By the same kind of logic, peace is an important prerequisite, because without it, daily existence will be characterized by coercion and violence, which are counterproductive in terms of achieving individual and social goals.

Nondemocracies in contrast are seen as untrustworthy because they seek other ends, such as the coercion of other states to achieve local or regional domination. They tend to assess outcomes in zero-sum terms and seek diplomatic and economic "victories" over other states in the system. Democracies will claim that fellow liberal democracies share their ends and that totalitarian states do not, although this may not always be a reasonable assumption. Liberal democrats will therefore expect an "appropriate" response during a war-threatening crisis, which will be characterized by attempts at deescalation if the other state is democratic, but by preparations for the use of force if the adversary is an authoritarian regime.

An example of the way the democratic peace appears to work occurred in the 1990s with the transition to democracy of the Russian Federation. In the

1990s there was a profound change in the way that the NATO states perceived Russia following its evolution from communism to democracy. The change in attitudes toward Russia after democratization was evidence of the crucial way in which the perceptions of liberal democracies are substantially shaped by the political composition of the states with which they interact. As a rule, democracies will trust states that they consider democratic and will be suspicious of those states that they see as illiberal. Because of this, when democracies observe a state becoming a democracy in terms of their own criteria, they will automatically expect relations with it to be friendly and cooperative. This happened quite quickly in the case of Russia, even though the population of that country had no history of civil society or democratic behavior.

Against this, in the Anglo-American relationship with Iraq during the 1990s the ideological hostility became a more crucial factor than empirical realities. Despite the imposition of massive disarmament on Iraq, and the establishment of a highly intrusive arms control verification regime, Britain and the United States proved incapable of being reassured by Iraqi statements or general behavior. Overall compliance with the Western-imposed restrictions on Iraqi policy proved insufficient to satisfy Britain and the United States, which eventually adopted the military-political objective of "regime change" in order to install a more compliant government. The ideological justification for this act was the extension of democracy to Iraq.

A crucial question that follows from this is, how do democracies "know" that other democracies are equally peaceful and can be trusted, and why do they feel potentially threatened by totalitarian regimes, thereby triggering the "security dilemma" with them? An answer can be provided in terms of a social constructivist interpretation of international relations, which forms part of the social construction of reality. Social structures, rather than material structures, form actors as social individuals and as agents that are mutually constitutive. It follows that anarchy and the resulting security dilemma are social constructs as well.

The structure of the international system has not somehow fallen from heaven, but has been created by states and their interactions. As a result, anarchy and self-help as fundamental characteristics of international relations are not unavoidable. Actors' interests and preferences are not fixed, nor given. They originate and change during the process of social interaction.

This has important implications for democratic peace theory. The starting point is perceptions. As noted above, democracies assume other democracies to be "just" and consensual. Authoritarian states, in contrast, are perceived as unjust and exhibiting aggressive behavior toward their own people. Crucially, these presumptions about friendliness or hostility in international relations are not the result of the distribution of power in the international system, as realists argue. But neither are they the result of the effects of domestic structures *as such,* as many liberals argue.

Instead, the democratic peace is socially constructed. The democratic peace, as well as the frequently aggressive behavior of democracies toward nondemocracies, results from a rule "learned" through the process of interaction, which is to infer aggressiveness or peacefulness from what is perceived to be the degree of violence inherent in the domestic political structure of the other state.

What is crucial about this interpretation is that it does not require the underlying assumption that all democracies are always peaceful and that all authoritarian systems are always aggressive. Instead, complicated intersubjective perceptions are at work. Democratic leaders work through peaceful conflict resolution domestically, and instinctively prefer this option in international relations. When dealing with fellow democracies they assume that this feeling is reciprocal. Actors who trust each other start behaving accordingly. They therefore create a peaceful and cooperative order through their mutually reinforcing interactions. There are clearly important parallels here with Deutsch's ideas about how a pluralistic security community comes into existence. The presumption that the other is predisposed toward peacefulness becomes a self-fulfilling prophecy if both sides act on this assumption.

Criticisms of the Theory

Critics such as Christopher Layne (1994: 8), argue that democratic peace theory must explain the anomaly that democracies are no less war-prone than other states. They do not fight democracies, but do fight any other form of regime. Actually there is no reason why democratic peace theory should stand or fall on whether it can explain this, as long as the correlation exists for relations between democracies. However, there might be a sense in which a marked difference in attitude toward the use of force in different circumstances would threaten a democracy's pacific reputation. At the turn of the twenty-first century, for example, Britain and the United States used military force to impose regime change during a number of crises, in Kosovo, Afghanistan, and Iraq, and declared their willingness to take similar steps against other enemies in the near future. Both demonstrated a willingness to use war as an instrument of policy in circumstances where the majority of the international community were highly uneasy about the necessity and legitimacy of such action. The ability to do so without effective domestic political opposition demonstrated a dominance of the national and international media, which raises doubts about the degree to which governments in a democracy genuinely need to be fully responsive to public opinion. In the contemporary era, with spin doctors and media manipulation, governments may well be able to so shape public attitudes that the clear distinctions in perspectives on regimes needed for democratic peace to operate might be overcome by a government determined to use force.

Neorealist opponents of the theory have argued that it is not only unproven, but also positively dangerous. It is seen as dangerous because it is a central component in the argument that there has been a qualitative change in international relations since 1989 (Layne, 1994: 48). With the end of the Cold War, many observers of international politics felt there had been a profound and historically fundamental change in the nature of international relations.

Therefore countries like the United States need not worry about future military challenges from countries such as Germany and Japan. Layne calls this "a peace of illusions," arguing that "there is no evidence that democracy at the unit level negates the structural effects of anarchy at the level of the international system" (1994: 48). This view is based upon a realist balance of power analysis, with the suggestion that if U.S. leaders believe in the validity of democratic peace theory, they will become reluctant to use force in circumstances where it is necessary, and that, for example, "The US will be ill prepared to formulate a grand strategy that will advance its interests in the emerging world of multi-polar great power competition" (1994: 49).

Some of the arguments put forward by realists on this issue are not at all convincing. For example, David Spiro argues that the democratic peace theory has not demonstrated "that zero is statistically significant" (1994: 50–51). It is argued that "there have been few instances when democracies have been in a position to fight each other." This is an argument that does not stand up to historical analysis. More significant is that it is possible to identify cases where two democracies were clearly prepared to go to war with each other, and were not prevented from doing so by the operation of democratic peace considerations—for example, Great Britain and the United States in 1861 at the time of the Trent crisis. Indeed, the outbreak of the war between the United States and Confederate States of America in 1861 is itself a major caveat, since the political structure of the two states was essentially identical (Layne, 1994: 16–22).

For others, the argument is that the absence of war between democracies may simply be a result of the fact that, historically, few democracies have existed and therefore opportunities for war between them have been rare. Thus the absence of war between them is simply the result of random chance. When Kant first proposed the idea, there were hardly any states that fitted the description of a functioning democracy, and the number remained very low for a century afterward. In the contemporary world, not only are there far more democracies, but their numbers are increasing as well. When 50 percent of the world's states are democracies, the "separate peace" will embrace 25 percent of the world's state-pairs, and the validity of the thesis will increasingly be put to the test. The correlation is also vulnerable to the criticism that proponents simply *define* the difficult cases away, by modulating their definitions in such a way that apparently anomalous cases can be excluded (Layne, 1994: 40).

Georg Sorensen (1992) agrees with the general arguments of democratic peace theory, but with an important caveat. Democracies may be unwilling to go to war with each other, but they do appear to be prepared to use *subversion* against other democracies, the effects of which, in many cases, may be very similar to those of a war. Examples include the numerous occasions when the United States has intervened to impose "regime change" on countries whose governments have opposed its policies, such as the U.S. activities that led to the overthrow of democracy in the Dominican Republic in the early 1960s and Chile a decade later. On these occasions, U.S. economic and political interests triumphed over democratic solidarity.

Conclusion

There are significant overlaps in the security community and democratic peace approaches to security building, and the norm against using the threat or practice of force in relations between democracies can itself be seen as placing such relationships within a security community (Russett, 1993: 42). For Adler and Barnett, there is nevertheless a key divide in that the democratic peace approach does not allow for the possibility of security communities emerging between states that are not democracies (1998: 12). The security community approach, by focusing on the emergence of community, does not require democracy as a necessity, though it is clear that the particular features of democratic societies make them stronger candidates, and the historical record of peaceful interaction between nondemocratic regimes lacks the statistical frequency that is shown by democracies interacting. Amitav Acharya, however, has made a cogent case for seeing the ASEAN states as a "nascent" security community, despite their differences in political systems (1998: 219).

The research into security communities and democratic peace demonstrates that it is possible to explore different understandings of security while still operating within a paradigm that does not challenge the view of the state as the central actor, or the existence of an international anarchy shaped by the security dilemma, and research into security communities is therefore close to realism in crucial respects. However, by accepting that security is a social construction, and that the domestic form of the state can be a major contributor to the nature of bilateral and regional security relationships, these approaches embody a conception of security that is implicitly critical of classical and structural realism. For some of the proponents of the idea of security communities, the approach offers the possibility of finding a "middle way" between realism and idealism, which combines a focus on the state and military power with an acceptance of the possibility of effective evolutionary change in governing norms and institutional arrangements to provide security (Adler and Barnett, 1998: 15).

In the post–Cold War period these processes have been strongly reinforced. To a significant extent the state has undergone a "legitimacy deficit," with its territorial integrity being eroded by new forms of transnational management and intergovernmental institutions that are more effective at dealing with problems that cut across national borders (Clark, 1999: 120). John Baylis and Steve Smith argue that the ambivalence of globalization processes "reinforces the search for *national* security, and at the same time leads states to seek greater *multilateral and global solutions* as they are less able to provide security for their own citizens" (1997: 272).

These approaches explicitly draw on the same positivist and rationalist methodologies that mainstream realism draws on. Their significance is that they are indicative of a move during the Cold War period to explore understandings of security and community building in a way that clearly departed from prevailing realist orthodoxy, but without abandoning the majority of realism's assumptions and methodology.

Ole Waever has pointed out that in its original Deutschian formulation, the idea of the "security" community operated with a very limited conception of what constituted security as such, so that in effect security could be more accurately described as "nonwar." To this extent it can be seen as being "at odds with most on-going efforts to redefine and broaden it" (Waever, 1998: 76).

This is true. However, in practice, the linking of ideas of security, community, and ideology has been important not only in terms of their interrelationships, but also because their confluence in particular regions of the world has helped construct emergent security communities. These groups of states are more open to reconceptualization of the meanings of "power" and "security" in ways that enable them to embrace a broader, multidimensional approach to security itself (Adler and Barnett, 1998: 4).

FOUR

The Broader Agenda

In trying to develop a better understanding of security, a major advance was the "broadening" of the concept to encompass additional sectors, a process that took place during the 1980s, though it had been anticipated to some extent by studies published in the previous decade. "Security" is a socially constructed concept. It has a specific meaning only within a particular social context. Its received meaning is therefore subject to change as a result of material charges in the external environment and changes in the ways in which we think about issues. This process of conceptual reevaluation was clearly evident in the thinking about security that occurred during the 1980s.

During that decade, the traditional approach to security came to be subjected to a barrage of criticism. It might be thought that this was a natural result of the winding down and eventual end of the Cold War. As the superpower military confrontation faded, so it became possible to address other, previously ignored, conceptions of security. This is not the case, however. There may have been a general sense in which, as the Cold War wound down, alternative conceptions gained easier acceptance, but it is a striking fact that the breakthrough contributions to what would be sustained debate came in 1983, at the height of the renewed Cold War. In the same year that the North Atlantic Treaty Organization (NATO) and the Warsaw Pact were deploying new generations of nuclear weapons in Europe, and President Ronald Reagan was announcing the Strategic Defense Initiative, two important critiques of traditional security thinking were published: Richard Ullman's article "Redefining Security" (1983) in the flagship realist journal *International Security,* and Barry Buzan's book *People, States, and Fear* (1983; 1st ed.). Their arguments had been anticipated to a certain degree by the UN's Brandt Commission, whose 1980 report *North-South: A Programme for Survival* had "called for a new concept of security that would transcend the narrow notions of military defence and look more towards the logic of a broader independence" (1980: 124).

Buzan himself noted in the second edition of his book that although the decline in military threats during the 1980s enabled other threats to be perceived, "other types of threat are rising in importance regardless of the decline of military concerns" (1991a: 369). It is arguable whether these threats were indeed rising in importance, or whether it was more the case that their significance was at last being fully realized. Some parts of the new security agenda, such as the environmental sector, probably were rising in importance in the sense that the scale and momentum of the damage being done to the regional and planetary biospheres were accelerating at an alarming rate. Other security issues, such as the suffering of the poor in the third world, were not new, but had not been seen as issues requiring an urgent or large-scale response during the Cold War era.

The contributions of Buzan and Ullman, and those that followed, would suggest that the concept of security needed to be opened up in two directions. First, the notion of security should no longer be limited to the military domain. Rather, it should have a more general meaning that could be applied not only to the military realm, but also to the economic, the societal, the environmental, and the political fields. Second, the referent object of "security," the thing that needed to be secured, should not be conceptualized solely in terms of the state, but should embrace the individual below the state, and the international system above it.

These changes in thinking about security offered the possibility of significantly extending the areas of social existence that could be considered to be security-affecting. However, the expansion of the concept could occur in different ways, with very different social and political implications. Broadening in itself can be a very radical exercise, but this is not inevitable. It can still be done in pursuit of a conservative political agenda. Much depends upon whether the objective of a particular securitization is to capture the concept for a radical, emancipatory political agenda, or whether the purpose is to militarize new areas of governmental action, to colonize wider areas of social policy with an essentially militaristic mind-set. It is not just what is being done that is crucial, but also how it is being done, and for what purpose.

The requirement to broaden the definition of security could be promoted in both academic and policy terms. In academic terms there was a definitional issue as well as a political issue. Security, it was argued, could have no single meaning, because its reality changes according to context. Helga Haftendorn argued that "there is no one concept of security; national security, international security and global security refer to different sets of issues and have their origins in different historical and philosophical contexts" (1991: 3). By the 1970s, issues such as regional environmental degradation were increasingly forcing themselves onto the national and international political agenda. These were not part of the traditional security agenda, yet they raised implications that were similar in many ways to traditional security issues. However, they lacked a conceptual framework into which a coherent policy response could be placed. Broadening the meaning of security offered a solution to this problem. By becoming "security" issues, they automatically gained a level of governmental attention and policy response previously limited to military issues.

It can be argued in this regard that some proponents of "securitizing" an issue do so to attract resources for their favorite causes. However, as Daniel Deudney notes, it has always been the case that "new phrases are coined and old terms are appropriated for new purposes" (1990: 264). Evolution of the meaning of a crucial term such as "security" was therefore to be expected to some extent.

There was also a political aspect. The traditional limited definition of security was not ideologically neutral as its proponents claimed. On the contrary, by carefully delimiting what security was and who it could apply to, it delineated acceptable reality and acceptable discourse. This in turn raised the question of who benefits from what is commonly taken to be sensible. As Robert Cox pointed out, "theory is always for someone and some purpose" (1986: 207). The established conception of security could be seen as favoring the interests of certain states rather than others, and even of particular groups within those states.

Traditional approaches to security had identified it with order, predictability, and stability. During the Cold War, this approach was strongly criticized by peace researchers, who argued among other things that peace can only be achieved with one's adversary, not against. However, it was not until the final years of the Cold War that new thinking in security politics began to accelerate.

With the end of the Cold War a more radical critique emerged. Feminists, critical theorists, and postmodernists argued not just that the earlier approaches were inadequate. They also insisted that they were a deliberate and important part of the way in which the dominant groups within societies imposed particular interpretations of "reality." These have the effect of promoting the interests of some sections of society at the expense of others, underpinning a fundamentally unjust political and economic order.

Read with the benefit of hindsight, Ullman's article is not particularly radical. In many ways it is as important for when and where it appeared as it is for the details of what it actually said. It did challenge the prevailing military-centered conception of security by calling for attention to environmental issues, arguing that "since the onset of the Cold War in the late 1940s, every administration in Washington has defined American security in excessively narrow and excessively military terms" (1983: 19–20). Perhaps the greatest significance of the article was that it appeared in *International Security,* the flagship journal of realist security studies, initiating a requirement to reflect upon previously unstated assumptions that was both healthy and long overdue.

There were nevertheless problems with Ullman's attempt to move beyond the military conception of security. Ullman defined a security threat as "an action or sequence of events that (1) threatens drastically and over a relatively brief period of time to degrade the quality of life for the inhabitants of a state or (2) threatens significantly to narrow the range of policy choices available to the government of a state or to private, non-governmental entities (persons, groups, corporations) within a state" (1983: 133).

Although an attempt to move beyond a purely military definition of security, this interpretation illustrates the problems involved with the process of widening the definition. The narrowing of the policy choices of a multinational corporation, while inconvenient, hardly seems to be a security threat in the same way that the possibility of starvation to an impoverished peasant would be, or the collapse of a regional environment, or a military attack on a state. It is an example of the fact that in broadening the concept of security, care needs to be taken if the concept is not to be divested of all meaning.

Ullman's contribution was significant, but represented only a partial move in the direction of a more holistic definition of security. Ullman argued that defining security in traditional military terms is unhelpful in two ways. On the one hand it leads to an underestimation of other security threats, and on the other hand it contributes to the militarization of international relations. However, Ullman himself found it hard to make a decisive break with the military conception of international relations. His proposed alternative agenda still consisted of threats that were clearly related to the military security agenda in some way.

One danger in the enthusiasm for reworking the concept of security in the early 1990s was that its use was being broadened before its meaning had been properly deconstructed and reworked. The risk involved in putting the cart before the horse in this manner was that its extension would carry with it earlier meanings that were fundamentally realist and that therefore would not represent a major advance on earlier thinking on the subject.

Buzan's Five Sectors

It has been argued that, for European security specialists, Buzan's book has been so influential that it has become "the canon and indispensable reference point for students of security" (McSweeney, 1996: 81). Buzan, in *People, States, and Fear,* stressed the fact that security as a concept had come to be dominated by the idea of "national security." Thinking about security through a national approach easily led to a perspective that only identified military issues with security, whereas in the real world of everyday human existence, people were affected by threats in the political, economic, societal, and environmental areas as well (1991a: 15). Therefore, he argued, in today's world the national security problem needed to be seen in terms of a general systemic security problem in which individuals, states, and the system all play a part, and in which economic, societal, and environmental factors can be as important as political and military ones (1991a: 368).

Buzan's book was highly influential because it opened up a debate about security in two dimensions. First, it raised questions about the appropriate level at which security should be assessed, whether individual, national, or international level. Second, it proposed a broadening of the number of the domains in which security threats should be perceived. According to Buzan, the security of human collectivities was affected by factors in five major sectors:

- Military security concerns the two-level interplay of the armed offensive and defensive capabilities of states and states' perceptions of each other's intentions.

- Political security concerns the organizational stability of states, systems of government and the ideologies that give them legitimacy.

- Economic security concerns access to the resources, finance and markets necessary to sustain acceptable levels of welfare and state power.

- Societal security concerns the sustainability, within acceptable conditions for evolution, of traditional patterns of language, culture and religious and national identity and custom.

- Environmental security concerns the maintenance of the local and the planetary biosphere as the essential support system on which all other human enterprises depend. (Buzan, 1991a: 19–20)

A crucial point is that these five sectors are not seen as operating in isolation from each other. Each defines a focal point for concern and analysis, and a way of ranking priorities, but the sectors inevitably interrelate and overlap in a variety of ways. As Buzan noted, "Relations of coercion do not exist apart from relations of exchange, authority, identity or environment. Sectors might identify distinctive patterns, but they remain inseparable parts of complex wholes" (Buzan, Waever, and De Wilde, 1998: 8). While these five domains have become the key concepts, in terms of both governmental practice and scholarly analysis, they do not exhaust the list of possible contenders. Many feminist scholars, for example, have called for a focus on gender relations and female-specific or female-dominated security concerns.

Buzan suggested that there were three main reasons for wanting to broaden the concept of security. First, broadening was needed in order to capture the changing realities of the world. Second, he argued that the concept had useful political qualities. Various groups in society would want to "securitize" particular issues in order to make governments prioritize them. Third, security had potential as an integrative concept for international relations as a field of inquiry that had notoriously fluid boundaries. Buzan argued that the "rising density" of the international system was producing new realities. By "density" he meant the frequency and complexity of the networks of interaction that tie the international system together. In other words, the continuing effects of interdependence and globalization.

This growing interaction and interdependence could be seen across all the dimensions of the broader concept of security. Advances in military capabilities, for example, had made possible mutual assured destruction, planetwide war and the possible elimination of the human species through nuclear war, or even the elimination of all life on Earth through the "nuclear winter." Political ideas such as democracy now circulated globally, many issues were discussed in planetary forums such as the United Nations, and the model of the Western industrial democracies emerged as a standard route to development. Economically the world was characterized by the concept of globalization, with a global market of production, trade, and finance (Sheehan, 1996b).

Societally, the international system remained profoundly parochial, though superficial elements of a global society emerged—for example, the increasing use of English as a common second language. However, while there was little sign of a true global society, there were broad patterns of similarity in terms of the problems societies faced in a globalizing era. The breakup of the Cold War empire of the Soviet Union, the revival of aggressive national self-determination, and the impact of globalization left many peoples feeling societally insecure. Examples include both the Russian minorities and the ethnic majorities in Estonia and Latvia, the Hungarian minorities in Romania, Slovakia, and Yugoslavia, and nonwhite or non-Christian immigrants in many countries in Western Europe. Environmentally, human activities were increasingly having a dramatic impact at both the regional and global levels in a way that was "creating both common fates and a need for collective action" (Buzan, 1991b: 42). Examples include the problems of global warming, rising sea levels, ozone depletion, atmospheric pollution, soil erosion, and depletion of plant and animal species.

The broadening of the concept of security to encompass additional sectors was an important development in both intellectual and policy terms. Opening up security to embrace new sectors was valuable in itself, but more importantly it served to break the intellectual stranglehold of the "national security" concept. Once it had been recognized that security did not have a single, fixed meaning, then the potential breadth of its meaning was subjected to a process of analysis and negotiation. And this process was by no means limited to the categorization initially created by Buzan.

Buzan's proposals to open up the subject of security were a radical and important departure. However, although Buzan criticized much Cold War security theory, he himself continued to maintain an essentially structural realist position, but during the 1990s this steadily evolved, moving him further and further from an automatic acceptance of realist tenets. His 1998 collaboration began with the statement: "our approach is based on the work of those who for well over a decade have sought to question the primacy of the military element and the state in the conceptualization of security" (Buzan, Waever, and De Wilde, 1998: 1).

The existence of the "international anarchy" is the basic ontological premise of his work. The idea is that there is no overall world government and therefore states must promote and defend their interests in competition. This is an essentially realist position. Security was defined as "pursuit of freedom from threat" (Buzan, 1991: 18). In this conception, states were seen as the key focus for security because, in the absence of world government, "they are both the framework of order and the highest source of governing authority." Anarchy ensures that "security can only be relative, never absolute" (Buzan, 1991a: 22–23).

These caveats shape Buzan's examination of levels of analysis. The relationship between individual and national security is recognized as being a complex one in which states themselves can pose significant threats to the security of individuals. Social groups are recognized as being important security actors in themselves, with the potential to destabilize their states. Despite this, Buzan sees individual security as "essentially subordinate to higher levels" (1991a: 5). Individual security, according to Buzan, cannot be the basis of security analysis, "because the state cannot be reassembled from individual-level attributes; it has *sui generis* state-level attributes and one has to see the state itself as a unit of reality" (Buzan and Waever, 1997: 241).

His systemic perspective on the state includes "territory, government, and society" (Buzan, 1991a: 60). The state is defined in terms of a clearly realist perspective. The state is seen as needing to have a strong and widely held conception of itself (sociopolitical cohesion) and a clear institutional structure (sometimes substituting for national identity). It also needs physical resources. When these are all clearly present, strong states are produced, "a necessary but not sufficient condition for improving international security" (Buzan, 1991a: 106).

Buzan's systemic level of security analysis is developed through the concepts of "immature" and "mature" anarchy. Immature anarchies are lacking in effective structural constraints and are characterized by fragmentation, competition, and a limited framework of norm-regulated behavior. A mature anarchy—for example, the North Atlantic states—limits instability through widespread acceptance of codes of behavior by strong states.

Buzan also placed considerable emphasis on regional security. This allows an intermediate level of analysis, where highly interdependent "security complexes" operate between the state and system levels. A security complex represents a group of states whose interests and destinies are sufficiently interlinked that each state's security cannot be understood except in relation to the other states in the complex. Such complexes are held together not by the positive influences of shared interest, but by shared rivalries. The dynamics of security contained within these levels operate across a broad spectrum of sectors—military, political, economic, societal, and environmental.

Subsequent work within the Copenhagen school developed this approach in relation to post–Cold War European security. Waever analyzed sociopolitical change and superpower decline leading to competing organizing principles concerning concepts of Europe (1998: 89–90). The "security complex" concept was reworked in favor of a conceptual sliding scale denoting change, ranging through security community, self-help balance of power, mutual security regime, and nonviolent conflict culture.

This research program represented an attempt to remain within an essentially neorealist framework of analysis, while developing a more nuanced and sophisticated explanation of the way in which security dynamics operate at the suprastate level, though the implications of the conclusions reached have led both Buzan and Waever steadily away from the simplistic verities of orthodox neorealism.

The developing trajectory of this work led to increased emphasis being focused on "societal security." It was clear that in the 1990s, while there still remained military security threats in the new Europe, the major source of European insecurity operated at the level of society rather than necessarily the state. Integration in Western Europe had transformed the permeability of traditional state boundaries, so that societies were less able to use the state to protect themselves from threatening external cultural and political forces. Fragmentation in Eastern Europe, combined with the homogenizing pressure of economic and political transition, in turn produced relatively weak states with little historical experience of nation-statehood upon which to draw. The concept of societal security, manifested in the problems of identity and migration, relied largely upon the resolution of contested identities.

Critics of Buzan and Waever have welcomed their attempts to expand the definition of security, but take issue with a number of their assumptions, particularly with the realist-inspired ontological preference for the state. Steve Smith criticized Buzan's 1991 definition of security as "vague and restricted" (1991: 333), being related only to the existence of conflict or violence. The Buzan schema, it was argued, made little effort to explore the implications of questioning the assumption that security is just for states.

Martin Shaw also criticized Buzan's conceptual framework. Despite Buzan's sensitivity to nonstate security actors and notwithstanding his major attempt to redefine the security "issue agenda," he argued that much of Buzan's work is nothing more than "caveats to a state-centred nation of security. Buzan has effectively ruled out any referents other than states or quasi-state collectivities as a serious basis for security studies" (1994: 90).

In the groundbreaking *People, States, and Fear,* Buzan continued to give the state the pivotal place in conceptions of security. As other authors took the agenda forward, however, the state-centric approach was often found to be inadequate in dealing with specific issues. Buzan, in his publications after 1991, showed himself increasingly open to the centrality of nonstate security actors in particular sectors (Waever et al., 1993: 23–27). As he himself noted, having established the existence of society as a second possible referent object for security alongside the state, it became very difficult to refuse to accept the possibility of other potential referents emerging (Buzan and Waever, 2003: 70–71).

Buzan's thinking on this subject, like Waever's, has been evolutionary. In 2003 the two published another major contribution, focusing on the study of regional security complexes, in which the centrality of the state was brought clearly into question, though its importance continued to be seen as crucial, and in which Buzan explicitly distanced himself from a purely neo-realist approach to security analysis. The regional security framework was seen as drawing on neorealism's materialist concepts of bounded territoriality and power centrism, but using social constructivist ideas to elaborate the mechanisms that allow security issues to become constituted (Buzan and Waever, 2003: 4). This effectively placed them "outside the neo-realist project" (2003: 11).

Buzan and Waever, along with a number of other collaborators, are often collectively described as the "Copenhagen school," but this designation, while helpful in some respects, also suggests a unity of approach among its members that, in important respects, is more apparent than real. Buzan and Waever, for example, have significantly different tolerances of the centrality of the state to security discourse. There is a tension in Buzan's writings. In a 1991 work, he argues strongly for the state-centric approach, declaring that it is only against the reality of state security that threats to other referents such as the individual make sense (1991b: 54). In contrast, in the 2003 work it is argued that "we have designed our theory so that it can accommodate non-state actors and even allow them to be dominant" (Buzan and Waever, 2003: 12), and there is a recognition that in at least certain parts of the world, in the post–Cold War era, security communities have emerged for whom security is largely perceived in nonmilitary terms (2003: 19). Indeed, Waever argued elsewhere that Western Europe was a security community that could be thought of as having gone through successive stages of insecurity, security, desecuritization, and resecuritization. The penultimate stage was reached as the military security threat diminished with the waning of the Cold War, but the final stage emerged as new security sectors such as the environment came to dominate the security discourse (Waever, 1998: 69). In the end, Buzan and Waever leave the question open, declaring that it is for history to decide how central the state is to security compared with other possible referents; their own structure does not assume that the state must be dominant, but neither does it insist that it is not (2003: 44–45), that it is possible to operate with a theory that "is not dogmatically state-centric in its premises, but is often somewhat state-centric in its findings" (2003: 71).

It is hard to make comparisons between Karl Deutsch's value-driven notion of security communities, and Buzan's system-driven analysis. However, the latter's acknowledgment that anarchy is to some extent what states make of it suggests that security is not just about power or peace, but is also closely connected to, or constitutive of, identity. If security is defined as "the pursuit of freedom from threat, and is primarily about the fate of human collectivities" (Buzan, 1991a: 19), it is reasonable to assume that such security is related to the strength and stability of particular forms of social and political organization. Indeed, Buzan argues, *contra* neorealism, that security dynamics are inevitably affected by the nature of the types of states found in particular regions (Buzan and Waever, 2003: 21).

Simon Dalby argues that Buzan's conceptualization, while employing a novel terminology and sectoralization, is still essentially a defense of the post-1989 Western-dominated modernist status quo, and that Buzan calls "for the triumph of Westernisation, liberal capitalism, territorial states, and the inevitability of technological progress, backed up by the willingness to use force to maintain this international order" (Dalby, 1992: 102).

The Meaning of Securitization

In the debates about the necessity and purpose of broadening the concept of security that would take place from the 1980s onward, values would be central to the critique. Those who called for an expansion of security to embrace new sectors such as threats to the environment, or economic security, were challenging the existing value-hierarchy of society. To "securitize" an issue not previously deemed to be a security issue was to challenge society to promote it higher in its scale of values and to commit greater resources to solving the related problems. For the postpositivist critics, both the value-hierarchy and the nature of unstated assumptions were being challenged. Traditional approaches to security were being unpacked in order to expose to critical scrutiny the unstated normative and political commitments that underpinned them.

The invocation of the word "security" creates priorities for action and the use of exceptional measures. It has the capacity to bring increased political attention to certain issue areas. For many who have sought to broaden the definition, this has perhaps been the most important reason for wanting to do so. Traditional security areas have benefited from high levels of assured state funding in a way that has not been true for other areas such as health policy, job creation, education, and so on. Most of the security threats identified by those who have called for a redefintion of security have involved aspects of human health and welfare, social problems, internal sources of instability, and the impact of the disruption of traditional customs (Lipschutz, 1995: 6). When an individual or group has called for something to be made a security issue, their purpose has been to cause it to receive the same political attention and the same access to problem-solving resources that military issues have traditionally received.

What quality is it that causes something to be accepted as being a security issue in international relations? Ole Waever argues that in classical security thinking, security was about *survival*. Something is a security issue when it appears to pose an existential threat to a particular group or institution, usually though not necessarily the state. This life-or-death aspect of security threats in turn justifies the use of extraordinary measures to deal with them (Waever, cited in Lipshutz, 1995: 54). Traditionally, to make something a security issue has legitimized the use of force, and allowed the state to take special powers. Invariably, it has justified the commitment of a substantial proportion of a state's resources to address the problem.

In a sense, therefore, securitization is simply a stronger instance of the phenomenon of politicization. Something is designated as a security issue because a convincing argument can be made that this issue is more important than other issues on the political agenda, and that it should therefore take absolute priority. Security is therefore self-referential. An issue becomes a security issue not necessarily because there is a real existential threat in an objective sense, but because the issue can be constructed as an existential threat and is then accepted as such by the political establishment (Buzan, Waever, and De Wilde, 1998: 24).

Analysts as far back as Arnold Wolfers (1962: 151) have noted that security can be approached both objectively (there is a real threat) and subjectively (there is a perceived threat), and that it is not inevitable that both will be true at the same time. When an actor securitizes an issue, "correctly" or not, this will make its subsequent behavior different. What may seem a legitimate securitization within a political community may appear paranoid to those outside it—for example, Islamic fears of Western cultural icons like pop music, clothing, and so on. Security is thus a structured field where some actors are in positions of power by being generally accepted voices of security, by having the power to *define* it.

Security discourse is used to identify some threats as being existential, as being fundamental because they are clearly related to survival. The conception of security needs to be expanded because politicians already use a broader approach. Therefore, analysts must investigate how and why they do this. But Waever also seems to accept some of the misgivings of critics like Daniel Deudney and Jef Huysmans, who suggest that securitizing certain issues such as the environment and migration is likely to be counterproductive, because they will end up being colonized by a military mind-set rather than being addressed in a holistic and politically progressive manner.

According to Waever, security, as with any concept, carries with it a history and a set of connotations that it cannot escape. At the heart of the concept there still remains an essential essence related to defense and the state. As a result, addressing an issue in security terms still evokes an image of military defense-related threat perception, which gives the state an important role in addressing it. This is not always a helpful development (1995b: 47).

Because he sees the effects of attaching the security label as fixed, Waever argues that "a conservative approach to security is an intrinsic element in the logic of both our national and international political organising principles" (1995b: 56–57), and advocates the *desecuritization* of as many issues as possible. For Waever, securitization is a development that moves a particular issue beyond the normal rules of the game "and frames the issue either as a special kind of politics or as above politics" (Buzan, Waever, and De Wilde, 1998: 23). To desecuritize an issue, in contrast, is seen as removing it from the realm of the politics of existential survival and, by doing so, making it easier to resolve using more cooperative forms of problem solving.

In a sense, therefore, Waever, like the neorealists, also wants to restrict the use of the term "security." But doing so would mean that groups would lose the ability to mobilize support for their agenda, which undoubtedly exists when they can associate it with security. All kinds of social groups, at both the substate and suprastate levels, securitize different types of issues, often with profound sociocultural, political, and economic implications.

Another problem with Waever's approach is that he appears more concerned with the broadening of the security concept than with deepening it. Security is a concept that can be applied in a number of different sectors, but its essential meaning is seen as being unaffected by its transposition away from the military sector. For the Copenhagen school, the meaning of security can be determined not so much by analyzing the term as a concept, but by investigating the empirical meaning of its everyday use. "The meaning lies not in what people consciously think the concept means, but in how they implicitly use it in some ways but not others" (Buzan, Waever, and De Wilde, 1998: 24). Security is described as "a generic term that has a distinct meaning but varies in form" (1998: 27).

However, this would clearly suggest that, contrary to what Waever (or Deudney) suggests, the meaning of security is not necessarily fixed to statist, militarized mind-sets. It is open to argumentation and dispute. However, Buzan makes the argument that this can only be taken so far, that while it is true that security as a concept and as a practice is intersubjective and socially constructed, nevertheless there is a core understanding of both that has remained constant for so long that in practice it dramatically limits the parameters of the concept. For Buzan and his colleagues, "even the socially constituted is often sedimented as structure and becomes so relatively stable as practice that one must do analysis also on the basis that it continues" (1998: 31).

The work of Jurgen Habermas can be useful here. Usually language is thought of as a description exercise, a factual representation, whereas Habermas sees it in terms of three "validity claims"—truth, normative rightness, and expressive truthfulness—that are given equal importance (Outhwaite, 1994: 131). This understanding of "speech acts" can be applied to concepts of security to provide a basis for understanding their purpose and practice.

Thus, when something is deemed to be about "security," a claim is being made, and this claim can be subjected to analysis through reasoned argument. Any claim by a government that a particular issue is in fact a threat to "national security" can be put to the test in terms of the three criteria of truth, rightness, and sincerity. The government's claim that it is indeed a security issue can therefore be disputed. This then becomes crucial in making it possible to question whether in fact specific interests appear to benefit by identifying this particular issue as a threat to "national security."

The debate triggered by Buzan and Ullman in 1983 did lead in time to a broader working definition of security at both the academic and governmental/intergovernmental levels. However, they in turn triggered two other sets of questions. First, while the issues on the new, broader agenda are clearly important, are they truly "security" threats in a way that meaningfully relates them to the other parts of the security agenda? Are all the various elements of the expanded security agenda sufficiently similar in their impact upon human beings to justify designating them with a common terminology? Moreover, what are the implications for issues such as the environment and societal problems when they are securitized? Securitizing is never an innocent act. The history of the concept of security at the intellectual and policy levels has endowed it with very particular implications. It inhabits a thought-realm that has traditionally associated it with specific and unrepresentative elements of society as a whole, the military and government national defense sectors and their perspectives and ethos. These sectors have traditionally been able to dominate the national policy agenda in terms of their ability to take precedence over other national objectives and to make claims on a limited budget. Introducing a new sector to this thought-world has profound implications not just for the meaning of security, but also for the sector that is being securitized, and the possibility of this being a positive step cannot simply be taken for granted.

The "broadening" of the agenda need not necessarily produce a new conception of security; it could merely lead to the application of fairly traditional military security thinking to a wider range of subject areas such as the economy and the environment. Martin Shaw, for example, argues that the latter is the case, that "the recognition of additional dimensions of security—however welcome this may be—may be an ad hoc enlargement of a still state-centred concept of security" (1994: 90).

▨ Advantages of Broadening

Broadening has to be justified on conceptual and policy grounds. Jessica Tuchman Matthews argued at the end of the 1980s that global developments revealed the need for the concept of national security to include resource, environmental, and demographic issues. The logic behind her argument was clear: the world was going through one of its periodic phases of major political evolution and "the assumptions and institutions that have governed international relations in the postwar era are a poor fit for these new realities" (1989: 162).

These calls were welcomed by many and helped open up a debate on security as a concept. Ronnie Lipschutz asserted that Buzan and others who called for a broadening of the security agenda still left the concept unexplained, for it still seemed "self-evident" to many (Lipschutz, 1995: 5). It is one thing to say that the environment, for example, is a security issue, but this still leaves unexplained what exactly "security" is, or for that matter, what the "environment" is in this context. This therefore made it fairly easy "to shift the allocation of resources from one threat to another, so long as the new threat was conceptualized in terms of the state and couched in the language of 'national security'" (Lipschutz, 1995: 6).

Traditional approaches to security focused on particular conceptions of security and therefore on specific views of who was to be made secure and how. This meant in practice that the security needs of some groups in society were largely ignored, often those who were most adversely affected by military security (Tickner, 1995: 191).

The advantages of broadening the concept include the fact that governments are able to use emergency measures to address a wider range of issues and that the usual constraints on action are overcome. All that is required for an issue to be securitized is that its proponents convince the relevant decisionmakers that it is indeed a security issue (Buzan, Waever, and De Wilde, 1998: 25). This is particularly important in areas where existential concerns have been marginalized by the prevailing political agenda—for example, in terms of addressing the issue of world poverty.

A second advantage is that the security concerns of the individual can be directly addressed, rather than having to be addressed via the state. The individual becomes the direct focus of attention and can be protected from newly securitized threats such as the effects of inadequate health provision, poor education, political oppression, and violence of various forms. This involves treating people as "ends and not means" and, crucially, treating the state as a means and not an end (Booth, 1991b: 319).

Broadening the approach also has the advantage of encouraging a more holistic mind-set in which security is seen in terms of more than just the interests of a particular state or population. With the traditional narrow analysis, security specialists were compelled to ignore many of the factors that create and accentuate conflict, because they were outside the parameters of the definition. For example, the dynamics of the (military) security situation in the former Yugoslavia are impossible to fully understand without reference to the processes of identity formation in the region.

Between the 1940s and 1980s, thinking about security was excessively concentrated in the subfield of strategic studies. This was unfortunate for two reasons, according to Buzan (1991a). Strategic studies specialists generally tend to have a narrow degree of expertise. They are essentially military specialists and not surprisingly interpret security through the military dimension. In addition, a great deal of strategic analysis is specifically meant to be policy-relevant for national governments and therefore tends to be highly ethnocentric. This leads it to have an overwhelmingly national security perspective. This in turn discourages analysis of security interdependence and the more broadly systemic aspects of the concept, which is necessary when, for example, an issue such as the environment is under investigation.

All the "broadeners" argue that the security of states and populations should be seen as being crucially affected by a range of issues, not merely the military capabilities of other states. In addition, it is argued that these new "threats" should be addressed with the same sense of urgency and commitment of resources previously limited to the maintenance of military balances of power and the projection of military force. The broadening of the security agenda therefore makes it possible to take account of threats that are not currently met by state policies, but that are nevertheless encountered by individuals, social groups, and movements.

Ken Booth, an advocate of a more "critical" approach to security, accepts that with the broadening of the security concept, there is a risk of the concept becoming less coherent and the security agenda becoming overloaded, but sees this as a cause for celebration rather than concern. "To maintain the traditionalist ('intellectually coherent') concept of security simply perpetuates statist, militarized, and masculinized definitions of what should have priority in security terms, and to do that leaves the agenda in the hands of the traditional strategic/security specialists" (1997: 111).

The issue of securitization is not simply one of conceptual coherence or academic definition. Security issues dominate governmental policy agendas and generate political action and resource allocation in a way that other aspects of the policy agenda do not. Yet for billions of ordinary human beings worldwide, the everyday struggle for survival, for "existential security," is dominated by issues of healthcare, poverty, human rights, environmental degradation, and many other concerns that do not form part of the traditional military security agenda. If a government is a means to an end—the protection and improvement of the well-being of its citizens—then the central issue concerns how this should be done, how people can be made secure.

For Booth and other critical security proponents, the objective should be not just "broadening" the understanding of security by extending its logic to new sectors. It should also be about "deepening" the meaning of security. Deepening involves challenging existing conceptions that limit its application and instead exploring the implications of working with a richer concept of security that would alter the practice of politics itself (Booth, 1997: 111).

In the contemporary world there are obvious limitations to working with a very narrow definition of security. Broadening its meaning offers advantages in terms of addressing new issues, such as the degradation of the environment, or gaining deeper understandings of older ones, such as the relationship between the economy and military security. However, if security is a concept that can be applied to many different realms, such as the military, economic, and environmental, and at many different levels, such as the individual and the international, it clearly runs the risk of becoming no more than a synonym for international relations generally.

The efforts to produce a new conception of security in the 1980s had the effect of revealing the inadequacies of the existing, limited definition, without producing a new concensus on a broader understanding. Critics argued quite reasonably that if expanded too far, the concept would cease to have any clear meaning at all. Stephen Walt, for example, argued that broad definitions of security should be resisted, because although a case could be made for including such things as pollution, disease, and economic failure as security threats, this would represent an excessive expansion of the definition. If the field was defined too widely, its intellectual coherence would be destroyed (1991: 213).

As a result, the 1990s saw an attempt to build a consensus around a definition that could embrace many sectors, but that was grounded in threats to the existence of human beings. Buzan and later collaborators defined international security as being about how "human collectivities relate to each other in terms of threats and vulnerabilities" (Buzan, Waever, and De Wilde, 1998: 10). Security was seen as being fundamentally about survival. When a collectivity sees an issue as posing an existential threat, this is seen as justifying extraordinary measures to handle the threat (Buzan, Waever, and De Wilde, 1998: 21). Other writers such as Lothar Brock (1991: 418) also argued that what ultimately defines security is an existential threat.

However, in many ways even "existential" is a minimalist criterion. Clearly, it is obvious that any threat that could end the physical existence of an entity is a security threat. But for human beings, life is about more than simple survival. Humans live in complex social organizations, devise elaborate belief systems for which they may be willing to sacrifice their existence, and constantly aspire to a quality of life greater than they currently have, or that their forebears had. It is legitimate therefore to expect a concept of security to have embedded within it assumptions about a certain quality of existence and the protection of ideas and values as well as lives and structures. As the United Nations put it in 1994, "human security is not a concern with weapons—it is a concern with human life and dignity" (1995: 229).

The "existential" approach, while offering the possibility of preventing the definition from becoming unworkably broad, is not without problems itself. Security can be defined very broadly so that it means anything that affects the well-being of human beings. But this would force the inclusion of things such as natural disasters and illness. Volcanic eruptions and cholera epidemics are obviously serious problems, but are they *security* issues? Clearly for many populations they are, and are much more immediate dangers than the highly unlikely possibility of being attacked by the armed forces of another country. Yet if they are security issues, then where does one draw the line? Any serious illness would need to be included, as well as transport policy, insofar as it related to safety issues, food quality controls—almost anything might be deemed a security issue. But if this were the case, the term would lose most of its value, since it would not describe anything in particular. Nobody picking up a book on "international security" would be able to guess, with reasonable accuracy, what kinds of issues would be likely to be addressed by the author.

The problem faced in widening the meaning of security is that to retain its value as a specific concept within international relations it needs to have a restricted meaning. But this meaning must not be so restricted that it effectively excludes most of the tangible threats to human collectivities. Using the standard of the "existential threat," as Buzan and Waever suggest, offers one way out of this dilemma.

Security can be seen as relating to dangers to human collectivities that are of a life-threatening nature. The danger itself emerges not from the natural environment or the natural process of life, but from the calculated activities and policies of other human beings. Human agency is fundamental to the definition of security threat. The danger may not be immediate, but it is apparent and is likely to manifest itself within a foreseeable time scale.

Within this definition, all traditional military threats can be encapsulated. Other threats may or may not be, dependent on their nature. Thus, environmental threats are included if they are human in origin—thereby embracing global warming and pollution, but not earthquakes or typhoons. Societal threats count if the collectivity is placed in physical danger, but not if only cultural distinctiveness is threatened. The Kosovo crisis of 1999 counts, the danger of Gaelic disappearing as a language in Scotland does not. The ups and downs of national or regional economic performance count only if economic crisis or failure threatens political stability or survival, or the physical survival of human beings.

Even with this kind of restricted definition there are significant problems. One area where the definition clearly remains unsatisfactory concerns the meaning of "survival," which cannot simply mean "not dead" or "not physically maimed." A minimum level of well-being, of quality of life, must be included. And where does this address Johan Galtung's concept of "structural violence" (1971), the idea that institutional behavior—for example, the former South African policy of apartheid—when it unjustly constrains human rights and opportunities, is itself a form of violence?

Criticisms of Broadening

Although Buzan began by criticizing traditional state-centric understandings of security, he ended up by stressing the continuing primacy of the state as the central referent for security. Martin Shaw, among others, took issue with Buzan on this point and argued that unless the state-centric assumptions of traditional security thinking were challenged, the broadening move, while a valuable step forward, would have only a limited impact in terms of deepening our understanding and practice of security (Shaw, 1994: 90).

However, it is important to recognize that there are possible disadvantages as well as potential benefits involved in the act of securitizing an issue. War has not disappeared from the international realm and military dangers continue to confront communities and states in various parts of the world (Booth, 1991a: 338). New threats may be too far in the future to justify securitization now (Deudney, 1990: 467). The traditional military security agenda tended to operate in terms of threats that were immediate, or at the very least, clearly urgent. The public could be mobilized to confront such a threat with relative ease. Threats on other sectoral agendas, such as the environment, may be real, and may be years or even decades away from reaching crisis point. Mobilizing public opinion against such threats using a traditional vocabulary may be counterproductive, because the public's attention span and commitment (and perhaps that of the government as well) will wane well before the critical time period is entered. If broadened too far, the concept of security might lose its significance. This is important in the sense that the political effectiveness is determined by security issues being seen as exceptional. If too much is securitized, security might become unexceptional and therefore securitization would not be politically effective.

Some traditionalists, however, have suggested that an expanded security definition will lead to a loss of focus. This has been argued forcefully by Stephen Walt, who suggests that introducing nonmilitary issues onto the security agenda undermines the field's "intellectual coherence" (1991: 213). He called instead for a return to a more restricted meaning of security. Security studies should be limited to analyzing "the conditions that make the use of force more likely, the ways that the use of force affects individuals, states and societies, and the specific policies that states adopt in order to prepare for, prevent, or engage in war" (1991: 212).

However, Walt's views are inconsistent. While wanting to restrict the conception of security, Walt's own proposed agenda is broad enough to include issues such as the role of domestic politics, the power of ideas, and the influence of economic issues. However, this is inevitable because of the inherent weaknesses of a narrow conception of security.

A further criticism of Buzan's expanded definition was that of those like Deudney (1990) and Huysmans (1995), who object to the securitization of problems such as the environment and migration. For these critics, the danger involved in "hyphenating security" lies in the militarization and confrontation–orientation attitude produced by the traditional conception of national security. However, others, like Robert Walker, argue that security will inevitably expand to include issues that are not military in nature. This is because of the way questions regarding security are so closely implicated in the whole legitimization of the sovereign state (Walker, 1997: 76).

Is securitizing an issue necessarily a positive step? As noted earlier, bringing a new issue onto the security agenda can be seen as an effective strategy for groups wishing to prioritize issues. However, doing so may also have consequences that are harmful in various ways. Security in this sense comes equipped with a traditional confrontational and militaristic national-security mind-set that may be totally inappropriate to the issue at hand. Deudney (1990) and Huysmans (1995) have warned against importing such a mind-set into analysis of issues of environmental degradation and international migration, respectively.

This is an important reservation. It may well be unhelpful to securitize in this way since it provides the security forces with a claim to act in the resolution of such wider issues. This can be seen in NATO's increasing interest in environmental security and the U.S. government's decision to give the intelligence services an overt and public role in the collection of economic intelligence to support U.S. competition with its trading rivals, as well as the UK government's decision to give M16 a lead role in efforts to counter the international trade in narcotics. British foreign secretary Robin Cook told Parliament in 1998 that the British intelligence services had been given new priorities to combat terrorism and the international drug trade (Cook, 1998: 579).

Critics of a broadened security definition have argued that if the concept is widened, it would become meaningless, that in fact anything could be put forward as a security issue. To an important degree, however, the redefinition of security in the post–Cold War era did not seem to bring about much change, because in important respects statist notions continued to reign. Simply broadening the agenda only presents a broader range of threats in traditional competitive terms.

Although the fading of the Cold War allowed a broadening of the security agenda, it did not produce a consensus on where the boundaries of the

broader definition should be (Buzan, 1991a: 14). It is a political and normative act to choose which issues should be security issues. Must new issues
have effects on the military sector, or be as "dangerous" as war, as Deudney
suggests? Should they have what has been called "stun value"? Gregory Treverton suggests that the Cold War nuclear threat, with its potential for almost
instantaneous genocide, had a shock capacity that is not true of the threats
identified by the expanding security agenda. Contemporary threats are more
localized in their actual or potential effects and therefore do not provide a
comparable catalyst for policy response (1995). For Steven Walt and other traditionalists, broadening would lead to a drastic loss of focus and undermine
the field's coherence. For Walt and other neorealists, security is synonymous
with strategic studies and the analysis of the use or threat of military force.
Other issues might well be important *problems,* but that does not in itself
make them security threats (Walt, 1991).

Conclusion

Deudney's arguments illustrate one of the key difficulties arising if a static
concept of security is simply applied to a broader range of sectors. Traditional
security involves security against another group, on behalf of a particular
group. However, the purpose of broadening beyond traditional military threats
is to be able to address security issues without necessarily triggering a traditional military-type response (Wyn Jones, 1996: 198). For Wyn Jones, moving away from a state-centric perception for thinking about security is crucial
because it encourages adoption of an approach centered around ideas of common security, where security is pursued in cooperation with others rather than
in opposition to them (1996: 209).

Moreover, the argument against the securitization of certain issues cannot
be sustained for the simple reason that it is not only states that securitize.
Other groups, at both the substate and interstate levels, already securitize
many different types of issues in this manner, often with far-reaching implications and effects (Wyn Jones, 1996: 209). To this extent the security agenda
needs to be broadened simply in order to take account of what are already the
realities of world politics.

The key to a legitimate criteria set is the acceptance of the idea of security as an intersubjective understanding. Securitization is about constructing a
shared understanding of what are to be considered security issues, and what
should be seen as threats. Security means survival in the face of existential
threats, but what constitutes an existential threat is not the same across different sectors, nor is it perceived in the same way by different societies at the
same time, nor even by the same society at different periods in its history.

Many social groups are already securitizing a diverse range of issues, so
analysts *must* broaden their use of the concept in order to capture the emer-

gent realities of the contemporary world. Rather than leaving the terrain of security to outdated notions, it is important to dispute what it means to securitize an issue. Given the importance of words and concepts in defining realities, it is vital that the political potential of the concept of security be used for a range of purposes. It is essential that a concern with others and a breaking down of domestic and international barriers are implicit in the broader approach to security.

FIVE

Economic Security

The sectoral approach to broadening the security agenda moves it beyond the traditional focus on military and state security to embrace new areas. For many of the sectors, there is no single analytical approach; rather, a number of significantly different interpretations exist under the same heading. This is certainly the case with the economic security domain, where even after twenty years of discussion of the idea, "no clear definition of what is meant by that phrase seems to have emerged" (Neu and Wolff, 1994: 11).

Economics and national security have always been seen as being linked to some extent. Adam Smith in *The Wealth of Nations,* for example, discussed the link between "defense" and "opulence" (Hitsch, 1960: 434). The relationship between economics and security has traditionally been one in which the former is seen as being subordinate to the latter. Security is centrally related to the practice of politics and there is an economic dimension to the successful practice of security politics. An absolute distinction can never in any case be made between political and economic power, since each is always present in the other. Although it was given some consideration as a concept during the early Cold War period, it can be argued that it was the economic and political shock of the 1973 Organization of Petroleum-Exporting Countries (OPEC) oil embargo that placed the idea of economic security firmly on the Western policy agenda. The shock waves of that period were still reverberating at the end of the decade, when Robert Keohane and Joseph Nye's *Power and Interdependence* was published. This became the crucial text for the neoliberal approach; the authors argued, among other things, that military security issues were not always the primary concern for states and that under certain conditions economic issues might supersede military matters (1977: 99).

In traditional realist approaches to security, the economic dimension is crucial among other reasons because it is seen as one of the key criteria by which great powers are defined. Economic resources are one of the ways in which the power of a state can be estimated. The concept of economic security raises a number of important issues, and it is important to explore its contribution to a broadened approach to security.

It is a much older concept than other elements of the broadened security agenda, such as environmental or societal security, and in some ways is a centuries-old approach to thinking about security. It was one of the five sectors identified by Barry Buzan in 1983 and his definition declared that "economic security concerns access to the resources, finance and markets necessary to sustain acceptable levels of welfare and state power" (1991a: 19).

The definition is interesting because it attempts to embrace two quite different approaches to the concept of economic security, which, while they may not be antithetical, are certainly in a state of tension. The reference to sustaining state power relates to an approach to economic security that is centuries old, the basic belief that a prospering economy and healthy tax base are necessary in order to purchase military and diplomatic capabilities. Armed forces and diplomatic networks are expensive to acquire and maintain.

The reference to acceptable levels of welfare, however, suggests a quite different understanding—that the material well-being of a country's citizens is in and of itself a security issue. This opens up a quite different agenda relating to issues of poverty, health levels, employment levels, and overall economic and political stability. It is an economic security agenda of particular resonance for the countries of what used to be called the "second" and "third" worlds, the former communist transition states and the developing countries.

It is open to exploration in security terms in the sense that under a broader interpretation, questions of existential survival and structural violence can be equated with questions of poverty and economic issues. In addition, the confrontation with the global economic structure can be seen as being disciplinary, in the sense that it operates to maintain the privileged position of elites within national societies, and of the hegemonic West against the less developed states of the world.

There are indeed a number of different ways in which economic security can be understood, and Buzan himself, while favoring the widening of the security agenda, has been skeptical about the likelihood of clearly defining "economic security," as has Giacomo Luciani (1989). Moreover, while the 1990s produced a large literature on "economic" security, much of it was merely promoting the concept of "geoeconomics" as an adjunct to neorealist military security theory.

Buzan and the Copenhagen school have argued that the contending camps in the economic security debate can be divided into three groups. However, their categorization is not particularly helpful in appreciating the way contending approaches to economic security have played themselves out since the end of the Cold War. This approach divides the economic security debate into the views of the mercantilists, the liberals, and the socialists. Mercantilists are those who prioritize politics and see the state as the key actor, providing the necessary security for the operation of firms and markets. The economic realm is self-contained and the role of the state is simply to protect the state's frontiers and regulate a secure internal market and pursue an external environment where business can operate efficiently. Economic liberals, in contrast, are seen as putting economics first and believe that the market should operate as free from state interference as possible. The state here is seen in a minimalist perspective, required only to provide law and external military protection and to support the social fabric in a strictly limited number of areas where the market fails to do so.

The final group are the socialists, who, following Karl Marx, argue that economics underpins the entire social and political reality and that states should therefore interfere in and organize the economic system in order to direct its results toward achieving the social and political goals of justice and equality. In this perspective there is a security bias toward advancing the interests of the economically weak as against the strong.

Both mercantilism and socialism are types of economic nationalism, but the historical reality is that the outcome of the Cold War left the values of economic liberalism dominant. Together with accelerating processes of globalization (Sheehan, 1996b), this has increasingly shaped a world characterized by a global economy underpinned by liberal market values, with the emphasis on achieving a situation where there are as few restraints as possible on the movement of goods, capital, services, and people.

For the foreseeable future, it will be the liberal agenda that dominates the debates on what economic security is, and its place within the broader meaning of security itself. From the liberal perpective, the emphasis is on achieving an unfettered international market, but there is also a recognition that pursuing the liberal agenda creates major social and political difficulties for developing and transition states and that the problem of the widening gap between the rich states and the very poor states needs to be addressed. This is reflected in the economic agenda of human security. It is important to recognize that the triumph of the West has also put capitalism on trial. For the failure of the liberal market system to provide security for millions of the world's poor must be laid at the feet of a global economic system that is currently unchallenged.

In the context of a broadened approach to security, the concept of economic security opens up a number of crucial areas of international relations to analysis within the security context. However, it is important to raise a number of significant challenges here, without necessarily condemning economic security totally as an analytical tool.

On the negative side, "economic security" is a phrase that covers a multitude of sins. Much of the economic security agenda is a neorealist research program with no novel or radical content whatsoever. Moreover, economic analysis is usually grounded in the same positivist methodology that has proven so problematic in international relations and security studies. In both the theory and the practice of international economics there has been a commitment to statist scientism that has been profoundly damaging to the interests of the world's poor. On the positive side there are elements of the economic security spectrum, at the human security end, that open up the understanding of security dramatically, but in order to clarify them it is necessary to develop an alternative conceptualization of the economic security spectrum.

There are at least four quite distinct ways in which economic security has come to be analyzed since the end of the Cold War. The first is the traditional historical sense in which it is recognized that economic strength is generally a necessary prerequisite for military power. Vincent Cable further subdivides this category into those elements relevant to a state's ability to defend itself and those needed for power projection (1995: 306–307).

This category overlaps with the idea of economic instruments of foreign policy more generally. J. Kirschner (1988) discusses the use of such economic instruments for the purposes of coercion and punishment, influence, and dependence creation. The volume of goods, services, resources, and capital traded internationally continues to grow, and because of the existence of economic interdependencies this creates opportunities for political leverage. Techniques such as trade embargoes, quotas, most-favored-nation status, foreign aid, and so on, can be used as both rewards and punishments to induce favorable policies in other states and, as punishments, may be employed as a first resort against states with which a government is in dispute. For four decades, for example, the member states of the North Atlantic Treaty Organization (NATO) alliance imposed a comprehensive embargo on goods that might be of military use to the Soviet Union or China. Similarly, after Fidel Castro came to power in Cuba, the United States used a wide range of restrictive economic instruments in an effort to encourage the Cuban government to modify its policies. This category embraces the various kinds of economic sanctions, which involve the deliberate interference with the economy of another state in order to coercively enforce its compliance. The purpose of the sanctions is to produce economic deprivation in the target state, thereby triggering political resentment and protest against the government (Oudraat, 2000: 105). A relevant consideration vis-à-vis the issue of human security is that such sanctions may have a seriously detrimental effect on the lives and well-being of the ordinary people of a country, without necessarily triggering the desired policy change from their government. This was clearly the case with the economic sanctions imposed on Iraq during the 1990s.

The second version of economic security as an approach is the neo-Darwinist approach of the "geoeconomics" school, which identifies threats and enemies in the international economic environment. Third, there are those whose focus is on "human security" or emancipation and who emphasize the idea of human welfare needs as a security issue in itself, rather than an adjunct to a military security agenda. Finally, there are those whose emphasis is on the argument that war and conflict in postmodern international relations is diminished by the positive effects of economic development and economic integration. There is clearly scope for a novel approach to economic security, but the degree to which it is realizable within these alternative conceptualizations depends crucially upon whether the state or the human being is seen as being the referent object of security. Economic security can simply mean new economic threats to the political and military integrity of the state, or it can refer to economic vulnerabilities imposed on populations by the workings of the market system.

The Defense Industrial Base

The 1990s saw a revival of a concept that had been prominent in the early Cold War period and that itself reflected a much older way of thinking about the relationship between the economy and security; this was the so-called, defense industrial base. In its pre-twentieth-century form, this approach simply reflected the truism that military spending has to be sustained by an economy that is generating the necessary financial resources. By the twentieth century, with the industrialization of warfare, the concept was expanded to embrace the idea that a national economy also needed to include an industrial infrastructure capable of producing the matériel of modern warfare in large quantities. For the developed states this meant a capability to produce weapons such as fighter and bomber aircraft, tanks, self-propelled guns, missiles, submarines, and large warships.

While these issues were debated during the 1990s under the "economic security" rubric, they do not really reflect the idea of economic security as a distinctive domain. Rather, they are simply part of a traditional military security agenda, where there is a concern that a national economy might fail to produce the necessities required to equip sufficiently powerful armed forces.

The technological element of this problem has been described as the "economic security dilemma." This is deemed to arise out of the paradoxical situation that for certain highly advanced states, there is a perception that while military *threats* have been reduced in the new world economic order, fears of economic vulnerability have actually increased (Crawford, 1995). This is because in the modern, high-technology, globalized economy, states find it increasingly difficult to procure everything they need militarily through national production. For many highly advanced technologies, the production source lies abroad and not necessarily in companies owned or operated by one's own nationals.

Richard Rosecrance has described as "virtual states" those countries that have transferred much of their manufacturing capability abroad in order to benefit from lower labor costs and to concentrate on high-level services at home (2002: 443). Every advanced industrial state has moved in this direction to a greater or lesser extent as domestic labor costs have escalated. While this suggests that states would become less secure as they become more vulnerable to potential disruptions of crucial supplies, Rosecrance argues contrarily that, in an increasingly interdependent world, potential rivals will not be able to exploit such security vulnerabilities, because they will themselves be adopting the same strategy and exposing themselves to the same vulnerabilities as the existing "virtual" states.

Nevertheless, in the specific area of defense production, such fears have become evident. As countries such as the United States become increasingly dependent for supply of crucial military components on countries such as Japan, so there is a growing sense of vulnerability. Allocation of these important goods and services is driven by international market forces. As globalization accelerates this trend, states become materially dependent on essential production over which they have little or no control. They are therefore made vulnerable to the effects of any disruption in the flow of raw materials, goods, and services. But as Buzan notes, market forces do not operate with national security concerns in mind; they are about the maximization of profit in a highly competitive supply-and-demand situation. Firms that are inefficient in these terms may become extinct, no matter the sophistication of their product or its importance to the armed forces of another state (Buzan, 1991a: 124–131). Not surprisingly, the modern state feels nervous about leaving its vital military security function to the vagaries of the marketplace (Crawford, 1995: 154).

To the extent that the link between economics and security has been theorized in the past, it has tended to be in these terms—as a straightforward assumption that a country's security was affected by its ability to generate sufficient economic growth to enable it to purchase the quantity and quality of armed forces it deemed necessary to protect its interests, and also that it required access to certain resources and markets beyond its own borders. Even this basic assumption did not go entirely unchallenged. Charles Schultze argued in the middle of the Cold War that, in fact, U.S. military strength was not dependent to any significant degree on the size or growth rate of the U.S. economy, that the U.S. economy was not dependent on a healthy defense sector, and that overseas markets and resources were not significant for the United States either (1972–1973: 523). As a result, considerations of this kind ought not to underpin U.S. foreign and defense policy. What was more important, it was argued, was the manner in which the United States conducted its trade and financial relationships with other states, so as to be a positive and stabilizing factor in the international economy generally.

Between 1945 and 1990 the field of security studies did not make the link between economic interdependence and national security. For all intents and purposes, it focused on strategy, on the problem of war, and more generally, on the threat, use, and control of military force. National security was seen as a specifically limited field and was the responsibility of the state. Although interdependence was recognized as restricting the autonomy of the state in various areas, there was a presumption that the military sector remained unaffected because states saw this as a crucial national responsibility. Until the end of the Cold War this did in fact remain largely the case. The most powerful states produced what they needed themselves and those concerned by national military deficiencies sought the benefits of joining military alliances such as NATO. Market forces did not play a major part.

By the closing years of the Cold War the concept of the "defense industrial base" was being revived. This was defined as "any good, service component or input to the national economy necessary to the security interests of the state" (Crawford, 1995: 160). In this definition, "security" is clearly understood in the limited military sense of the word.

For the countries that rely on the most advanced military technologies to meet their military security requirements, a particular problem is that much of the necessary technology is no longer specifically military in application or origin. Microchip technology, for example, is produced by civilian industries for an overwhelmingly civilian market, but such technologies are crucially important for modern advanced weapons and sensor technologies. This means that, in effect, military technology is being traded freely on the international market.

Moreover, it is precisely these forms of advanced military technologies that are seen as the basis of contemporary military power. Merely possessing very large armed forces is no longer sufficient; it is the quality of the technologies with which these forces are equipped that now determines their military effectiveness and their political utility. In the same way, it is the most advanced civilian technologies that define the world's leading economic powers; and economic capability, by generating resources, underpins military capability in a more general sense. Thus it can be argued that countries such as Japan, with advanced high-technology economies that produce crucial military components for the armed forces of other countries, are becoming increasingly powerful. Therefore, states in the "economic security dilemma" see a decline in the threats they face, because of global political developments and the relative military superiority conferred on them by their advanced military systems. Yet at the same time they feel more vulnerable, because those systems depend on components whose external production is beyond their absolute control. For neorealists, "there is a legitimate concern about American vulnerability as local industries crucial to defense disappear, and high-tech firms are acquired by foreigners" (Moran, 1990–1991: 80–81).

States can try to counter this vulnerability by supporting their own defense industries. However, this may weaken overall economic and technological competitiveness by diverting intellectual talent into the defense industrial sector. In addition, the products of these national programs may be under national control, but may be technologically inferior to alternatives that could have been procured on the international market.

The scale of this threat can be exaggerated. In many cases, there may be a number of competing producers of the same or similar products, with all or most of them located in states that are friendly to one's own. In this case the national security threat is minimal and any economic response, if needed, can be channeled into areas where a genuine concern might exist.

By including thinking of this kind, the width of the debate and analysis of economic security is made to seem broader than it actually is. Arguments of the sort noted above are simply refined versions of an aspect of traditional military security logic that has existed for a considerable period.

Geoeconomics

Another perspective on the relationship between economics and security that has emerged in the post–Cold War period has been described as geoeconomics, and as "an economic agenda for neo-realists" (Moran, 1993). Governments do not always see economic growth purely in terms of its likely effect on the well-being of their citizens. Economic capability is itself an instrument of policy available to states and is capable of being applied as a force.

The Cold War period had been characterized by military confrontation, arms races, and security paranoia, and much of the time by a zero-sum outlook. In the post–Cold War period, many realists, confronting an obvious reduction in measurable *military* threats and confrontations, simply transferred their mind-set to the economic domain. Samuel Huntington stated that "in a world in which military conflict between major states is unlikely, economic power will be increasingly important in determining the primacy or subordination of states" (1993: 72). This is at first sight a statement that seems uncontroversial. In the absence of military confrontation, economic criteria will primarily determine the pecking order in the international community.

For the geoeconomics school, however, the implications are deeper and more sinister. Economic competition is envisaged as a war fought with other tools. Huntington constantly uses military metaphors in his discussion of the trading relationship between Japan and the United States. Thus, "Japanese strategy is a strategy of economic warfare. . . . Japanese strategy, behavior and declarations all point to the existence of a Cold War between Japan and the United States" (1993: 76). In the geoeconomic perspective, a trade deficit is intrinsically undesirable not because of its domestic employment effects, but because the state becomes dependent on the imports of goods and money and therefore vulnerable to foreign threats.

For economic "hawks" the post–Cold War era has not meant the end of the fundamentally antagonistic basis of interstate relations. States are seen as continuing to measure their relative military power against that of other states, and continue to want to minimize their strategic dependence on resources controlled by other states. Under this logic also, economic interdependence is not something to be welcomed, because the more intertwined the economic destinies of states are, the less individual states are in a position to dominate outcomes.

There are particular concerns with the possibilities of economic dependencies within the global market and security of supply generally, particularly when they relate to products such as oil, whose levels of production and distribution can be manipulated for political purposes. Geoeconomic thinking encourages the idea that international trade is a zero-sum conflict and emphasizes factors that relate to the "threat" of relative economic decline vis-à-vis other countries, rather than a concern with the national welfare effects of absolute economic performance.

At the center of this perspective is a continuing adherence to the idea of the state as the focus of analysis, and of trade and financial movements being seen in almost zero-sum terms. It is the health of the state and its economic and political structures that is the cause for analytical concern, rather than the existential well-being of the human beings who compose the state's population.

In relation to international politics, it is a perspective with significant policy implications, since it promotes economic confrontation and protectionism. It would weaken the security of states with transitional economies in the former communist world, by denying them the opportunity to exploit their relative advantages in order to achieve sustainable economic growth. In addition, it would place additional obstacles in the way of developing states attempting to close the gap with the West, thereby perpetuating international poverty and injustice.

Economic Integration and Conflict

Economic security, as with all the security sectors, is not a free-standing and clearly distinctive security domain. It overlaps with various other approaches to security and to methods of reducing insecurity, including societal security and efforts at regional economic integration. However, while such effects are usually seen as security-building if successful, there are analysts who have questioned whether this is in fact the case.

Some have suggested that international interdependence threatens national security in ways that are indirect and not easily countered by military force (Ullman, 1983). If the idea of security is expanded to embrace both territorial integrity and societal well-being, then interdependence can be seen as threatening national security.

Interdependence necessarily erodes the absolute autonomy of states and therefore their capacity to maintain territorial integrity. However, it is possible for interdependence to enhance the security of society, in the sense of societal well-being, even as it undermines the autonomy and capacity of the state as an institution and a political actor. For example, considerable levels of high-technology foreign investment in a country might encourage technological innovation and provide well-paid employment—but at the potential cost to the host state of loss of control over strategic parts of its economy.

The idea of complex interdependence reinforces the need to distinguish between the security of the state and the security of society. Policy-oriented debates about the redefinition of security tend to overlook this point, since they continue to characterize economic security largely in terms of a state's ability to marshal resources in order to counter specifically military threats. But the ability to make a meaningful distinction between society and the state is central to broader approaches to security.

Economic "doves" take issue with the idea that interdependence should be seen as having a negative impact on security. In contrast, they suggest a number of ways in which it might increase international cooperation and stability and reduce potential military threats. Keohane and Nye argue that economic interdependence among advanced industrial states can minimize threats directly by reducing the incentives to use force against each other in settling disputes (1977: 27–29). When economic well-being is tied up in complex linkages with other states, then disrupting those linkages through the resort to force imposes considerable social and economic costs. The more integrated the economies are, the higher the potential costs involved in disruption.

Second, states have created international regimes in order to better manage their international trading relations. The rules and procedures of these regimes enforce the norm of reciprocity and ensure a convergence of expectations that can lead to compromise. Governments know that if their own country acquires a reputation for failing to live up to its international legal obligations, then this will make it difficult to conclude future agreements with other states, will threaten their continuing adherence to agreements that are highly valued by one's own state, and may impact upon other important aspects of relations with other states. This encourages the pursuit of compromise.

Globalization of production and exchange increases competition and makes the factors of production more mobile. Governments are aware that companies invest and establish themselves where their costs are lowest, where an appropriate work force is available, and where the country concerned is seen as being politically and economically stable. Investment tends to shy away from war zones and from unstable countries. Again, this encourages states to pursue nonviolent compromise in their dealings with neighboring countries. The key to economic success is no longer territory, or traditional heavy industry; rather it is technological innovation and knowledge-based production. This also reduces incentives for territorial expansion and aggression.

Globalization of production and technology has internationalized the Cold War defense industries. David Held and Anthony McGrew note that with the increase in licensing, coproduction agreements, joint ventures, corporate alliances, and subcontracting, institutions of defense have been shifted from state to multinational control with few countries laying claim to having a "wholly autonomous military production capacity" (2001: 12).

The interdependence-generating effects of the global international economy may seem positive from various perspectives, but they are clearly threatening to regimes that have sought to maintain themselves through economic autarchy, and the responses of those regimes to this situation may have negative security consequences. The classic example of this dilemma is North Korea, whose government sees no possibility of the current authoritarian communist regime surviving if the country were to be fully exposed to the workings of the liberal international economy. In trying to increase its domestic legitimacy in the face of this challenge, it has increasingly turned to an aggressive form of nationalism and cultural chauvinism in order to sustain itself (Zoellick, 1997: 42).

The evolution of the international economy and simultaneous opening up of the debate about what constitutes security raises one other candidate for inclusion in this category: the effects of transnational organized crime. As with multinational corporations in the interdependence context, transnational criminal organizations can be seen as important nonstate actors within the economic security framework. This is a result of their involvement in various forms of illegal trade, particularly in weapons and drugs. Whereas nineteenth- and twentieth-century economic liberals always welcomed the increased freedom of international trade as inevitably representing a positive force in historical development, globalization has "facilitated the movement of dirty money, as well as the transportation of drugs, counterfeit goods, arms, illegal aliens and nuclear material" (Godson and Williams, 1998: 67). These can be seen as representing threats to security at all levels, from the individual to the stability of the international system. They also impact upon various elements of the broader security agenda. Fears about illegal aliens and their alleged links with organized crime can trigger national resentment of legal immigration of ethnic or other minorities, for example, producing societal security problems within states.

Human Security

The 1990s saw the end of the Cold War, which had dominated the previous half century. The Cold War as an epiphenomenon had many guises, but it represented, among many other things, a competition between major powers with very different economic systems. The end of the Cold War has been portrayed as the "end of history" in the sense that it represented the final triumph of liberal democracy. While this is clearly a fundamentally flawed thesis, since it posits an ahistorical telos for a species whose fundamental characteristic is evolutionary change, nevertheless it is significant. In the contemporary world, human populations are enmeshed in the psychological and physical structures of liberal capitalism, and will remain so enmeshed in the foreseeable future. The destiny of most of the planet's human population is therefore dependent upon the advantages and disadvantages of this particular way of organizing national and regional economies. Capitalism is a social invention, a way of organizing economic life that produces winners and losers. The central issue is, who are the losers under this system, how far is this a clear "security" issue, and what can be done to increase security within this paradigm?

Poverty, and the problem of global development, can be seen as a security issue both in its own right and because it may lie behind many conflicts. Most modern conflicts take place within states, rather than between them, so that internal explanations become crucial. If security is to be defined on an existential basis, then it is clearly legitimate to understand economic security in terms of basic human needs. An individual's survival and development as a human being is crucially dependent upon the provision of certain basic needs for sustaining life, such as adequate food, water, clothing, shelter, education, and healthcare.

This is important because in many areas of the world the prevailing economic orthodoxies, as implemented by organizations such as the International Monetary Fund (IMF) and World Bank, seem to have operated in a manner that has not only failed to advance emancipation, but has actually had the opposite effect. The structural adjustment programs imposed on many developing countries have resulted in rising unemployment, falling healthcare and welfare provision, and a general decline in living standards and opportunities.

"Food security" and calls to eradicate mass starvation are clearly within the realm of meeting basic human needs, as is disaster relief. Other issues may or may not be, depending on their severity, the number of people affected, and the impact on other sectors of the security agenda. Thus, for example, issues such as relative welfare levels or unemployment in developed states may matter vitally to individuals, and so to societies, but in economic security terms they are not (usually) about existential survival.

However, the scale of such problems might threaten economic, social, or political collapse and place these problems on the economic security agenda. European security in the early 1990s appeared more at threat from such issues than from the traditional military agenda, with economic crisis being identified as the most immediate danger to most central and eastern European states and threatening to open the way to authoritarian and belligerent governments.

Economic security is also clearly relevant in the poverty issue area if we accept Galtung's concept of "structural violence"; or, as Senator Robert F.

Kennedy once put it, "there is another kind of violence in its way as destructive as the bullet or the bomb. This is the violence of institutions; indifference, inaction and slow decay. This is the violence that afflicts the poor . . . this is the slow destruction of a child by hunger, and schools without books and homes without heat in the winter" (Kennedy, 1998: 59). The United Nations came to a similar conclusion a quarter of a century later, declaring in 1994 that "in the final analysis human security is a child who did not die, a disease that did not spread, a job that was not cut, an ethnic tension that did not explode in violence, a dissident who was not silenced" (United Nations Development Programme, 1995: 229).

Implicit in the poverty-related element of economic security is the "Kantian idea that we should treat people as ends and not means. States however, should be treated as means, not ends" (Booth, 1991b: 319). In this perspective, security is viewed holistically and the linkages between different elements are emphasized—"for people, states and the global community there will be no predictable peace without justice, no justice without security and no permanent security without peace" (Booth, 1991a: 342).

Since 1945 the world has seen unprecedented economic development, yet almost one-third of the planet's human population live in conditions of abject poverty and over 14 million people die of hunger each year. In the majority of third world countries the main security threats take the form of issues such as population growth, social instability, disease, lack of proper healthcare, and inadequate access to drinking water. The United Nations in the post–Cold War era has argued that true human security has a military dimension, but also has, and has always had, an equally important nonmilitary dimension. Human security requires both freedom from fear and freedom from want. And in vast areas of the world, the workings of the international economy impose structural violence by denying access to basic needs. "If security is defined broadly to incorporate threats to safety, then the majority of humankind is obviously highly insecure in the sense that the global political economy renders so many vulnerable" (Dalby, 1992: 104).

Many of these problems do not reflect an absolute lack of resources. Global hunger and starvation, for example, continues to exist despite the fact that the countries of the world actually produce enough grain to provide every person on Earth with 3,400 calories a day. And this does not take into account production levels of other commonly eaten foodstuffs such as vegetables, beans, nuts, root crops, fruits, meat, and fish. Taken together, these could provide over forty pounds of food per person, per day. Global hunger is the result of lack of access and maldistribution of food, not the result of an absolute shortage of food as such.

Governments and international organizations operate with a specific view of what poverty consists of, what factors contribute to it, and what methods are most like to ameliorate it. In the Western, capitalist worldview, what defines poverty is the working of the cash economy and the ability or inability of people to purchase adequate quantities of food and other necessities. The impact of Westernization and globalization has led to this conception of poverty becoming universalized. Ideas like poverty and development reflect particular ways of thinking about reality and social values, and are ideological constructions that have crucial political effects.

During the 1970s, developing countries borrowed heavily in order to achieve high levels of economic growth. However, in the 1980s and 1990s they suffered badly as interest rates on loans rose, while commodity prices fell. The IMF and World Bank responded with policies of structural adjustment lending designed to encourage third world states to emphasize market-oriented policies and open up to foreign investment. The policy achieved Western governments' goal of preventing wide-scale debt defaulting, but the price paid by the populations of many developing countries was devastating. Government spending cutbacks on healthcare, education, agriculture, social welfare, and so on, all impacted hardest on the poorest and most vulnerable groups in society.

The treatment of security in the West during the Cold War era was dominated by U.S. perceptions of what was, and was not, a security threat. Yet the Cold War itself, though often described as the struggle between East and West, was largely fought out in the battleground of the uncommitted South, "where the poor and underdeveloped countries were rendered as a security threat as soon as questions of unrestricted US access to their resources were raised" (Dalby, 1992: 100).

Perceptions of the first world–third world relationship invariably assume a flow of wealth from the former to the latter. Yet the reality is the opposite. There is a massive flow of wealth each year from the poor to the rich. The enormous debt burdens borne by many third world states seriously threaten their internal stability. By the late 1990s it was increasingly recognized that economic growth reduces poverty only if accompanied by specific economic and social policies directed to that end, and it was these policies that were absent.

Provision of food is a vital element in the security of third world countries. If countries are dependent on tied aid or international charity for a commodity so basic and essential as food, then there is little real sense in which they or their populations can be said to be secure.

The traditional explanation of global hunger relates the available food supply to population growth. The human population of the planet is continuing to grow very rapidly. In 1991 it was around 5.4 billion. By 2002 it had reached 6.2 billion and by 2050 it is expected to reach 10 billion. The world's human population will have doubled in less than a century, and over half of the increase will be concentrated in only seven countries—Bangladesh, Brazil, China, India, Indonesia, Nigeria, and Pakistan.

From a food security perspective, one very notable fact is that, notwithstanding the increase in human population, there has been a simultaneously massive increase in per capita food production, which has made little impact on the enormous numbers of people in the world who experience chronic hunger. The third world, where the majority of the planet's starving people are found, also produces much of the world's food, while those who consume it are located in the developed West. Countries like China and India, despite their enormous agricultural outputs, consume far less grain and livestock products per capita than do Italy and the United States. Such evidence leads critics of the orthodox approach to poverty and food security to argue that we need to look much more closely at the social, economic, and political factors that determine how food is distributed and why it is that access to food is achieved by some and denied to others.

Amartyn Sen's research into the causes of famines concluded that "hunger is due to people not having enough to eat, rather than there not being enough to eat." He found that famines have frequently taken place when there has been no significant reduction in per capita food availability and that some famines have occurred during years of peak food availability. For example, the Bangladesh famine of 1974 occurred in a year of maximum food availability, but because floods left many rural laborers unemployed, they could not afford to buy the available food, and huge numbers therefore starved. It was the cash economy that killed them, not a shortage of food as such. Thus, what determines whether somebody eats their fill or starves is not a question of the amount of available food, but whether or not they can establish an entitlement to that food. The key, therefore, is not food availability, but the distribution of food. In the contemporary world, purchasing power is what determines this entitlement, and this gives rise to a reality in which many "will go hungry amidst a world of plenty" (Sen, 1981: 193).

This distinction between the tangible elements required for someone to survive and be secure, such as food, clothing, education, and so on, and the ability to pay for them in a globalized market economy, is reflected in the UN approach. The United Nations makes a distinction between "income poverty" and "human poverty," with the former relating to monetary measures of poverty and the latter to the tangible elements needed for an adequate quality of existence.

Bangladesh is a country that exemplifies many of these human economic security issues. With a population of more than 125 million, it is one of the most densely populated countries in the world (Kamaluddin, 2000). About 49 percent of the total population are defined by the United Nations as living in absolute poverty. Twenty-two million people live in urban areas and 50 percent of them live in poverty. Twenty percent of children never receive any formal education of any kind. In Bangladesh, 30,000 children go blind each year because of vitamin A deficiency and lack of pure drinking water. Of the twenty poorest countries in the world, Bangladesh has the largest number of poor people (93 million). Yet there are forty-three countries in the world even poorer than Bangladesh. The low income of the poor makes it impossible to procure necessary food for themselves or for their dependants. Healthcare facilities are inadequate and are concentrated in the large urban areas. Thousands of children die each day from preventable diseases. About 55 percent of children under age five are moderately or severely malnourished. Anemia caused by malnutrition affects 77 percent of pregnant and lactating mothers (Kamaluddin, 2000: 4). Yet Bangladesh is a fertile country with rich fisheries. In 1999 it produced more than 22 million tons of food grains, enough to make it self-sufficient in terms of food quantity.

Nevertheless, two-thirds of the population are malnourished. The causes of food insecurity in Bangladesh include unequal distribution of wealth, lack of access to food and resources, lack of purchasing capacity and job opportunities, the transformation of croplands into industrial zones and housing, government policies that favor a small, privileged elite, and international influence that prioritizes debt repayment rather than human welfare.

Bangladesh has no significant border disputes, has no neighbors that aspire to control its territory, has no significant insurgency, and is not targeted by nuclear weapons. Under the traditional realist definition, the population of Bangladesh enjoy enormous security. Even with a focus on the economic dimensions of security, such as the traditional "defense industrial base" approach, Bangladesh might appear secure, since its weaknesses in terms of national defense production are offset by a low level of military threats. But such an assessment flies in the face of the human reality.

Conclusion

What the case of Bangladesh, and many other poorer countries, demonstrates is the need to exercise a degree of caution in assessing the literature on economic security. Economic security is an important element in the broader definition of security.

But economic security is a broad church. There are many different ways of interpreting and operationalizing this idea. Even a cursory analysis of these approaches makes it clear that while economic security can be deemed a part of a broader security analysis, this is true only if there are boundaries placed between the various economic security approaches.

The traditional manner of linking economic issues to security, whether in terms of the defense industrial base or in terms of economic instruments of foreign policy (such as the various forms of economic sanctions), is merely a subset of the orthodox realist approach to security that prevailed during the Cold War era. The same is true of geoeconomics, which is likewise emerging from the realist worldview and simply substituting economic for military terminology.

The interdependence school can make more of a claim for inclusion within a broader security perspective. There is clearly a sense in which this approach acts as a major critique of the two earlier economic security approaches. However, it is also the case that much of this literature self-consciously attempts to relate its arguments to the traditional military security agenda, in order to argue that interdependence has a confidence- and security-building aspect in relation to the dangers of the resort to force in international relations. Moreover, liberalism, while it has some minor ontological differences with realism, also shares a great deal of its worldview, and epistemologically is essentially identical to realism. In addition, since its proponents are wedded to the virtues of the liberal market economy system, they have found it difficult to react positively to the flaws in that system evidenced by the enormous structural disparities within the global economy and the scandalous levels of poverty it sustains.

It is thus only the "human security" approach to economic security that can be placed unambiguously in the broader security domain. The meeting of basic human material needs must logically be considered the starting point for any meaningful understanding of human security. As noted in Chapter 1, realism argues that the securing of the independence of the state must take priority over other social objectives, because otherwise a state and people are not at liberty to decide what goals they wish to prioritize. By the same logic, unless a human being's basic existential survival needs are met, all other considerations become moot, so that the human security dimension clearly needs to be placed at the center of a meaningful concept of security. For societies that call themselves civilized, it is also important that human security is not pursued simply in terms of providing the minimum necessary for a person to physically survive. Quality of life is important and the standard aimed at must be much higher than basic survival if people are to be able to play their part as full members of society.

SIX

Societal Security

Of the various security domains identified by Barry Buzan in his 1983 book *People, States, and Fear,* societal security initially received far less attention than other areas such as economic and environmental security. Yet the realities of the nature of conflict in the post–Cold War world, particularly in Europe and Africa, raised societal security concerns to the forefront of the international security agenda. Societal security has been defined by Buzan as "the sustainability, within conditions for evolution, of traditional patterns of language, culture and religious and national identity and custom" (Buzan, Waever, and De Wilde, 1998: 8). As a security sector, societal security suffers from weaknesses similar to those affecting other sectors such as the economic and environmental. It clearly expands the concept of security away from the traditional state-centric military interpretation, but it is not necessarily a radical break. It is capable of being interpreted and employed through a neorealist perspective, and when the model of society employed is an objectivist, one-dimensional one, it has limitations similar to the state-centric model.

The logic of exploring the societal dimension points toward an approach to security that is grounded on the individual. This lends itself to a radical rethinking of security, but at the same time, the particular way in which the societal security agenda has been interpreted and operationalized since 1990 also demonstrates the dangers involved in the broadening exercise, as exemplified by the securitization of the migration issue. Societal security is seen as being closely related to, but distinct from, political security, which in Buzan's schema is about the organizational stability of states and of systems of government protection and sustenance, and the ideologies that give governments and states their legitimacy.

In the contemporary international system it is only rarely that state and societal boundaries are identical. Examples are Iceland and Portugal. Even countries like Japan and Italy, which are unusually homogeneous, have small national minorities. In the rest of the international system the more usual pattern is the existence of various minorities within states. This is one reason for taking societal security seriously. It provides a way of thinking about security issues when the referent object is not the state, but rather a people, whose boundaries may cross two or more states—for example, the Kurdish people, who are found in large numbers in Turkey, Iraq, Iran, and Syria. Or they may be fully contained within a particular country, but represent a minority of that state's population.

Even when the state and the society of the same people have the same boundaries, they are not the same thing and generate two different logics of security. The state is an administrative structure, based on fixed territory and formal membership. Society in contrast, is about identity, the way that communities think about and define themselves and the way that individuals identify themselves as members of a particular community. Societal insecurity exists when communities of whatever kind define a development or potentiality as a threat to their survival *as a community.* Ole Waever argues that a striking but largely unremarked change in the European security problematic after the end of the Cold War was "a change in forms of community as referents of the security discourse—away from 'state' and towards 'nation'" (1995a: 404). It is therefore perfectly possible for the state to remain secure in a military and political sense, and yet for a significant degree of subjective societal insecurity to exist. Iranians, for example, might feel that the Iranian state is secure, but that their Islamic values and belief-system are under threat from the challenge of Western cultural imperialism.

The particular society does not need to be as large as that of the Kurds. Societal security is about large, self-sustaining identity groups. What these actually might be varies in both time and space. It could be national groups, but might just as easily be religious, racial, or other groupings. The concept could therefore also be understood as "identity security." Identity communities are self-constructed "imagined communities" (Anderson, 1989). Objective factors such as language or location might be involved in the construction of identity, but it nevertheless remains a personal and political choice to identify with some community by emphasizing some factor or factors in contrast to others, particularly when more than one option is available, or when there are political pressures *not* to identify with a particular group. Waever refers to societal security as being "security analysis in the field of cultural identity" (1995a: 395).

There is a problem here, which is highlighted by Bill McSweeney. Buzan and Waever bring forward the concept of "societal" security in order to achieve a number of objectives. One of these is to move away from a purely state-centric conception of security, and allow for the fact that the referent actor of security threats is not always, or even often, going to be the state as such. A second objective was to provide purchase on a crucial part of the international agenda in the 1990s. In most of the conflicts that characterized that decade, traditional state-to-state military conflict was not the essence of the problems that the international community found itself being mobilized to take action on. Invariably it was state disintegration, civil war, and insurgencies of various kinds. In many cases what was being contested was not the control of a particular state's levers of power, but rather the identity of that state and the shape of its borders. The conflict was societal rather than state-centric and this type of insecurity manifested itself in the Baltic republics, the former Yugoslavia, Moldava, Sri Lanka, Kurdistan, Central Africa, and elsewhere. What this situation clearly required, therefore, was a view of security that was more nuanced and could explain how conflict could arise within societies between majorities and minorities, between groups with different conceptions of what the cultural and historical icons of "the nation" should be, or the values that should underpin it, and whose arguments might be applicable across the borders of more than one state.

One of the criticisms that can be leveled at classical approaches to security is not just that they were overly state-centric, but that they also operated with a one-dimensional understanding of the state. The state was seen as the central actor in the security field throughout recorded history and little attention was paid to the reality of the state in different eras. The nature of the entity about which Thucydides wrote when he analyzed the struggle between Athens and Sparta was very different from the Soviet and U.S. states during the Cold War, or from the Roman, Napoleonic, or Habsburg empires. The differences between forms of state in different historical epochs is important in understanding how the security problematic was constructed for those particular actors and the instruments available to them for addressing it. Operating with an unsophisticated model of the state is a major constraint in understanding and explaining the dynamics of international security.

However the Buzan/Waever development of "societal" security is not entirely successful, because it can be accused of making the same mistake with society that was earlier made with the state—that is, to treat it as a single, fully formed, unproblematic entity. So threats to society are identified, which that society can respond to in various ways. Waever's conception of society draws on Ferdinand Tonnies's classic distinction between *gemeinschaft* (an organic sense of community) and *gesellschaft* (a contractual sense), but it is not always clear in which sense Waever understands "society" in relation to his use of the societal security concept. However, the fact that he refers to the existence of a "societal security dilemma" (1989: 190) suggests that society is being seen as a highly coherent, organic entity.

Martin Shaw (1993) also criticizes Waever's work on societal security, on the grounds that the model of society used was a simplistic Durkheimian one that places far too much stress on the assumed existence of a coherent national identity. A further criticism made by McSweeney is that Buzan's idea of "sedimented structure" is effectively applied as much to the idea of society as it is to the state. "Society is conceived as a social fact, with the same objectivity and ontological status as the state" (McSweeney, 1996: 90). In reality, society is as fluid and intersubjectively constituted as is security itself. The same is true of the identities related to it. Societal security is therefore a much more problematic and plastic reality than is allowed for in the Copenhagen school's approach. In addition, the idea of identity being pluralistic or contested is not prominent in this approach. A society's identity is seen as being capable of being threatened as if its nature is stable and singular.

In defense of the Copenhagen school, it should be pointed out that to introduce the societal security concept at all represents a step forward, and a means by which additional forms of insecurity can be explored. That the concept was not fully developed in its initial incarnation is hardly surprising, and it therefore gains from the insights of the critics who note the way that society itself needs to be broken down for the purposes of analysis. This does not invalidate the idea of taking society and culture as a point of departure in terms of identifying referents for security in contradistinction to the state. Society is a fairly flexible concept. The advantage of the Buzan/Waever contribution is that it enables a number of new issues to be analyzed as issues of security.

Threats to identity are always a question of the construction of something as threatening some "we/us." This often contributes to the construction or reproduction of "us." It can be argued that some societies have defined themselves as much by what they are not as by what they are—for example, Poland and Scotland, whose identities are strengthened by the effort to avoid becoming overwhelmed by a powerful neighboring culture. Indeed, as will be discussed in Chapter 9, in David Campbell's poststructuralist analysis (1992), U.S. foreign and defense policy are seen as playing a crucial role in creating the very identity they defend.

Any "we" identity can be constructed in many different ways, and often the main issue that decides whether security conflicts will emerge is whether one or another self-definition wins out in a society. To engage in self-redefinition will in many cases be an important security strategy—for example, Slovenia, which successfully redefined itself as a central European rather than a Balkan country in order that its image might become like that of the settled and stable central European states, or Mozambique, which became a member of the British commonwealth, despite having no history as a British colony. The preference of states like Libya to be referred to as "southern Mediterranean" rather than "North African" springs from a similar desire to project one kind of identity rather than another.

Limitations of the Objectivist Model

One problem with the analysis of identity politics within the societal security model is that the nature of the relationship between society and identity is not always clear. Waever, for example, argues that a nation, as distinct from a state, "will only allow integration when it is secure that its national identity will not be threatened" (1995a: 404). This suggests a Durkheimian image of a homogeneous people. Indeed, elsewhere Waever stresses that his approach is founded upon a Durkheimian conception of society that is a *sui generis* phenomenon (1995b: 67). But Waever goes on immediately to argue that if its identity is secure, "it may even be strengthened by its exposure to different identities" (1995a: 404). It is not clear whether this is a recognition that identity is something that is continuously evolving, or that the idea of cultural "reproduction" with simultaneous evolution through cultural interchange with other societies is under way, or perhaps that a society defines itself partly in *opposition* to the pressure of other cultures, as with Poland or Scotland.

While using society rather than the state provides a fuller analysis of the issues at stake in such examples, the way in which the concept of security is being employed is itself problematic. There is an assumption at work, which is that societies are coherent, homogeneous entities with effective mechanisms for choosing spokespersons who can speak accurately and effectively for society as a whole. However, Waever himself recognizes this problem, and raises the issue of who speaks for a society in the way that a government leader speaks for the state (1995b: 69).

But this is a vision of society that does not reflect contemporary sociology or the realities of contemporary international relations. Societies are imagined communities. Many modern societies are multiethnic, multiracial, and multireligious. There are few common indicators to which all members of the society will fully or automatically subscribe. In many of the conflicts during the 1990s, it was the very definition of society that was being contested through force of arms. The Copenhagen school sees social construction as operating within certain limits produced by "sedimented" structures, and this concept is applied to society as well as to the state.

McSweeney argues that in the Copenhagen school's perspective, "Society is conceived as a social fact, with the same objectivity and ontological status as the state" (1996: 90). This seems an unfair criticism, since Waever himself has been at pains to recognize the problem, noting that, "societies are of course, highly differentiated, full of hierarchies and institutions, with some better placed than others to speak on behalf of 'their' societies" (1995b: 70). Waever himself seems to suggest that society has both continuities and an evolutionary aspect. Society is seen as being distinct from the state, but at the same time more than the sum of its parts.

For McSweeney, "identity is not a fact of society, it is a process of negotiation among people and interest groups" (1999: 73). For Buzan and Waever, in contrast, identity and society are treated as ontological givens. There is a working assumption that all the individuals within a particular society largely share a common culture. There is an objectivist approach to society, with society and the identity that underpins it seen as external, observable realities (Buzan, Waever, and De Wilde, 1998). But when society is being treated in this way as a natural, automatic, or inevitable association, then the idea of society as a social construction is being weakened (McSweeney, 1996: 83). Rather than being seen as a contested process, the identity upon which the Copenhagen school sees society as being founded is relatively stable and coherent, which allows it to be the subject of security threats. The level at which one chooses to identify "society" here is also important. In the early 1990s it became clear that "Bosnian" society was not sufficiently powerful as an integrating idea in comparison to the competing claims of Croat, Serbian, and Bosnian Muslim identities.

Societal security issues are always ultimately about identity. Societies that feel themselves under threat can react by making more energetic efforts to sustain and promote their distinctive cultural traits. They can do this if the state and the majority culture do not themselves feel threatened by such moves. However, if such a strategy is not possible, or if it is deliberately blocked, the group that feels threatened may transform the cultural claims into a political agenda or, in the face of repression by the state apparatus, may resort to the use of force.

However, society is not a single, homogeneous reality. It is composed of numerous subgroups engaged in a continuous process of social construction. While focusing on "societal" rather than "state" security concerns can be a very useful step, the logic of understanding the dynamics of threat construction in this context "would force the level of analysis down from society as a whole to its social-group components" (McSweeney, 1999: 72).

This is a crucial move, because it provides the handle for understanding the real-world problems of the post–Cold War era. To understand the latter it is necessary to adopt an approach "in which the apparent fact of societal identity was exposed as an integral, political aspect of the security problem, rather than a taken-for-granted reality which defined the problem" (McSweeney, 1999: 73).

Horizontal and Vertical Competition

Buzan cites the concepts of horizontal and vertical competition as examples of societal security threats. In the horizontal competition case, a situation exists in which, although the community living in a particular place is still the original community, it is changing because of the overwhelming cultural and linguistic influence of a neighboring culture. Such fears were evident in francophone Quebec province in the 1960s and 1970s, and fears of the cultural pressures from anglophone Canada and the United States led to the dramatic rise to power of the Parti Quebecois in the 1970s.

There is invariably a degree of interaction between neighboring cultures of different size, and this may generate feelings of societal insecurity among members of the smaller culture. A small society like the Welsh may feel threatened by a much larger neighbor such as England. In Mexico there is the poignant saying, "Poor Mexico, so far from God, so close to the United States!"

Integration projects, whether democratic or imperial, that try to impose the dominant state culture will attempt to do this by manipulating the institutions of cultural reproduction, as with the deliberate discouragement of the use of the Welsh language in Wales during the nineteenth and early twentieth centuries. In more repressive states there will be a deliberate effort to crush a separate culture by using all the state's access to educational, media, and other systems to solely promote the majority culture, possibly even denying the existence of a minority culture, as with the Turkish denial of the existence of a Kurdish minority, which raises inevitable fears about physical as well as cultural survival.

In the case of vertical competition, the pressures on a particular culture emerge because there is an integrating project, such as the attempt to create a multinational Federal Republic of Yugoslavia, or the rolling political and economic integration represented by the European Union (EU). The pressures may also come from attempts by one area to secede from a country. These examples also seem predicated on a simple objectivist notion of society and of threat construction. Vertical competition posits a situation in which a previously stable and apparently homogeneous society is transformed, in a negative way, by integrationist or secessionist pressures. But if one takes the example of the European Union, the threat construction and homogenizing pressure are not as straightforward as they might appear. Countries and societies, as collective entities, invariably face many threats of different kinds. Among other things, they have to prioritize threats in terms of scale, immediacy, and other factors. In the period after 1945, a number of West European countries decided that the division of Europe into competing "national" states and particularly the century-old rivalry between France and Germany represented a threat that overshadowed all others. The solution pursued, economic and political integration, generated a societal security threat to the countries as they were then constituted, but this was accepted as a price worth paying in terms of the greater threat represented by the possibility of a third European-centered world war. In part, the effort involved a deliberate attempt to create and sustain new societal loyalties at the pan-European level. As the loss of cultural diversity and richness became an issue in later decades, the union sought to develop a political strategy that would emphasize and sustain Europe's regions and "nations," even as the states were gradually divested of absolute sovereignty.

Such a threat can also materialize as a result of a secessionist movement to break away from a larger political and cultural entity, such as the francophone support for an independent Quebec and the regionalist pressures to unite the Kurdish minorities of the Middle East into a single Kurdish nation-state, or pressures for a Tamil state in Southwest Asia. Such struggles draw a population toward a primary loyalty and cultural designation at a level higher or lower than the currently existing one.

How particular societies perceive feelings of societal insecurity will depend to a significant extent on how their societies are constructed. Societies of countries like the United States and United Kingdom, even though they may resent certain economic migrants seen as competitors for employment, are essentially immigrant societies, with a long-term tolerance for the infusions of novelty and energy that immigration brings. Tension occurs when immigrants appear to resist assimilation into the existing culture and are felt to threaten it in some way. Because they are distinct in racial, religious, or some other characteristic, they may seem to threaten the original population's sense of identity, however ill-defined. Countries with a strong sense of cultural identity may feel threatened by the forces of globalization and resent even comparatively small groups of representatives of the threatening culture. Iran and Saudi Arabia are examples of this dilemma.

The early 1990s saw the disintegration of a number of states that had been constructed over time through the integration of a number of ethnic groups who had previous histories of their own distinct national existences, which were capable of being restored. For a state constructed on this basis, the rise of nationalism and reemergence of a sense of historical continuity with these earlier identities can be fatal to the continuity of the state. The Soviet Union rapidly collapsed in the face of such pressures, and despite a furious and violent rearguard action, so did the former Republic of Yugoslavia. Czechoslovakia also failed to hold together, although in its case, the separation of the country into two successor states was a peaceful and essentially amicable one, the so-called velvet divorce.

Migration as a Security Issue

People may decide to migrate for many reasons—for example, economic opportunity or religious freedom. But they may also move as part of a political program to homogenize the population of the state. Buzan cites the Sinification of Tibet, and the Russification of Central Asia and the Baltic states, as examples of this kind of process.

But if the Russification of the Baltic states is taken as an example of a societal security threat, the problems of using a simple, Durkheimian conception of society become clear. As the Soviet Union entered its death throes, the Baltic states successfully regained their independence, an independence recognized by the Soviets following the results of referenda in the three Baltic republics. Countries like Estonia, with very large Russian minorities, became independent. This was seen by many Estonian and other commentators as representing a clear societal security threat. The Estonian people, having regained national sovereignty, felt threatened by the presence within Estonia of a very large Russian minority (more than 40 percent of the total population) who did not speak Estonian, who did not relate to Estonian culture and history, and who rather looked to neighboring Russia when identifying their national and cultural affinity.

Yet the reality was much more complex. In the referendum on the question of independence from the Soviet Union, the majority in favor was larger than could be accounted for by the ethnic Estonian majority. It was clear that a substantial proportion of the Russians living in Estonia had voted in favor of Estonia breaking away from the Soviet Union (and therefore Russia) to become an independent state. They did this knowing that the new state would be overwhelmingly Estonian in character. Clearly, many Russians had placed a belief in their common Estonian citizenship and the hope of a higher standard of living above their loyalty to their cultural roots in Russia. It was clear also that the strength of this commitment varied in terms of a number of factors, such as age (older Russians tended to be less enthusiastic about Estonian independence) and employment history (former members of the Soviet security and armed forces were also less enthusiastic). There was no single, homogeneous population of "Russians" living in Estonia.

Nevertheless, the Estonian authorities reacted to the perceived societal security threat by attempting to marginalize and politically emasculate the Russian-speaking minority in the new state. Those who were not ethnically Estonian at the time of independence were denied citizenship and the process of gaining citizenship was made unreasonably difficult for the Russian population. It was only when Estonia sought membership of the European Union that external political pressure from the EU forced it to amend its citizenship policies to restore the human rights that had been denied to the Russian minority.

The significance of this example is that the Durkheimian model fails to recognize that while the presence of the Russian population represented a form of societal (and political) security threat to the Estonian majority, the postindependence policies of the Estonian government were a societal security threat to the Russians themselves. They were being forced to deny their own culture and embrace another in order to become citizens of the country in which many of them had been born. This difficulty would reappear in later crises in post–Cold War Europe, such as the Kosovo conflict, where the understandable desire of the international community to defend the human and political rights of the Albanian population threatened its collusion in the postconflict denial of those same rights to the Serbian minority.

The "societal" security concept employed in the broader approach is therefore not enough in itself to provide accurate purchase on these types of non-state-centric problems, though it is clearly a major step in the right direction. And this weakness points toward the desirability of a genuinely comprehensive approach to security, capable of conceptualizing and dealing with such complex, multidimensional security issues.

In the Copenhagen school model, migration is defined as a societal security threat in terms of one society being "overrun" or "diluted" by influxes of another people, or when the identity of the first group is being altered by a significant change in the composition of the population. But this insight also suggests how the securitization of societal questions may be seen as a negative effort of broadening the security agenda into new sectors, and as a development that is in conflict with a commitment to the enhancement of individual and group security. Buzan, Waever, and De Wilde, for example, cite migration as being a significant threat to societal security, where nations that dominate a state thanks to the possession of a small numerical majority will be vulnerable to significant population influxes (1998: 121).

Concern about the impact of migration is not new; resentment of "foreigners" has been notable even in the history of countries, like England and the United States, that have been profoundly shaped by successive waves of immigration. But by the 1990s such concerns had become overlaid with the security label. European leaders, in particular, repeatedly referred to actual or potential migrations as a significant security threat. The language of traditional security began to be appropriated, so that it could be argued: "In many countries, citizens have become fearful that they are now being invaded not by armies and tanks, but by migrants who speak other languages, worship other gods, belong to other cultures and, they fear, will take their jobs, occupy their land, live off their welfare system and threaten their way of life" (Weiner, 1995: 2).

By broadening the definition of security, it has become possible to include a wider range of categories as security threats, allowing refugees and migrants to be seen in this way. This is not necessarily a positive step. At the end of the Cold War, there was a major fear among West European governments, that the collapse of communism and the opening of the international frontiers in Europe would see a massive flood of economic migrants moving west in order to share in the blessings of capitalism.

Buzan sees migration as a threat to society rather than to the state. It is seen as being existential because it threatens the self identity of the existing population. How great a threat migrants are in this regard depends upon factors such as the scale of the immigration, the adaptive capacity of society, and the way in which that society's identity is constructed (Buzan, Waever, and De Wilde, 1998: 124).

In this regard, Arnold Wolfers's (1952) distinction between objective and subjective security threats is clearly relevant. A significant migration may be important for the receiving country because the key features of its culture are genuinely being dramatically impacted upon by the alternative values and behaviors of the immigrant population. A small national population may feel particularly vulnerable in this regard. Jewish immigration with Palestine in the 1930s triggered such fears in the resident Palestinian population, prompting serious violence.

Even if the level of immigration is objectively on too small a scale to meaningfully affect the character of the existing population, the issue can still be successfully securitized by politicians seeking to raise such fears in order to promote their own political agenda. The security "threat" of migration is very much a matter of perception in which the exaggeration or calming of fears is a crucial factor. The issue can be politicized and securitized through the use of inflammatory rhetoric promoting images of a society being "overrun" or "swamped" by the migrants.

When immigration is politicized in this way it may generate security threats in a number of directions. The Buzan/Waever objectivist conception of society is limiting because it only allows for the discussion of threats to a preexisting homogeneous totality. But societies often contain several minorities, and an objectivist conception does not provide a purchase on understanding of threats posed in different areas simultaneously. When attention is focused upon a new generation of immigrants, it may focus attention upon other minorities in the country whose presence had been unproblematic up until that point, but who now find themselves being targeted by the rising xenophobia in the country.

The migration issue highlights the importance of the concept of identity to the societal security sector. Immigration may be seen as threatening by a population because of straightforward concerns about economic security—a perception of increasing numbers of people competing for limited numbers of jobs, with the migrants resented because they are perceived as being willing to work in poorer conditions or for less pay, giving them an advantage in job competition. Here the societal security sector overlaps with the economic security agenda.

But the concern posed by migration can be the result of a more general perception of threat to cultural identity. In the classical security dilemma, the foreigner is constructed as the actual or potential enemy, the threatening "other" against whom the resources of the state must be mobilized and against whom the national identity is to some extent built.

Toward the end of the Cold War in Europe the issue of migration appeared to undergo a significant transformation. Until then, European governments had tended to see it as a purely economic issue. The value of immigration was therefore assessed in terms of the trade-off between the benefits that migrant workers brought to the country in various ways, and the additional burden on existing social security provision that they might represent. As the broader agenda encouraged a reassessment of such questions as security issues, the terms in which the issue was framed changed in a negative direction, with the question increasingly being seen as the extent to which migrants would threaten the established culture and values of the receiving state and the degree to which they would expose the state to international networks of organized crime. Simply framing the issue as a *security* problem, rather than, as previously, an economic issue, significantly reduced the security of such migrants themselves, because of the negative images with which they were now associated. This became particularly noticeable as increased attention was given to *illegal* immigration and its links with organized crime.

In the societal security sector, the migrant can also be successfully characterized as the threatening cultural "other" who endangers the way of life of the existing population (Huysmans, 1995: 61). This is problematic in terms of comprehensive security approaches, because the fears being generated operate on the level of the individual as well as society as a whole. The problem is "not only in insecure individuals threatened by 'foreigners,' but also one of an insecure collective identity which unites the insecure individuals" (Huysmans, 1995: 53).

The perception of migrants as a threat to cultural identity is clearly closely linked to the definition of the host community. Populations may fear an alteration in their ethnic, religious, or cultural composition, while governments may fear that migration might generate a rise in xenophobia among the population and an increase in the size and influence of racist political parties. In the face of such perceptions, governments invariably opt for restrictions on immigration.

The political and economic effects of migration are a possible source of insecurity to the state as well as society, to the extent that they generate instabilities by overloading the capacity of the government to cope with resulting problems. The degree of instability and insecurity generated will depend on "the capacity of social, economic, political and administrative institutions to integrate large numbers of immigrants, and the resistance of some immigrant families to assimilation" (Heisler and Layton-Henry, 1993: 162).

A number of factors encouraged the promotion of migration as a societal security issue in Western Europe during the 1990s. The process of European integration itself contributed to this development by removing the EU states' sovereign control over the regulation of migration. Article 8A of the Single European Act of 1986 provided for the creation of "an area without internal frontiers in which the free movement of goods, persons, services and capital is ensured." This was to take effect by December 31, 1992. Member states thereby lost their absolute control over national borders.

Concerns over migration were also encouraged by the end of the Cold War and the dismantling of the "iron curtain" that had divided East and West for decades. This triggered Western fears of a massive influx of economic migrants from the former communist states of Eastern Europe. Several southern European states also perceived pressure from large-scale immigration, both legal and illegal, from the Maghreb countries of North Africa. Buzan argued that "Europeans are often sensitive to Islamic immigrants, whose strong, visible and alien culture can be seen as a defiance of integration, and therefore as a kind of invasion" (1993: 44).

While attention in the North Atlantic Treaty Organization and the European Union in the 1990s was understandably focused on actual and potential refugee and migrant flows in Western Europe, this presented a misleading picture of the actual international situation. The reality was that only a relatively small proportion of global refugee flows moved from east to west on the continent, or from the developing world to the developed. In the early 1990s, immediately after the end of the Cold War, there were 15–17 million refugees. Their reasons for becoming migrants varied, and included fleeing from the dangers of war zones, political persecution, hunger and poverty, or unbearable environmental conditions. More than 90 percent of these refugees were moving from one developing country to another (Stewart, 1992: 19). Far from the poor flooding into the rich nations, they were overwhelmingly fleeing to countries that were little or no richer than their own, and it was these developing countries that were having to bear the social and economic costs of coping with the refugee flows. Some of the largest refugee populations were to be found in Africa (Weiner, 1992–1993: 94). In contrast, the numbers moving to Europe were much smaller and included a large proportion of migrants with a legal right to settle because they possessed dual citizenship, or were nationals of former colonies who had made special arrangements with the former colonial powers.

Yet as Myron Weiner noted, in Europe the migrant issue was often presented in dramatic terms, in which the migrants clearly constituted a societal threat to countries perceived as being "invaded" by people "who speak other languages, worship other gods, belong to other cultures, and they fear, will take their jobs, occupy their land, live off their welfare system, and threaten their way of life, their environment, and even their polity" (1995: 2).

The process of securitization can be seen as a useful act in which human concerns that need addressing are brought into a framework that allows them to be treated with greater urgency and purpose. But it can also result in issues being constructed as part of a threat spectrum, where the consequences are by no means positive. Securitization of the issue of migration comes into the latter category. European politicians in the early 1990s allowed migration to come to be seen as an issue that could threaten domestic social and political cohesion, and subsequent political developments such as the Gulf wars and Al-Qaida terrorist attacks made it comparatively easy to manipulate sentiments and securitize the migration issue in a negative manner. As Wolfers (1952) noted, security has both an objective and a subjective dimension, so that it is not necessary for a genuine threat to a culture to exist for a population to *perceive* this as being the case and react accordingly.

The focus on the cultural threat dimension of this issue is necessary in order to explore the implications for societal security, because the migrants are seen as threatening the society rather than the individual or the state. The threat is to a particular way of life. The scale of immigration is relevant, since if the population flow is small in relation to the size of the existing population, the sense of threat may not be triggered. However, if a culture sees itself as highly distinctive, even small but highly visible numbers of immigrations may produce a sense of cultural threat.

Securitization of this issue marked a change from the way it had usually been constructed in the past, when it was invariably presented as an economic question. The presence of migrants could be presented as economically beneficial to a state, because of the labor and skills they brought, or as detrimental, because they competed for scarce jobs and burdened the social security, health, and housing systems (Loescher, 1992). But there is no sense of existential threat to a community or a culture in this conception. It is the addition of the cultural dimension and threat to identity that transforms the issue into one of societal insecurity, in which the scale of the perceived crisis may be much greater than is justified by the reality of the cultural subversion actually or potentially possible.

Regional Examples

In the analysis of the broadened security agenda, a fundamental question is that of why a new sector should be seen as analogous to existing ones. Most authors have resolved this question by relating security to questions of existential survival. In the societal sector, however, the definition has not focused on existential survival in the same manner that it is conceived of in the military and economic realms, for example. Waever argues that in the societal sector the issues are still existential, although the meaning of "survival" is different: "if a state loses sovereignty, it has not survived as a state, if a society loses its identity, it has not survived as itself" (1995a: 405).

This is not entirely satisfactory in that it suggests that "survival" is the same thing in different categories, when a "commonsense" interpretation of the word would suggest the opposite. It could be suggested that through exposure to Western culture over two centuries, the traditional Aboriginal culture has not "survived" in Australia. This may or may not be true in an absolute sense, but it is clearly a different issue from the fate of the Aboriginal population of Tasmania, who were physically hunted down and exterminated.

However, the examples of societal security explored by Buzan and Waever, while clearly relating to the concepts of migration and vertical and horizontal security threats, do not fit easily into the idea of a genuine existential threat as defining the existence of societal insecurity. In Africa, both modern and premodern societal referents continue to exist simultaneously. The continent is divided into a large number of states, but hardly any of them are nation-states in the classical European definition of that term. Rather they are state-nations, countries that have come into existence with defined borders, but great cultural and linguistic diversity, and in which governing elites have subsequently attempted to generate popular loyalty to a new cultural and political identity—"Kenyan," "Nigerian," and so on—in the face of continuing strong loyalties to tribe and clan.

Few states in Africa are threatened by traditional interstate violence. Wars between African states have been very rare. Military threats have more typically emerged from within states. These have taken the form of coups, insurgencies, and civil wars, which have had a devastating impact upon the political and economic development of the continent.

Thus, in the African societal security sector the "threat" invariably comes from within. However, in discussing it, Buzan, Waever, and De Wilde make clear that what they are actually concerned with are threats to the state, rather than to the society or the nation (1998: 127). States are threatened by vertically competing loyalties from tribal groups, such as the Ibo in Nigeria. This is reflected in tribal-based party and military competition for political power.

But what is not discussed is a societal threat to the cultural identity of particular groups in Africa. The threat is to the political integrity of the state, or to the political power of a group, or the physical survival of peoples in the face of military threats from within the state. This is a traditional security agenda, not a "societal" one in the sense originally defined.

A similar problem is evident in the discussion of societal security concerns in Southwest Asia. India and Pakistan are correctly identified as states with very specifically constructed national identities. In the breakup of the British Indian Empire, two successor states emerged, one as a homeland for Muslim Indians (Pakistan), the other as a home for Indians who wished to live in a multiconfessional secular republic. This basis for state creation has explained the decades-long difficulty in resolving the Kashmir dispute, where Kashmir's accession to India as a Muslim state would threaten Pakistan's claim to be the natural political homeland for Muslims on the subcontinent and therefore threaten Pakistan's raison d'être. However, if Kashmir were now to be incorporated into Pakistan, India fears that other parts of India where there are substantial Muslim populations might press to do the same, thereby threatening India's territorial and political integrity in turn.

Again, the examples given by Buzan, Waever, and De Wilde of "societal" conflict on the subcontinent are either threats to the state, in the sense of the founding basis of the republics, or threats to the political power or physical existence of various groups. They are not discussed in terms of a threat to the cultural identity of those groups. "Societal" is thereby being used to allow discussion of nonstate threats (though not entirely), but does not emerge as a sector clearly distinct from the military and political. This does not mean that it has no utility or value as a category; it clearly does, but it has proven extremely difficult to operationalize it as a category limited entirely to existential threats to cultural identity, rather than a receptacle for threats to society of a more general kind, including cultural identity.

Conclusion

In the broader security spectrum, societal security remains a highly problematic concept. Its distinctiveness from other sectors is not at all clear, and it lends itself to appropriation by forms of security analysis and political discourse that can place groups in situations of reduced rather than increased security. It remains a potentially valuable extension of security conceptualization, but clearly needs to be developed further conceptually to confirm its distinctiveness from other security categories and approaches.

SEVEN

Environmental Security

L ike the economic sector, the environmental sector potentially falls clearly within the broader security agenda, but equally it has proved vulnerable to colonization by neorealist research programs. Arguments about whether the environment should be seen as a security issue range from those who believe that the securitization of the environment is the most important step to securing the survival of humanity, to those who believe that its advocates are simply environmentalists cynically attempting to grab part of the governmental attention and spending that traditionally attaches to security issues. It has been called both the "ultimate security" (Myers, 1993) and a "pollution" of true security (Deudney, 1990).

Most contributions to the debate lie somewhere between these extreme positions. The environmental issue has probably received more attention than any of the other domains in the broadened security concept and there is a large and growing literature devoted to the intellectual and policy implications of the concept of environmental security.

The environment as a policy issue has been on the international agenda for a long time. Fears about the accelerating damage to the environment were being voiced in the 1960s and early 1970s, but both because of a lack of convincing data and because of the understandably overwhelming international focus on the dangers posed by nuclear war, environmental issues did not assume any kind of priority for governmental attention. Nevertheless, concern steadily increased. The United Nations held a conference on the human environment in Stockholm in 1972, and this event can be seen as having begun a process "that has resulted in the piecemeal construction of a number of environmental institutions, the steady expansion of the security agenda, and increasing acceptance by states of international monitoring of environmental standards" (Mingst and Karns, 1995: 127).

On January 31, 1992, the United Nations Security Council declared that threats to international peace and security could come from "non military sources of instability in the economic, social, humanitarian and ecological fields." So far had this steady increase in political attention progressed that by 1995 one writer could argue that since the late 1980s, "a groundswell of support for the core proposition that environmental degradation constitutes a security risk has encountered hardly any voices of dissent" (Levy, 1995: 35).

Environmental security has been defined as concerning "the maintenance of the local and planetary biosphere as the essential support system on which all other human enterprises depend" (Buzan, 1991a: 19). Defined thus, it clearly falls within the scope of a security issue, since it encompasses the same dangers that focused so much attention on the issue of nuclear weapons during the Cold War—that is, a possibility of events unfolding that could trigger a complete collapse of human civilization. Robert Kaplan (1994) has made just such a correlation, arguing that accelerating environmental collapse will trigger increases in crime and ethnic conflict that will plunge the world into conflict-ridden anarchy.

That the environment emerged on the broadened security agenda in the past twenty years is hardly surprising. For many states and populations there are obvious environmental threats that outweigh any traditional military threats that a particular group faces. Many developing countries, for example, are more immediately threatened by issues such as deforestation or desertification than they are by the threat of external military forces. A good example is Tunisia. Desertification clearly threatens the core values and existence of those who farm on the land that the Sahara threatens to envelop (Nester, 1995: 441). Tunisia has reflected this reality in its national security doctrine by defining the struggle against desertification as a key part of its national defense efforts, and by allocating specific military units to a continuing effort to contain and reverse the advance of the Sahara (Sheehan, 1999).

There may also be a sense in which the advent of environmental security is an example of the development of the postmaterialistic era. Societies can be seen as operating in terms of a "hierarchy of needs," so that once basic needs are met, there is a movement up the hierarchy, and as this happens, new "needs" emerge. In this sense, a "hierarchy of security needs" may be operating, so that developments such as economic development, economic globalization, and the end of the Cold War have encouraged the development of an environmental security "need" that was not previously seen to be present.

Thus, while environmental security may have emerged as a vital issue for many states, the nature of the issues, and the developments that triggered concern about them, may be quite different for different countries. Tunisia's concern is being driven by direct environmental impact for example, while U.S. interest may be more a result of the progress of a developing needs hierarchy.

▓ Human or Natural Environment?

In theory there are two possible kinds of environmental security threats. The first are those that emanate from the natural environment, such as volcanic eruptions and earthquakes. The second are those that are the result of human agency impacting on the natural environment, such as greenhouse gas emissions and damage to the planetary ozone layer. There is a consensus that it is the latter category that is the proper concern of environmental security. These are threats resulting from the way that the process of civilization has come to involve a manipulation of nature that has reached self-defeating proportions as a result of massive population increase and the enormous growth of economic activity in the twentieth century. Much of the wider "environmental" agenda is not part of the "environmental security" agenda, which is an important distinction to make.

The question of the referent object for environmental security is an interesting one (Buzan, Waever, and De Wilde, 1998). The answer would appear to be the environment. In reality it is more complicated than that. There have been attempts to propose the environment at the system level as an appropriate referent of security—for example, by Dennis Pirages (1997) and K. Rogers (1997)—but these have been exceptional in the security literature. Much of the environmental security literature, however, can be equated with environmental protection in the sense that the threats being identified and solutions proposed are attempts to protect the planet's natural biophysical systems and processes. However, when the term is being used in this sense it does not relate to a novel conception of security, but is simply applying a novel term in this context to an existing problem area. Protection of the environment is a concern of groups, organizations, and governments that do not necessarily use the term "environmental security" to describe this policy domain and, in some cases, actively oppose such a linkage.

Buzan, Waever, and De Wilde argue that the environmental debate is really about preserving existing levels of human civilization. The real concern is whether or not the ecosystems needed to preserve and further develop human civilization are sustainable. This means that the environmental coalition is a very broad one that is divided at some points between those who wish to preserve the environment as such—for example, the survival or well-being of certain animal or plant species, in the interest of environmental diversity—and those whose interest is purely in sustaining what is required in order to allow humanity to progress economically.

Environmental security is thus not about humanity's struggle with nature as such, but a problem of coping with the dynamics of its own postindustrial cultures. This perspective on the meaning of environmental security allows a distinction between threats from the environment that have human origins, and those that do not. The greatest tragedy for Colombia in the late twentieth century was the floods and mudslides of 1999, which killed tens of thousands. While this would not be deemed a legitimate environmental security issue unless a link with human agency could be proved, for the people themselves it would already be the central security crisis of their lifetimes.

Buzan, Waever, and De Wilde point out that environmental security is not really about threats to nature, or to the planet as such. The "security" problem is therefore really one for human civilization. Can this civilization devise solutions for the problems it has created for itself? How does humanity adapt to the new constraints that its activities clearly place on the environment? It is the environment as the sustainer of humanity that is the point, and therefore human civilization may require the survival of certain elements of the natural environment, but not necessarily all.

Environmental security addresses threats to humanity posed by human impact upon the "natural" environment. It is about the effects of atmospheric change, deforestation, chemical pollution, soil erosion, and so on. These are all problems primarily induced by human activity. They may be the result of deliberate acts, or they may be caused by the unintended side effects of the pursuit of other objectives. It is not about dealing with natural disasters such as earthquakes or hurricanes. It is the result, not of humanity's struggle against the unpredictable effects of nature, but of humanity's struggle against itself. This is important, because it has been suggested that environmental threats, unlike military threats, are "threats without enemies" (Prins, 1993). Unlike military threats, environmental dangers are not deliberately created, and no one is in that sense specifically to blame for their existence. Seen from this civilizational perspective, it is clear that in terms of nature, scale, and effect, not every environmental problem can be considered a threat to national or international security, and there is a danger that claiming so would trivialize the genuine problems.

An important aspect of this way of looking at environmental security is that it does not make or require any link with war or violent conflict between human groups, as do the arguments of some other interpretations of environmental security threats. Environmental degradation is seen as a security problem because it impacts negatively on the health and well-being of humans. It represents a direct existential threat to humans in certain respects and therefore encourages a mind-set that sees human welfare and the welfare of natural systems as being crucially linked (Mische, 1989: 393).

The Environmental Security Agenda

A wide variety of issues can potentially be seen as environmental security concerns. They can be grouped into a number of subcategories, including those stemming from the disruption of ecosystems, such as climate change, loss of biodiversity, deforestation, desertification and other erosion problems, depletion of the ozone layer, and various forms of pollution. In these cases the natural environmental balance of local to global ecologies is being damaged by the activities of the human population, usually through the effects of agricultural or industrial production.

Second, there is a set of issues related to energy, including the depletion of natural resources, various forms of pollution, particularly those involved in the storage and transportation of chemicals, oil, and nuclear materials, and problems of energy scarcities and uneven distribution. Many of these kinds of concerns have been present on the national and international security agenda since the early 1970s. The third category comprises problems stemming from the effects of human population growth, such as pressures caused by major population movements, excessive consumption and waste, pollution, and overuse of limited natural resources.

Fourth, there is a group of issues related to food scarcities and uneven food distribution, including famine and the loss of fertile soils and water resources in many parts of the world. These issues overlap with questions of poverty and with certain elements of the economic security agenda. Not all of these issues are permanently securitized, nor is there consensus about what should be on the list and what should not. Much of the literature on environmental security has focused on this interpretation of the issue, in which growing populations, usually identified in the third world, are seen as being the cause of environmental degradation, which may in turn cause them to become migrants and result in their being perceived as a problematic area of societal security. Simon Dalby (1998) has strongly criticized this approach, arguing that it fails to place the real problem at the center of the discussion. For Dalby, it is the pressures of globalization, and the operation of postmodern capitalism, that are the culprit, rather than population growth per se, because of "the accelerating processes of globalisation that are interconnecting the world's economies and cultures in ways that often operate to undercut traditional economies and challenge the sustainability of agricultural and survival practices" (1998: 13).

Environmental security is not entirely a case of "threats without enemies," as Gwyn Prins (1993) has described it. The basic logic of environmental security is that, globally, humanity is living beyond the carrying capacity of the planet. The exact meaning of "carrying capacity" is disputed, but it has been defined as "the total patterns of consumption that the Earth's natural systems can support without undergoing degradation" (Buzan, Waever, and De Wilde, 1998: 81).

These patterns of consumption involve a wide range of variables, including the total global human population, the dominant modes of production, and gross per capita consumption levels. Carrying capacity is influenced by numbers, technology, and lifestyle. With so many variables, it is not that easy to estimate exactly what the carrying capacity of the planet actually is, and this lends itself to arguments about precisely how urgent some of the environmental dangers are. It is also important to note that the impact of the planet's human population on the environment is very far from being uniform. In the highly developed economies of the "West," the advanced consumer lifestyles of the population make much greater demands upon the planet's resources than do the lifestyles of the populations of poorer countries. The world's poorer countries are not the most to blame for global environmental problems, in that their lifestyles are far less demanding on global resources, but they are the most vulnerable to its consequences. Industrialized countries use ten times as much energy per person as do the poorer countries. Realities like these generate complicated political and economic problems in that, while raising the living standards of the world's poor would require a growth in consumption by the populations of the poorer countries, unless this were accompanied by reductions in Western levels the damaging impact upon the environment regionally and globally would simply be accelerated still further.

Although the damage to the environment is often described as a planetary problem, the realities are somewhat different and problems tend to be regional rather than global. Most of the global pollution problems, for example, require joint action only by the highly industrialized states. Most "global" environmental crises have uneven effects and involvements. Some countries are far more at risk than others from the effects of specific environmental problems. Some countries are far more to blame than others for causing those problems. Some countries are far better placed than others in financial or technological terms to deal with the problems.

This raises crucial issues for international relations. Who is responsible for damaging the environment? Who should take the lead in dealing with the problem? Who is going to pay the huge costs involved? The diplomatic difficulties arise because it is often the countries that suffer most that are least able in technological and financial terms to deal with the problems. These countries are often the most at risk from the problems and are not necessarily those most to blame for causing them in the first place. "Those who have to pay the price for prevention are different from those who pay the price of failure" (Buzan, Waever, and De Wilde, 1998: 86).

One interesting feature of this aspect of environmental security is that it has major implications in terms of identifying the providers of security. In the traditional Cold War discourse, the provider of security was clearly the state, and the instrumental providers were the armed forces. But when damage to the environment per se becomes part of the security problematic, it remains partly and crucially a responsibility of the state to seek to maximize security in this area, and yet it also becomes possible for nongovernmental organizations, epistemic communities such as scientists, and even individuals to take on an important responsibility for enhancing environmental security for society as a whole. Where global economic production processes are a part of the problem, then the individual choices of consumers can become part of the solution, in terms of distinguishing between those products that have a significant negative impact on the environment and those that do not. Through ecologically responsible actions, individuals can become security providers, in a general sense, for themselves and others.

Should the Environment Be Securitized?

The case for including environmental issues on the security agenda has been made by numerous authors. Peter Gleick (1991), for example, argues for a conception in which the "environment" is linked to a number of other sectors, including the military and societal sectors, where security thinking embraces problems of population growth, transnational pollution, widespread poverty, and inequitable social systems. A responsible international community would be obliged to rethink the way that states interact with the natural environment, and rethink also the way in which energy use is costed, so that, for example, national energy policies would need to take account not just of the price and supply of fuel, but also of the global environmental consequences of certain forms of energy use.

Critics of the idea of environmental security have argued that it is too amorphous. As this book shows, security can have many different meanings. The same is true of "the environment," which Marc Levy argues "can refer to anything in which something takes place or which affects what people do; in other words, almost anything at all" (1995: 37). He therefore argues that the term should be reserved for those issues that involve ecological feedback and equilibria, or are critical to the sustenance of human life (1995: 38).

Daniel Deudney presented a coherent set of arguments against the securitization of environmental issues in 1991. Deudney argued that environmental degradation and threats to military security were fundamentally different issues, for four main reasons. First, they were different kinds of threats. Many kinds of things kill human beings, such as accidents, aging, and illness, but these are not seen as "security" threats. When an earthquake or hurricane strikes, it may cause death and destruction, but it is considered a "natural disaster." If everything that could cause death or a decline in human well-being were to be labeled a "security threat," the term would lose any analytical usefulness it possessed.

Second, the scope and the source of threats to environmental and military security are very different. Few environmental threats are purely "national" in character, in terms of their causes, their consequences, or their solutions. In the traditional military security realm, a particular country may be seen as the "enemy" and its aggression may be directed specifically against one's own country. In the environmental realm, threats generally emerge over a large area and threaten more than one country simultaneously.

Third, threats to environmental and military security involve greatly differing degrees of intention. Threats of violence are generally highly intentional. They are planned, organized, deliberate acts by human collectivities. Environmental threats, in contrast, are largely unintentional. They are the side effects of other activities. Environmental problems are largely the result of the processes of industrialization and population increase. The degree of damage that the environment suffers has steadily increased as the industrialization process has intensified, but such environmental degradation has not been the objective of the process, but rather an unintended by-product of it. Environmental degradation is an unfortunate result of human development and progress.

Finally, the organizations that provide protection from violence differ greatly from those engaged in environmental protection. National security is delivered by organizations very different from those of civil society, characterized by hierarchy and centralization and willing to use high levels of violence, death, and destruction to achieve their goals. Environmental issues, in contrast, tend to involve a wider spectrum of society, and a quite different ethos motivates the individuals and groups concerned. The emphasis is on ideas like stewardship, respect, and protection (Deudney, 1991). Therefore, linking organized violence and environmental habitability might create a conceptual confusion, leading to a "militarisation of our thinking about the relationship between humanity and the environment" (Graeger, 1996: 111).

Deudney also argues that there is a risk of stirring up unhelpful nationalistic feelings. Those who propose the idea of "environmental security" are using a rhetorical device to make threats to the environment seem urgent and important. They are recognizing that in recent history, calling something a "security" issue has had the effect of propelling it to the top of the national policy agenda.

But the sentiments associated with national security are those of violence and war. It is not obvious how appealing to such sentiments will help create a national or international consensus in favor of protecting the environment. In contrast, it might encourage a movement toward scapegoating in which countries place the blame for serious international environmental crisis on a limited number of states, rather than accepting mutual responsibility for the protection of the environment. Given that the countries with the worst records are often the largest and most powerful, and the ones that other states therefore fear to antagonize, it is not even obvious that the countries blamed would really be those most at fault.

The national security mind-set creates an inappropriate "us/them" attitude. The kind of zero-sum thinking characteristic of the national security mind-set is simply not appropriate for dealing with environmental protection issues. There is no specific "enemy" as such in the sense of a hostile "other." If there is a culprit at all, it is "us." The attitudes and economic demands that characterize our civilization are the problem, not the activities of any particular group of humans.

Intense nationalism is also in conflict with one of the most important insights of environmentalism—the global, holistic perspective. Environmentalists tend to pay scant regard to the political significance of borders, seeing environmental problems as transnational in scope and requiring concerted international cooperation if they are to be overcome. If, on the contrary, specific environmental issues such as pollution were seen as a security threat, it is possible that the citizens of a particular country might resent the pollution caused by foreigners more than they would resent the pollution produced by their own country. At worst, this might trigger various types of interventionism and imperialism. In addition, because other countries may be seen as enemies, agreements between states may come to be viewed through an inappropriate realist mind-set, where they are not pursued or valued unless they serve an immediate national interest, no matter how crucial an international consensus might be to resolving the problem at the regional or planetary level (Deudney, 1990: 467).

In addition, national security policies often reflect a sense of urgency and crisis, but this may not be the most appropriate attitude for the kind of steady, long-term commitment that is required for effective protection of the environment. Because a requirement for ecological protection is the alteration of everyday behavior over the long term, it may be better to keep the environment as an unsecuritized "low politics" issue rather than emphasizing crash solutions that would not necessarily produce the lasting commitment required for success. In military operations, the desire is usually for a quick resolution of the issue and a rapid return to postconflict normality. In environmental matters, the problems may be slow to develop or to be detected, and require the adoption of lengthy, perhaps permanent, compromises and policies if they are to be successful. In the absence of dangers that do not produce an immediate sense of threat, environmental problems on the security agenda may receive an initial burst of attention and public concern, followed by a return to complacency when no immediate results are perceived and a consequent failure to sustain the momentum needed for eventual success.

Solutions to environmental problems require a focus on common benefits and cooperation. They are in that sense naturally "federative," almost automatically requiring states to think in terms of international cooperation and institution or regime building. Environmental issues encourage such an approach because of the transboundary nature of most of the problems involved. Issues such as acid rain and pollution do not respect national boundaries and are therefore difficult to deal with through the perspective of state-centered national security (Graeger, 1996: 112). It is argued, therefore, that in environmental matters, the traditional "war against the enemy" mind-set needs to be replaced by the idea of a "war of us all against us all" (Myers, 1993: 12), an idea that is virtually impossible to fit into a traditional military security approach. In any case, the use of terminology like "war" is not a positive step despite its seductive attraction as a tool for mobilizing support.

Linking environment and security has a further disadvantage. Given the nature of environmental consequences, "which are not distributed equally" (Porter and Brown, 1991: 121), no one state can single-handedly protect the environment. In the absence of world government, states are required to voluntarily cooperate to deal with environmental problems. However, states are notoriously reluctant to compromise their autonomy and sovereignty until circumstances force them to do so. The nature of environmental threats compels states to cooperate with countries with which they may have very poor relations. They may feel disinclined to join forces with such countries in the face of common environmental problems if they feel that the matter is in some way associated with the traditional military agenda. Securitizing the environment would therefore be a counterproductive step in these circumstances.

Deudney (1990) argues that instead of seizing upon "environmental security," environmentalists should emphasize that ecological problems call into question the status of the nation-state, as well as nationalist thinking. The ecological approach has positive virtues in terms of conceptualizing planetary and regional problems and encouraging attitudes of national and international "stewardship" of the planetary environment. Because these ways of thinking about the issue can engender greater contributions to environmental stability and protection, it would be a counterproductive step for environmentalists to embrace the environmental security paradigm and terminology if their own rich symbolism were to be replaced with the narrower militaristic and nationalistic mind-set traditionally associated with security. It would therefore be better to promote a rich ecological worldview, rather than simply to take the term "security" and attempt to use it in a quite different context.

Varieties of Environmental Security Approaches

In reality, the case for securitizing the environment has not been universally accepted and remains controversial in some quarters, despite its broad acceptance at the policy level by most states and key international organizations. The apparent lack of opposition has arisen partly because many traditional military analysts have largely ignored the idea, particularly among the conservative realist academic community in the United States, and partly because the common rubric "environmental security issues" conceals important differences in the way the concept is envisaged.

At least three distinct components of the environmental security spectrum can be identified. The first group is composed of military security specialists who have become aware of environmental issues in the form of resource shortage problems. This group has simply focused on natural resources as a potential course of future interstate conflict and war. There is nothing particularly novel about this approach as a way of explaining insecurity and war—Thucydides, writing 2,400 years ago, described the struggle between the Thasians and the Athenians for control of disputed mineral resources (Gleick, 1991). This approach has been present in traditional realist analyses of military security for decades, and there is nothing particularly "critical" about this perspective. An example of this kind of approach is the argument that the relative shortage of water in the Middle East is a major contributor to tensions in the region, and as regional populations and levels of economic activity continue to increase, the disputes over water will be a cause of war between states in the region (Bulloch and Darwish, 1993).

This group also includes those who are concerned about the deliberate manipulation of the environment for military purposes. Concern about the potential manipulation of weather patterns as a weapon of war led the UN to create the Environmental Modification Convention in 1977. It has been suggested that technologically advanced states could covertly increase rainfall within their own borders in order to cause drought and agricultural damage elsewhere (el-Hinnawi and ul-Haque, 1982: 21). The control of water flow in regions where it is scarce can also be seen as a form of environmental manipulation. Turkey has used its control over the headwaters of the Euphrates to put pressure on the Syrian government to withdraw its support for Kurdish separatists in the east of Turkey. The deliberate burning of the Kuwaiti oil wells by Iraqi forces as they retreated during the 1990–1991 Gulf War was seen by many as an example of ecological warfare (Gleick, 1991).

One research group that has sought empirical evidence for this kind of environmental security approach is the "Toronto school," associated with Thomas Homer-Dixon. The Toronto school focuses on what it believes can be known about the links between renewable resource scarcities and violent conflict. For this reason, its research concentrates upon issues such as scarcities of cropland, forest, fish stocks, and water, rather than the broader range of environmental issues such as climate change or ozone depletion. For this reason also, its work fits a more traditional conception of what security is, rather than the broad interpretation, since it examines acute national and international violent conflict.

The concept of environmental scarcity underlying these investigations is defined in terms of three types. Supply-induced scarcity is caused by degradation and depletion of an environmental resource—for example, the erosion of cropland. Demand-induced scarcity results from population growth within a region or increased per capita consumption of a resource, either of which heightens the demands for a resource. Structural scarcity arises from an unequal social distribution of a resource that concentrates it in the hands of a relatively few people, while the remaining population suffers from serious shortages (Homer-Dixon and Blitt, 1998).

The questions that interest the Toronto school are whether or not environmental scarcities contribute to violence in developing countries, and if they do, how so. Their key conclusions, drawn from a wide range of case studies, are that under certain circumstances, scarcities of renewable resources, such as cropland and water, do produce conflict and instability. However, they argue that the mechanisms by which this happens are complex and that environmental scarcity essentially produces conflict by generating social effects, such as poverty and migrations, which are often subsequently mistaken for the immediate causes of a conflict. Significantly, they argue that environmental scarcity rarely contributes directly to interstate conflict, though the 1969 war between El Salvador and Honduras is described by Homer-Dixon as "a first class example of an ecologically driven conflict" (1991: 76).

The research carried out by the Toronto school demonstrates the complexities involved in these issues and the central roles played by both perceptions and politics. There is nothing inevitable about the link between environmental problems and conflict. It is possible for the former to result in conflict, but a number of other variables need to come into play for this to happen. The environmental effects need to trigger not only a sense of deprivation, but also and specifically a feeling of relative deprivation in a structured situation where the possibility to move beyond peaceful political action to violence is institutionally present.

Third world countries are seen as being particularly vulnerable to such pressures. In many such countries, population growth, desertification, water scarcity, and soil erosion may force inhabitants to move to towns and cities in an attempt to find work and basic resources. The mass migration of people to neighboring urban centers places enormous stress on the existing fragile infrastructure of these areas, and conflict can be seen to arise because of the inability of the system to cope with the increased demands made upon it. When migration occurs across international boundaries, such "environmental refugees" are placed in an even more vulnerable position in being forced to look to a foreign government for assistance.

However, for this school of thought, the resulting problems are a security issue "only to the extent that [they pose] a challenge to either the security of the state or to international peace and security, where there is a demonstrable link with violence or conflict, or when military intervention might be required or justified" (Elliott, 1998: 220). In other words, the suffering of the individual people is not a security issue as such, although it is clearly a social and economic problem; only the political dangers their presence might create in a particular state represents a genuine security threat.

The Toronto school takes a middle position in terms of how alarmed the international community should be about the linkage between environmental issues and national and international conflict. Environmental issues often play much more than a minimal role in the generation of conflict, but at the same time they should not be oversensationalized or exaggerated in their effects (Homer-Dixon and Blitt, 1998: 1). The work of the Toronto school has made an important and extremely valuable contribution in terms of the detailed empirical research into case studies that is the characteristic of their approach, demonstrating, for example, the contribution made by water shortages to political violence and feelings of social and political alienation in the Gaza Strip (Kelly and Homer-Dixon, 1998).

In Gleick's descriptions of forms of environmental security issues, the military link is equally very clear, although he treats conflict in fairly broad sociological terms. His definition of the linkage between the environment and security is that "threats to security include resource and environmental problems that reduce the quality of life and result in increased competition and tensions between subnational or national groups" (Gleick, 1993: 81–82). He cites, for example, attacks on dams, oil refineries, and nuclear reactors in wartime as actions with profound environmental consequences. Similarly, he speaks of environmental resources as military tools, pointing out that while in theory resources like water are renewable, in practice they are finite, unevenly distributed, and subject to national or regional control. For example, when Ethiopia proposed building dams on the Upper Nile in 1978, Egyptian officials said that their country was so dependent on the Nile that they were prepared to go to war to prevent the dams from being built. Using similar arguments, John Cooley (1984) argues that water scarcity was one of the main causes of the 1967 Arab-Israeli War.

For this group, therefore, environmental issues form an integral part of international and regional conflicts and as such are appropriate for consideration as security issues. It is important to note, however, that here the environment is simply being seen as an example of traditional security considerations. If this were the only group discussing the environment, the case for securitizing environmental issues would not be strong. Some of the examples cited, such as the destruction of Kuwaiti oil wells, could just as easily be described as "economic warfare" rather than as "environmental security." For many who follow this school of thought, the focus is rather more on conflict than it is on security, and upon identifying new causes of conflict in a fairly traditional sense rather than wishing to enunciate a novel or expanded interpretation of "security."

The argument that the environment is a present or future cause of war, seen in the realist-environmentalist school, is by no means an inevitable one. The same problems can encourage states and regions to cooperate, rather than to pursue violent solutions. For example, in the case of disputes over the

Tigris and Euphrates waters between Turkey, Iraq, and Syria, cooperation and coordination have been the outcome. In 1987, a protocol between Turkey and Syria guaranteed a minimum flow of water in the Euphrates at the Syrian-Turkish border. Similarly, Reidulf Molvaer (1991) argued that environmentally induced food shortages have been a major contributor to conflict in the Horn of Africa.

Deudney argues that this is likely to be a common development, that in fact it is less likely that problems like water shortages will lead to war than it is likely that the development of jointly owned water resources will reinforce peace. Exploitation of water resources typically requires expensive and vulnerable engineering projects that create a mutual hostage situation, reducing the incentives for states to employ violence to resolve conflicts.

Lothar Brock extends this line of reasoning by arguing that focusing on environmental issues promotes cooperation among states, which builds international confidence and thus ultimately functions as an integral mechanism of peacebuilding and security policy. It can go further and reduce sources of military insecurity in areas of high military tension (1991: 413). He suggests that the establishment of international parks between conflicting states could serve the interests of environmental conservation and at the same time act as a buffer zone between the parties by demilitarizing sensitive border areas. A possible example of this would be the border between Greece and Turkey along the waters of the Evros in Thrace.

Brock also draws attention to the historical ability of environmental issues to improve political security. An example was the cooperation between the East and West in protecting the Baltic Sea during the Cold War period. Brock argues that this conservation project not only addressed serious environmental issues, but also allowed the two sides to maintain functional lines of communication during times of high political tension (1991: 413).

A quite different group of analysts are those for whom the threat to the environment itself is the problem. Protection of the environment is seen as crucial for a variety of reasons related to the maintenance of the biosphere as a life-support system for the human race. This may relate to issues such as plant diversification, for example, where the loss of biodiversity might threaten the development of future medicinal drugs. This outlook retains a modernist connection to the potential for human emancipation.

A third group are those for whom environmental protection is crucial because of the way that environmental degradation impacts upon other areas of human security, notably living standards in the third world, where, for example, desertification leads to the loss of clean drinking water and arable land, the creation of economic refugees, and particular pressures on women in developing countries who are primarily responsible for food production and obtaining water supplies.

Gleick, for example, argues that disruptions to clean air, water, and the waste-absorbing capacities of natural ecosystems produce effects that need not relate directly to military security, but can trigger economic decline, societal disruption, and therefore conflict. Two examples of this are deforestation, which contributes to global climatic change, and the abuse of the "global commons," such as overuse of shared waters, creation of transborder pollution, and degradation of the atmosphere.

Some proponents appear to see the environmental agenda more in terms of job security than international security, in that it might provide a worthwhile set of objectives for the huge armed forces that otherwise could face a vastly diminished role in the post–Cold War era. U.S. senator Sam Nunn proposed this as a natural role for the military in the new world order. His reasoning was that the military has access to the necessary resources, including intelligence agencies, aircraft, ships, submarines, land forces, satellites, and highly advanced computer systems. In turn, this expensive array of resources might be opened up to nonmilitary scientists for the purpose of collecting information concerning environmental issues, such as the global climate and water and air quality (Brock, 1991: 419).

This linkage serves a double purpose. It grants scientists access to resources they otherwise might not have, and secures the military budget in an era of falling defense spending. It also provides opportunities for international organizations such as the North Atlantic Treaty Organization (NATO) to transform their roles for the new era. NATO in fact has had a low-level ecological security function since 1969. This line of reasoning proposes to modify traditional security in a fashion that is more appropriate for the post–Cold War world. It can be argued, of course, that traditional security is NATO's particular specialism, the "value added" it brings when appropriate. A new environmental security role might more appropriately be given to another, better-suited organization.

The nature of environmental threats has implications for the way that international security and indeed international relations are conceptualized. While the environment-conflict nexus draws the environmental agenda in the direction of realism, the nature of most environmental problems points in the opposite direction. The centrality of the Westphalian state is brought into question by environmental insecurities in the sense that the boundaries of ecosystems do not necessarily coincide with the political boundaries of the international state system.

Arthur Westing (1989) suggested that in this policy realm, it would make more sense to think and operate in terms of ecogeographical regions, such as the drainage basin of a river system, rather than the territorial divisions of the state system. The communities in such a region would pursue their environmental security cooperatively because of their ecological interdependence.

Such a move would have important political implications and cannot be reconciled with the traditional state-centric realist approach to security.

Conclusion

One aspect of the debate over environmental security that distinguishes it from other aspects of the broader agenda is the fact that many environmentalists do not favor linking the environment with the concept of security, because much of conventional security thinking is in direct contrast with the environmentalist worldview.

On the other hand, in many ways the environmental domain lends itself to a postrealist approach to security because, as Jessica Matthews noted (1989), many of the key issues are regional or even global in scope and cannot be neatly confined by sovereign territorial boundaries, so that traditional realist approaches to international relations distort, misunderstand, or ignore them.

In determining whether or not the environment is truly a security issue, the element of threat is important. Just as the threat of attack constituted the main reason for employing security strategies in the past, so continuing acts of environmental degradation can be seen to present "ecological threats to stability and peace" (Brown, 1989: 520). In the worst-case scenarios of this kind of thinking, environmental collapse is equated with the effects of a nuclear holocaust, producing a total breakdown of the natural system.

There is a case for not securitizing the environmental issue at all, because it would force environmentalists to contradict their appropriate methods and goals if they were to conform to state-centered national security approaches. However, the reality of the situation is that the debate over securitization was won by the proponents during the 1990s. The environment is now seen as a security issue by governments, international organizations, and general publics.

It could be argued that what happened in the 1980s was that the way in which the concept of security had traditionally been used came under attack. Its restriction to military threats to the state was no longer seen as adequate for understanding and explaining the contemporary world. So security was not employed to address issues such as environmental damage and societal problems. However, what was not really happening was a deeper unpacking of the meaning of security. What did it mean for different groups in the world? What might it mean? What would be the social and political implications of operating with a fundamentally different understanding or understandings of security? Some of the answers to these questions were given with the advent of postpositivist approaches such as feminism and critical theory.

EIGHT

Gender and Security

International relations as a field of study has only been subject to feminist critique for some twenty years; it is the last of the social sciences to benefit from feminist insights. The field has been marked by extreme male dominance, in terms of both the actors in international politics and the academics that study it. The implication has been that "one can study the course of relations between states without reference to questions of gender. Moreover, by neglecting the dimension of gender, international relations implicitly supports the thesis that international processes themselves are gender neutral" (Halliday, 1994: 149).

The basis of the feminist critique of international relations theory is the idea that there is a fundamental difference between the way that men and women experience and therefore see the world. "International Relations theory has overwhelmingly been constructed by men working with mental models of human activity and society seen through a male eye and apprehended through a male sensibility" (Grant and Newland, 1991: 1). The component ideas of international relations are therefore gendered because men and women experience societies and their interactions differently.

Knowledge and theory are built on experience; therefore, by being gender biased, the study of international relations has drawn on a selective set of sources to construct its model of the world, and its use of key concepts such as sovereignty, security, development, and power. Because women were left out of most of the historical classical texts of political theory on which it has traditionally drawn so heavily, the discipline of international relations has inevitably incorporated gender bias in its very definitions and theories of knowledge.

International relations as a discipline differed from other social sciences in being prescriptive and normative and stressing policy relevance from the very outset. The shadow of World War I led to the discipline being concerned above all with devising ways to help rational decisionmakers avoid war in the future. However, it can be argued that the exclusion of women's experiences from the conceptualization of international relations has had negative consequences both for the discipline and for male and female inhabitants of the world. It has resulted in an academic field excessively focused on conflict and anarchy, and a way of practicing statecraft and formulating strategy that is excessively focused on competition and fear.

International relations theory took as its basis political concepts articulated by classical thinkers such as Hobbes and Rousseau. Its concept of the state is heavily influenced by the historical example of the Greek city-states mediated through the ideas of Plato and Aristotle. Feminists argue that these ideas were gender biased and that when international relations adopted them into its own theory it duplicated the gender bias (Grant, 1991: 9). It also failed to acknowledge that the "political man" under discussion by Hobbes and Rousseau was indeed only a man. As Rebecca Grant points out, "women are invisible in the state of nature" (1991: 9). The characteristics of political man are masculine characteristics. Similarly, depictions of the Greek city-states are depictions of a male world in which women were relegated to the domestic sphere, leaving men in sole control of the national and international spheres.

By incorporating these perspectives into international relations theory without questioning how representative they were, the field gained a theory based on a truth that was not truth at all. International relations theory, shaped by the realist worldview, rests on the belief that states exist in an anarchical system where, in the absence of any higher authority, they will pursue their own self-interest and power. In order to protect their position, states must be autonomous, as dependency breeds weakness, and they must trust only themselves. This interpretation of Hobbes's "state of nature" is presented as fact or truth, but it rests on a narrow, masculinized interpretation of the world.

The issues that have been traditionally given priority in foreign policy are those with which men have a special affinity (Tickner, 1991: 27). Gender bias crucially influences the way that the world is perceived, interpreted, and organized, particularly on issues relating to international security. What is traditionally claimed to be universal often turns out to be true only of males. Obviously this reflects reality in the sense that most diplomats, ministers, and other decisionmakers are in fact male. What feminists argue is left out is analysis that asks how the fact of them being male affects their views and the decisionmaking processes of which they are a part. Feminists argue for "the presence of a specific political agenda at every level of social life. Simply put, this agenda involves the systematic exclusion of women from full participation in the constitution of that life" (Leonard, 1990: 216).

▨ The Feminist Critique of Realism

Feminists have a fundamental objection to the ontology and epistemology of realism and realist security theory. Realism's positivist methodology renders its masculinist underpinnings invisible (Tickner, 1992: 130). The realist approach is based on the positivist assumption that the universe being studied is directly accessible and representable by concepts that are shaped by logic and experiment (Tickner, 1992: 432–433). Therefore, the goal is to reveal the objective laws of the universe. A crucial aspect is the subject/object distinction. Realists regard themselves as being epistemologically outside the subject that they are studying. The observer or theorist is seen as being detached from the objective reality that he or she examines. This kind of "scientific objectivity" is associated with masculinity; separating the self from the other is essential in masculine gender development (Tickner, 1992: 432). For feminists there is no such archimedian point on which an abstract knower can reflect.

Feminists, like other postpositivists, challenge realism's claims to scientific objectivity, arguing that all knowledge and social reality are socially constructed (Tickner, 1992: 432). This rejects the neorealist account of states as unitary actors whose internal characteristics are largely irrelevant. Instead of existing as givens, states are constructed. Behind the supposedly "natural" states lie social institutions constantly made and remade by individual actions (Jones, 1996: 411). Gender is essentially socially constructed and produces subjective identities "through which we know and see the world" (Jones, 1996: 406). Feminists argue that "we reason from our history, and not to it from some abstract, disembodied point of view" (Leonard, 1990: 230). The world is shaped by gendered meanings and people experience the world as gendered beings. Therefore, in order to understand agents, the implications of "gendered states" must be recognized.

In one sense gender has always been incorporated in the study of international relations. State sovereignty has been accepted as a central constitutive political practice and gender identity has been incorporated into it as that of the universalizing abstraction of rational man (True, 1996). But this is a particularized gendered construction of reality.

The realist approach to security has been defined in terms of the need to ensure the survival of states. It has therefore been constructed as a guarantee of safety that necessitates "political arrangements which make war less likely, provide for negotiation rather than belligerence and which preserve peace as a normal condition among states" (Scruton, cited in Stearns, 1998: 106). The realist approach also emphasizes military power for the purposes of defense. It is for national security, defined in this way, that realists believe citizens should be prepared to make sacrifices, and governments should give priority in their political and budgetary strategies. This is not an amoral stance, because realists see the state as the ideal human community; they invest it with moral worth. In this sense realists are adopting a normatively driven perspective.

Realists usually define peace in negative terms—that is, as the absence of war. In classical realist terms, peace is to be achieved through the manipulation of alliances and balances of power. Barry Buzan has recognized, however, that in a "mature anarchy . . . states secure within themselves might recognise and uphold international norms of behaviour and this strengthens international security" (cited in Stearns, 1998: 107).

From the realist perspective the security of the individual is "inseparably entangled with that of the state" (Buzan, 1991a: 39). From this point of view, therefore, individuals are not the appropriate starting point for thinking about security, because most threats to individuals arise from societal issues, rather than from the military activities of other countries.

The inherent contradictions of the realist assumptions about security were demonstrated at the height of the Cold War, when "the military security of the state was deemed to be identical with the insecurity of individuals who were held hostage to nuclear deterrence" (Tickner, 1992: 177). At the same time, realists were skeptical about efforts to achieve security through disarmament, economic development, and respect for human rights.

Realists, however, do recognize that military strength incurs opportunity costs and that these might not be distributed equally among individuals and groups, and also that balance of power and arms race policies can lead to a spiral of insecurity. Some realists even accept that in certain circumstances a state may constitute a threat to people living within its jurisdiction. Buzan, for example, has argued that a "maximal state" might oppress its own people and a "minimal state" might fail to provide adequate levels of societal order. However, ultimately realists see the problem of war and insecurity as either due to man's aggressive nature, in the classical realist formulation, or due to the effects of the international anarchy in structural realism, though this can be mitigated under defensive realism.

The realist approach is based on a fundamental division of the domestic sphere of sovereign states and the international sphere of state interaction under anarchy. Realism has also tended to formulate its concepts in terms of opposed dualisms, such as security/insecurity and order/anarchy, which pose stark either/or choices. According to realism, international relations is governed by objective laws rooted in an immutable human nature.

The feminist argument is that realism promotes an extremely narrow understanding of security that is highly inconsistent with political realities and the experiences of most people in today's world. The critique of realist theory and practice flows from the feminist demonstration of "the link between the practices that oppress women and the theories and philosophical presuppositions that mirror and support these practices" (Leonard, 1990: 215).

▧ Varieties of Feminism

"Feminism" is a term that actually covers a wide variety of significantly different approaches and it is misleading to suggest that there is a single feminism or a single understanding of "security" that flows from it. These differences can fundamentally affect the approaches taken to security. For example, Joshua Goldstein (1994: 284ff.) distinguishes between three clear groupings, essentialist, liberal, and postmodern. Essentialist feminism believes that there are real differences between the genders that are not just social constructions and cultural indoctrination, that there is in fact a core biological essence to being male or female.

This has clear implications for the way we look at international relations and security. For example, for realists, the international system consists of separate, autonomous actors (states) that have complete control over their own territory and no right to infringe on another's territory. Is this approach based on a "masculine" view of the world? According to essentialist feminists it is. Psychological research shows that boys and girls grow up with different views of separateness and connection. Because the mother is the primary nurturer through childhood, girls form their identity from a perception of similarity with the mother, boys form theirs from a perception of difference. From this experience, boys develop social relations based on individual autonomy, but girls' relations are based on connection. Women fear abandonment, whereas men fear intimacy.

In moral reasoning, according to this research, boys tend to apply abstract rules and stress individual rights, whereas girls pay more attention to the contexts of different situations and the responsibility of group members for each other. Research by Carol Gilligan into playground behavior indicates that girls are less tolerant of high levels of conflict and that while boys prefer games taken to the point of conflict, girls prefer games in which players take turns and where the success of one is not dependent on the failure of another (1982). These kinds of findings suggest that gender does make a difference in the way that we try to deal with conflict, and this has implications for thinking about international conflict resolution and the construction of security.

Essentialist feminists argue that women would be less inclined to go to war than men and that therefore a world run by women would be a peaceful and secure world. This argument has been discounted by other types of feminists, who point out that historically women have often supported wars. In the past four decades, for example, Golda Meir led Israel to war in 1967, Indira Ghandi did the same for India in 1971, and Margaret Thatcher did so for the United Kingdom in 1982.

Feminist critiques of international relations are now more likely to argue about the dominance of "masculinity" rather than "men." The difference is the idea that it is not biological differences that are crucial, but rather the way in which society constructs the female and male identities. Grant asserts that the "real target is gender: not the anatomical difference between the female and the male sex but the complicated aspect of social being known as gender" (1991: 8). Thus gender does not refer to the biological differences between the sexes, but "to a set of culturally shaped and defined characteristics associated with masculinity and femininity" (Tickner, 1992: 7).

The crucial issue is not whether a person's reproductive organs happen to be inside or outside their body, but rather how the peculiar social construction of masculinity in Western thought influences the theory and practice of international relations. Feminists argue that "the social and political practices that issue in the domination of women by men are systematically linked with both received social theories and the metatheoretical assumptions that undergird those theories" (Leonard, 1990: 216).

Masculinity is defined in terms of power, strength, independence, rationality, and objectivity. These are all characteristics that are "projected onto the behavior of states, whose success as international actors is measured in terms of power capabilities and capacity for self-help and autonomy" (Tickner, 1992: 6–7). Feminine qualities have no place in this system. To be feminine is to be dependent, subjective, irrational, and therefore weak. A state that demonstrates feminine characteristics in international politics is doomed to be dominated by its masculine opponents.

The focus on masculine versus feminine, as opposed to man versus woman, allows us to see how men have been constrained by the gender bias in international relations as much as women have. The masculine qualities highlighted are not applicable to all men equally, just as feminine qualities are not applicable to all women. But traditional realist international relations theory taught that these are the qualities most required of states and therefore state leaders. The question therefore arises whether these masculinized qualities are "truths" or whether they rest on ideas about the world that, because they have excluded women and the majority of men, are not "truths" at all. By considering questions of gender, we are forced to question the basic concepts underlying postwar international relations theory and therefore the basic concepts underlying the theories of security that flowed from it.

Many feminists find in international relations hidden assumptions of masculinity. They suggest that an international system based on feminist principles might give greater importance to the interdependence of states than to their autonomy. It would stress the responsibility of people to care for each other regardless of abstractions like state borders. Where issues of sovereignty conflicted with human rights, the latter would take priority. The concept of security would be based on ideas of common security rather than narrow self-interest. It would reflect "a definition of security that is people-centred and transcends state and regional boundaries" (Tickner, 1995: 192).

In addition to autonomy and anarchy, realism stresses military force in international relations. Here, too, many feminists see a hidden assumption of masculinity. In this view, men are more warlike, women more peaceful, and warfare is seen as the quintessentially male occupation. Thus, though realism may accurately portray the importance of force in the contemporary world, this merely reflects the male domination of international politics to date—not a necessary, eternal, or inescapable logic of relations among states.

Historically, man has been the warrior sex. There may be biological as well as cultural reasons for this. Higher levels of particular sex hormones (primarily testosterone) are linked to aggressive behavior in males, notably in rats, apes, and humans. This doesn't mean that men necessarily have to fight, only that biologically they are better adapted to do so under certain circumstances.

In contrast, essentialist feminists portray women as more peaceful. Opinion poll research suggests that women are 10 percent less likely than men to support military action. Essentialists point to the motto of the UN Educational, Scientific, and Cultural Organization: "Since wars begin in the minds of men, it is in the minds of men that the foundations of peace should be sought." The motto itself is meant to suggest only that since human beings are rational, thinking creatures, they are capable of constructing social orders that are not underpinned by a war system. Essentialist feminists, however, prefer to take the sentence literally and argue from it that since wars begin in men's minds, it is in the minds of women that peace should be sought (Goldstein, 1994: 289).

Liberal feminists, in contrast, reject the essentialist claims on the grounds that they are based on stereotyped gender roles. Liberal feminists see the "essential" differences in the abilities and perspectives of men and women as trivial or nonexistent. They view men and women as equal in terms of their underlying beliefs and attitudes and their capacities for political and other forms of leadership. They object to the exclusion of women from positions of power and influence in the world, but do not believe that including women would fundamentally change the nature of the international system. They believe that when women are allowed to participate in international relations, they play the game basically the same way men do and with similar results.

Liberal feminists therefore tend to reject the critique of realism as masculine. They point to women who have become political leaders, such as Benazir Bhutto of Pakistan and Margaret Thatcher of the United Kingdom, and say that there was no distinctively "feminine" quality to their leadership.

A third approach is postmodern feminism. Postmodernist feminists find fault in both the essentialist and liberal feminist approaches. For postmodernist feminists the very concept of gender is itself highly problematic. Liberal feminists are criticized for adopting a fundamentally conservative analysis that accepts as valid virtually all the key features of the current international system, rather than condemning it for its manifest failings. Essentialist feminism is criticized for glorifying stereotypical "feminine" virtues, for condemning half of the human race out of hand, and for operating with a simplistic and flawed conception of identity and identity construction. Essentialism is treated with deep suspicion because of the biological determinism that underpins much of its analysis.

Postmodern feminists resist what they see as a tendency in other forms of feminism to work with simplistic categories of identity, such as "woman" itself. To some extent this is a wish to see the full range of identity attributes captured in discussion, such as race, class, sexuality, and so on, as well as gender. But the critique goes further than this, since simply adding on these attributes is not seen as sufficient. Even when the details are more specific, when it is accepted, for example, that the experiences of rich, white, healthy, American women are hardly the same as those of poor, black, disabled, African women, postmodernists warn against believing that identifying enough salient features has solved the problem. None of these categories are seen as being sedimented, unitary categories; all of them have understandings that can evolve over time and vary in their meaning and significance across regions and cultures (Peterson and Runyan, 1993: 120–121).

For similar reasons, postmodern feminists are critical of feminisms that draw on traditional Marxist analyses. Socialist feminists focus particularly on economic dimensions of patriarchy and on capitalism's failure to value reproductive as well as productive labor, the former including work that is done in the informal home setting. There is a focus on development issues and the comparative value of male and female labor in the contemporary international system that has led socialist feminists to strongly criticize the allocation of scarce resources to the military rather than the civilian economy. Postmodern feminists, however, criticize the socialist assumption that reproductive labor is unique to women simply because they are the mothers.

Whereas essentialist feminists locate the cause of war and insecurity in specific masculine traits and biological programming, postmodern feminists argue that there is no meaningful difference between the relative peacefulness or aggressiveness of men and women. They also make a crucial point in arguing that peace does not always equate with justice and that it is not necessarily always correct to prioritize the pursuit of peace over the pursuit of justice, so that there will be occasions when peace must be sacrificed in order to achieve justice and that this might involve the resort to violence by women as well as men (Peterson and Runyan, 1993: 119–121).

The challenge to the idea of a homogeneous feminist approach is also reflected in postcolonial feminism. Black and third world feminists were critical of much feminist argument in the 1980s, because the idea of a generalized female experience failed to reflect the specific differences that they felt their own experiences demonstrated. There was a suspicion of what was seen by many as "white" feminism. This was an important point because the colonial experience made third world women particularly sensitive to suspicions that they were being patronized or spoken for by white feminists (Mohanty, Russo, and Torres, 1991). For black feminists there was the specific issue of racialism, which could see white women alienating black women in ways that made a nonsense of the idea of a universal, undifferentiated sisterhood. Black feminists, while accepting the importance of gender discrimination, also see "white" as a privileged color, which has important social and political ramifications. Because of this, "relations between white women and colonised, ex-colonial and racialised women speak to historically constructed power relations. They immensely complicate attempts at feminist theorising" (Pettman, 1996: 43).

Gender and Security

Feminist writings have unsurprisingly concentrated on the gender variable in their analyses of international relations and security, but many of their general arguments are consistent with those of nonfeminist critical theorists. By questioning the realist assumption that the state of nature has no gender dimension, international relations theory is opened up to wider explanations and understandings. This has important implications for interpretations of security. With its emphasis on war and violence, international security has been the most thoroughly gender-biased of the various subdisciplines of international relations. It has also been the most difficult for feminists to intervene in, because it is so masculinized that women's voices have been considered "inauthentic" (Tickner, 1992: 4).

Feminists argue that the masculine construction of "security" emphasizes sovereign man and sovereign states defined not by connection or relationships, but by autonomy in decisionmaking. Security is understood not in terms of celebrating and sustaining life, but as safety and separateness from others, and possession of the ability to harm others. Believing that peace requires preparation for war generates an arms race mentality. This involves sacrificing social welfare objectives in favor of defense spending, and training people to risk lives and practice violence in the name of "higher" state objectives. As noted in the discussion of economic security, seeing security purely in terms of state-sponsored military threats produces opportunity costs in terms of lost or deferred government spending on other social objectives. Invariably it is the poor and marginalized elements of society who suffer most as a result of these opportunity costs.

In addition, the construction of security in military terms—understood as direct violence—may mask the systemic insecurity of indirect or structural violence. Structural violence refers to reduced life expectancy as a consequence of oppressive political and economic structures—for example, greater infant mortality among poor women who are denied access to healthcare services. Thus feminists argue that "structural violence especially affects the lives of women and other subordinated groups. When we ignore this fact we ignore the security of the majority of the planet's occupants" (Peterson and Runyan, 1993: 36).

Third world women, in particular, argue that poverty, environmental degradation, gross social inequality, exploitation, militarization, and violence are interconnected. Widening definitions of violence also widen our definitions of peace and security, so peace becomes more than "negative peace," more than just "not war." It becomes positive peace, where people's own security is built collectively in their everyday lives.

Most male-dominated societies have constructed elaborate sanctions and taboos against women fighting in war. As a result, men have acquired almost exclusive control over the means of destruction. Often this is done in the name of protecting women and children, who are discouraged from taking up arms, or not allowed to, in their own defense. In 1988 over half of the world's armed forces excluded women. The United States has one of the highest rates of female participation, at 11 percent. Given the low rate of female participation, it is obvious that most women are not direct recipients of military spending. However, women suffered disproportionately from the diversion of resources into military spending during the Cold War. For example, for the price of twenty Patriot missiles, the entire female population of Africa could have been immunized against tetanus.

Gender has always been present in understandings of international security, but this has rarely been acknowledged. While in wartime women are rarely involved in direct combat, they are frequently the majority of the victims. J. Ann Tickner argues that nearly 90 percent of the casualties from war suffered since 1945 have been suffered by women and children (1995: 191). Women and children make up 80 percent of all refugees. As an influx of refugees can cause major security problems for states, it makes sense to aim solutions for refugee problems at women.

However, while focusing on the gender variable is extremely important, there is a danger of stressing this variable so much that others are lost sight of. During the conflicts in Bosnia and Kosovo during the 1990s, it was strikingly obvious that the refugee columns were overwhelmingly composed of women and children. This focused understandable and justified attention on the status of women as the victims of such conflicts. But what was sometimes lost in such analysis was the fact that males were absent among the refugees because they were left behind fighting, or because they were already dead and lying in mass graves. They were just as much the victims of the conflict as were the women and children. For those who had been executed, their deaths were a striking example of the "gender variable" at work. The males of fighting age were murdered and the women, the old, and the young forced into exile. Discrimination in behavior on the grounds of gender was stark and deliberate.

Women also make up high percentages in other noncombatant areas of war. Amnesty International argues that in armed conflicts around the world, "women are particularly vulnerable to abuse, death, maiming and displacement" (1998: 1). These abuses are often not just examples of soldiers out of control, but also deliberate acts carried out as weapons of war. In the civil war in Afghanistan, for example, traditional Afghan norms of honor and shame that emphasize female purity allowed rival factions to use rape and sexual assault as part of a deliberate policy of terror. Systematic rape was used "to dishonour entire communities and reduce people's capacity to resist military advances" (Amnesty International, 1999: 1). By threatening to rape their wives and daughters, the male population is kept subdued and under control. This became the main security concern of Afghan women. Their government was not protecting their security interests, it was directly threatening them.

Afghanistan is by no means an isolated case. During the 1990s in Bosnia, rape was used as a deliberate policy of war by Serbian forces and the same tactic was employed by the forces of the Rassemblement Congolais pour la Démocratie in the Democratic Republic of Congo. In Bosnia rape was used as "a symbol of subjugation and humiliation, a means of propagating the superior race and a theme for mobilising ethnic rage" (Halliday, 1994: 153).

At the fourth United Nations Conference on Women, held in Beijing in 1995, governments declared that rape in armed conflict constitutes a war crime, and is sometimes also a crime against humanity and an act of genocide, as defined in the Convention on the Prevention of Genocide. This represented an advance, since at the war crimes trials held after World War II there were no charges based on rape.

That an issue like rape has been left out of constructions of "security" demonstrates how important it is to include a gender focus in this realm. Masculine concepts of what constitutes the "political" have left aspects that primarily affect women, such as rape, out of consideration. The examples from Afghanistan, Bosnia, and the Congo also make the point that citizens, particularly women, are often most at risk from the armed forces, or armed population, of their own country, not that of their neighbors, and that the state-centric realist assumption that a security dilemma arises because of the existence of armed forces whose purpose is to protect their citizens from external attack, is overly simplistic.

For feminists, the security of women is threatened by war and male violence at different levels, since the assumption of the supposedly secure domestic sphere is seen as hiding the masculinist social control of women. In this perspective, violence is seen as existing on a continuum, with war at one extreme. However, the continuum also encompasses direct violence such as murder and rape, and structural violence such as the ideological concept of "women's work" or the cult of motherhood (True, 1996: 232).

In addition, multiple forms of security from the broader agenda, such as economic and ecological forms, clearly question accounts of security that center on the state (Peterson, 1992: 31). The transformation toward a system of genuine global security is constrained by the system of sovereign states, despite the existence of the global security crisis. The contradictory nature of national security has particularly severe implications for women, who tend to be at the margins of many societies. The structural violence created by the gender hierarchy and women's resultant systematic insecurity are an internal and an external dimension of the operation of state systems. Constituting new visions of security is therefore seen as requiring the politicization of structural violence as contingent and not natural, and accepting that it can be changed (Peterson, 1992: 50). V. Spike Peterson examines the way state systems formulate security through a "lens of protection." States promise various forms of protection to the citizen. This creates an image of "shelter against danger," but the protection involves costs as well, although these are somewhat masked. Essentially what is created is a protection racket, in the sense that the threats against which a state protects its citizens are imaginary or are the consequence of its own activities.

The roles of the protector and protected are powerfully gendered, based on constitutions of masculine autonomy and feminine dependency. According to Jan Pettman, the dichotomy is easily turned into the idea of owned and controlled women. Furthermore, women are often under most threat from protectors and have limited protection from violence (Pettman, 1996: 26).

Locating security within state boundaries has been a significant project of much of international relations theory. Feminists question this by emphasizing the interrelatedness of all kinds of physical violence, varying from military combat to domestic violence in cultures where it is not effectively prevented by the legal system (Tickner, 1995: 193). Prioritizing order and the survival of states, it is argued, has served to hide and maintain various forms of domination and has restrained concern with other threats of security experienced by individuals. Thus, hierarchical social relations must be recognized and altered before it is possible to alleviate the multilevel insecurities. The goal of achieving peace and justice is indistinguishable from overcoming social relations of domination and subordination (Tickner, 1992: 128). In the final analysis, therefore, genuine security means the eradication of unjust social relations and divisive boundary distinctions.

International security is constrained by its realist underpinnings, which are rooted in gender bias and false truths. It is also constrained by its inability to adapt to a post–Cold War environment where interstate conflict is the exception and intrastate conflict the norm. Where a citizen is more likely to experience violence at the hands of her or his own government, rather than an outside aggressor, traditional security thinking that puts state security first clearly needs to be reassessed.

Feminist Approaches to Security

For feminists, the key concepts of security and sovereignty and units of analysis like "state" and "international system" are indistinguishable from the patriarchal divisions of public/private (True, 1996: 225). These are identified with men's experiences and forms of knowledge within the male-dominated public sphere as opposed to the private sphere, where women have traditionally been located. The private and the international realms are both subordinate to the domestic state and its sovereign order of justice. The private sphere is regarded as a natural realm of disorder where women must be controlled.

Many feminist political theorists have focused on the inside/outside approach typical of Western political thought, in which the conception of politics and the public realm can be characterized as a "barracks community." The *polis* is defined in opposition to the dangerous and disruptive forces that threaten its existence. This is seen as setting a hostile and combative dualism at the heart of the community that men construct and by which they live their lives (Stearns, 1998: 109).

Also, the provision of national security continues to be an almost exclusively male domain. Some liberal feminists have reacted to this by advocating the enlistment of far more women in the military, and allowing them to serve in all combat roles. However, the liberal "right to fight" campaign has been criticized because it advocates the politics of access, while accepting uncritically a profoundly gendered conception of security that legitimizes state violence. Critics also argue that liberal feminists have also failed to address the degree to which the military plays a central role in justifying the very social order that is responsible for the subordination of women.

Feminists argue that the military is an integral part of the institutions of the state and that therefore violence should not be seen as an unusual and limited act, but as an inevitable reflection of the way in which society is organized and the masculinist institutions that underpin it. Feminism's approach to the state and to patriarchy brings into question the view that the state is the mainstay of security and that security for the individual is adequately understood in terms of membership of a particular community. "This is because adopting a feminist perspective challenges the view of the military as a defender of a pre-given 'national interest'" (Stearns, 1998: 104).

Feminist approaches have also promoted new ways of thinking about the problems involved in achieving security. Postmodern feminism has encouraged a rethinking of dominant conceptions of identities and boundaries, in which traditional approaches to security have been framed. Feminists also argue that the degree to which people feel or actually are threatened varies according to their economic, political, social, or personal circumstances. The idea that "the state" or "the people" are threatened is a grotesque oversimplification of the political realities. Thus, a whole range of criteria, such as poverty, inequality, militarism, lack of development or underdevelopment, and the denial of human rights, ought to be taken into account when attempting to determine how secure individuals or groups actually feel.

From the perspective of a gender analysis, the development of the broader, multisectoral approach to security has been a major step forward, as has the recognition that the sectors overlap, because this has allowed mainstream security analysis to recognize the particular ways in which the social environment may generate severe vulnerabilities for women, who invariably earn less than men for doing comparable work and find that their work is not valued to the same extent as that of men. Moreover, women are often particularly exposed when environmental degradation or economic recession occurs.

The conception of security promoted by feminists is constructed in terms of a commitment to social justice, which is seen as essential for the development of an enduring peace. This replaces the realist priority of order as a guiding principle. For order to be just, the hegemonic masculinity that has resulted in insecurity for men as well as women must be overcome, and requires an approach that emphasizes the particular needs and circumstances of people (Tickner, 1992: 130).

One strand of feminist security thinking that is potentially rewarding for an approach to security based on social justice is the "impact on" approach, which holds that military expenditure imposes particular costs on women as a group. For example, during the 1980s as the United States increased its military spending dramatically, it simultaneously cut its social welfare spending. This led to the "feminization of poverty," as 34.6 percent of all women-headed households in the United States fell into the official category of "poor" (Stearns, 1998: 110–111). This figure increased to 50 percent among households headed by black and Hispanic women. Feminist scholars have also sought to show that, for example, low-paid workers and single mothers are less likely to benefit from military spending than are working-class men. Because defense spending was of minimal direct or indirect benefit to women, it could be characterized as "defeating the aims of the wider feminist movement to improve the status and position, health, welfare and security of women as a group" (Stearns, 1998: 111).

During the 1960s, advocates of third world development drew attention to the disparity in comparative resources allocated by the developed states to weapons acquisition and foreign aid, and to the fact that as defense spending increased, aid allocation tended to fall. In some years the total global amounts spent on weapons were greater than the combined incomes of all the poor on the planet. A detailed breakdown of the effects of this process revealed that it, too, was a highly gendered issue. Feminists argued that the transfer of resources from military spending to the civilian sector of the economy would benefit all sectors of society, but particularly women. The resources released could be spent on health, education, and development. This made disarmament a central feature of feminist approaches to international security, reinforcing the antimilitary attitudes that had been characteristic of the women's peace movement since the 1920s.

Building from an antipatriarchal perspective and taking a hostile stance toward war and high levels of defense spending, feminism has also critiqued militarism, using the existence of a militarist subculture within society as an explanation for the existence of large military establishments and governments willing to treat war and the projection of force as normal tools of state policy. In this reading, the proclivity for war is not simply the result of rational decisionmakers choosing from among a range of policy instruments. It is the outcome of the pervasive spread of militarist values through society, in particular through the decisionmaking elite. Because this elite is overwhelmingly male, the social construction of masculinity provides a ready breeding ground for the militarist mind-set and value system.

Of the great variety of diverse feminist approaches, postpositivist feminism presents the most significant challenge to the concept of security and the theoretical foundation underpinning it. This is because, like postmodernist approaches generally, it rejects the basic epistemological and ontological assumptions of realism as a positivist social science. Fundamentally, political realities are viewed only as social constructions and therefore have a history and a capacity for change. The classical approach to security emphasizes particular theoretical categories, while leaving others out of the picture. The overwhelming emphasis on the "national security" of states has had the effect of disguising the role of the state in legitimizing and maintaining other forms of insecurity for people.

The postpositivist feminist approach to security is reflected to a significant extent in the practice of many contemporary social movements. Social movements are fluid and transitional, and a large number have emerged in recent decades that are committed to pursuing human security in the economic, ecological, and political domains (Tickner, 1995: 190). Social movements largely disregard conventional assumptions of the political process and associated political space that have devalued the security of the less privileged in society. Hence security becomes not an objective, but a "process" that is initiated from the grassroots level. Social movements concerned with peace, the environment, and feminism promote a vision of global security based on people.

This is important in terms of developing a richer concept of security. The broadened security agenda is an attempt to promote the idea of security taking different forms in a variety of sectors. It necessarily critiques the traditional approach of seeing security in terms of one sector, the military, and one referent object, the state. It is a significant move, but to the extent that the state remains the primary referent throughout, it is only taken so far. Feminism operates with a primary objection to the division between the insecurities that are recognized and legitimated at the national and interstate levels, such as military threats from abroad, and the insecurities that are treated as private matters, such as domestic violence. For feminists, violence and insecurity exist on a continuum. This spectrum runs from the domestic to the international, and the explanation of and solution to both should be pursued on the basis of that continuum. Feminist theory, therefore, has the capacity to take the broader agenda, which it has always accepted, and deepen the understanding and practice of security.

All social theories are constructions. Even the currently hegemonic political paradigm, liberal metatheory, claims to be an innocent description of how things naturally are, but is instead an expression of a historically specific way of organizing society. The practice of feminism suggests an important alternative to prevailing security praxis. For feminists, the central issue is "less one of realizing theory in practice, than it is of realizing the practical demands theory must meet" (Leonard, 1990: 213).

Conclusion

The realist and positivist dominance of international relations theory has meant that the international system has been characterized by sharp and profound differences between the domestic sphere of sovereign states and the anarchic international sphere. This has had deep implications for formulating the theoretical agenda and the central categories of analysis.

Security has been tied to military strength and understood as the national security of territorial states. This has resulted in the constitution of theoretical approaches that have largely ignored the insecurities experienced by ordinary people. Postpositivist feminism has been one of the approaches that have questioned and challenged this simplistic notion of security based on privileging political regimes at the expense of marginalizing various forms of violence and threats to the security of individuals, which are arbitrarily excluded from the "high politics" agenda. Social and political realities are not "natural," but contingent and socially constructed and therefore not immutable. Feminism in particular is fundamentally concerned with revealing the inherently gendered nature of international relations as a discipline and how this has resulted in the marginalization of women from the theoretical agenda and the universalization of gender identity into that of rational man.

Furthermore, by concentrating on the gender variable in international relations theory, feminism shows the inadequacies of the realist security agenda in its failure to recognize the systematic social relations of domination that have made women vulnerable to security threats domestically and internationally. Feminists have taken the security of people, not states, as their point of departure, as well as a broader formulation of security that incorporates nonmilitary dimensions.

Feminist alternative understandings of security highlight the importance of recognizing and altering the gender inequalities within social relations as a prerequisite for envisioning a more secure world where security is based on the priority of justice. Not only are the experiences of women relevant, but all social relations of subordination must be eliminated.

States are a means to an end, not an end in themselves. Security theory clearly needs to evolve to address a changing world. This means acknowledging the importance of nonmilitary security issues and acknowledging the different security experiences of women, so that questions of poverty, rape, and refugee status are treated with the same seriousness as military strategy and nuclear weapons. Not only would this allow the experience of women to be incorporated into security thinking, but it would also open the way for effective consideration of other cultures' unique security needs.

NINE

Postmodernism and Security

P ostmodernist or poststructuralist approaches represent a fundamentally
different approach to security compared to the traditional approach, the
broader agenda, and even critical approaches such as feminism and critical
theory. For realists, the postmodernist contributions are beyond the pale, "a
prolix and self-indulgent discourse that is divorced from the real world"
(Walt, 1991: 223). That is not the view embraced here. Rather, postmodernism
is seen as an effective critique of traditional approaches to security and a perspective with valuable things to say about the nature of security and international relations.

The Impact of Modernity

In the years before the end of the Cold War, postmodernism became a leading
school of thought in Europe. It was a period in which many thinkers
responded to a growing sense of emptiness, a belief that what Jurgen Habermas called "the historical project of modernity"— the characteristic Western
ways of thinking that came into existence during the seventeenth and eighteenth centuries—was coming to an end. Previous centuries had been characterized by the dominance of the Catholic Church and a Christian worldview
and value system. However, the homogeneous worldview of Christendom
shattered under the pressures of the Renaissance and the Reformation and by
the middle decades of the seventeenth century, Christian Europe was undergoing a moral, political, and intellectual crisis as previous certainties were
undermined and almost everything was thrown into doubt.

The "scientific revolution" of the seventeenth century and the intellectual
revolution that accompanied it provided a way out of these dilemmas and
gave birth to the project of modernity. The Newtonian revolution in science
inaugurated a period dominated by the scientific method as a mode of

research and explanation, which could provide answers to the great questions for which religion had previously been the source of authority. Isaac Newton and the scientific community (in the broadest sense) provided a new epistemology, a way of validating the truth of particular claims and a new ontology, a wider world revealed by exploration rather than revealed wisdom.

This was the beginning of the "modern" era. It was characterized by a number of key features. The first was a belief in the power of human reason to uncover all the mysteries of the universe in time, and to solve all problems by force of intellect given enough research. Second was a view of history characterized by a belief in progress and a teleological assumption that history was moving humanity in a linear forward direction toward greater understanding and material well-being. Enlightenment thinkers sought to shape the future "through powers of scientific prediction, through social engineering and rational planning, and the institutionalisation of rational systems of social regulation and control" (Harvey, 1990: 249).

At the time of their inception, these were radical ideas, representing a fundamental break with the worldview that had characterized European thought for a thousand years. For the contemporary world they appear commonsensical only because over the succeeding centuries they have become the prevailing and usually unquestioned ideology. For most people in the "modern" world the approach is taken as valid and valuable, and the source of innumerable benefits to humanity in the past three centuries. It is an approach that has produced access to infinitely better healthcare, homes, and workplaces that are well-lit and warmed by electricity, the ability to travel and communicate rapidly throughout the world, the development of countless labor-saving devices that have reduced the drudgery of human existence, and the attainment of a far greater understanding of the nature and operation of the universe in which humanity lives. But for postmodernists there is also a dark side to these achievements and the way in which they were made possible. This has important implications for thinking about the concept and practice of security.

The Meaning of Postmodernism

It is important to recognize that there is more than one meaning of "postmodern" in terms of the analysis of international relations. There is a sense in which it is used that is in many ways at the heart of all contemporary "critical" approaches to the subject and that must therefore underlie any construction or interpretation of security relevant to contemporary politics. There is also a second sense, which is a very specific form of critique that contains elements antithetical to a fully critical theory of security.

Looked at in the first way, the postmodern age can be seen as the latest manifestation of the modern age, in which there have been revolutionary changes in global cultural practices as well as in economic and political processes. In particular, there has been a dramatic compression of space and time. Jet aircraft travel, e-mail, mobile phones, the Internet, and a host of other developments mean that in a very real sense the world is a much smaller place than it used to be, and the time available for people to cope with their responsibilities in life is dramatically less. In terms of human social, political, military, and economic activities, space and time do not mean what they did one hundred or even fifty years ago. International relations is not about billiard-ball states colliding in anarchy with the speed of horses or sailing ships; it is about almost instantaneous flows of information, capital, and ideas and the dramatically fast movement of trade, populations, and advanced military technology. This is the postmodern world, and any analysis of international relations or security that is not based on an understanding of these new structures and processes cannot possibly capture the realities of the present era. Even analysts who do not use a poststructuralist methodology have absorbed the language of postmodernity in this cultural and general sense. Barry Buzan and Ole Waever, for example, refer to the existence of "postmodern states" that have moved on from the Westphalian model and "desecuritised much of the traditional agenda of threats" (2003: 23).

The second sense in which postmodern is used is the focus for the rest of this chapter. This is the approach represented by individuals like Jean-François Lyotard, Michel Foucault, and Jacques Derrida, who reject modernity and the Enlightenment in favor of a perspective that refuses to adopt a normative position grounded in a modernist structure of privileged ethical assumptions and claims.

Postmodernism is notoriously difficult to define, all the more so since many postmodernist thinkers resist such categorization themselves. One useful definition of postmodernism is that put forward by Lyotard: "Simplifying to the extreme, I define postmodernism as incredulity towards metanarratives" (1984: xxiv). The term "metanarrative" refers to a general theory that asserts clear foundations for claiming the validity of particular knowledge. Metanarratives are the supposedly universal, absolute, or ultimate truths that are used to legitimize various political or scientific projects. The world's great religions and ideologies, such as Buddhism, Islam, Christianity, Marxism, anarchism, and fascism, are examples of such metanarratives. They are broad approaches to life that are composed of sets of interlocking concepts and explanations, which are largely internally consistent. For their adherents, they provide answers to questions concerning such topics as the meaning of past history, the nature of contemporary social and political relationships, and the future path of human development; they provide an explanation of which other societies should be seen as friends and which should be seen as enemies, a moral code by which to judge right and wrong actions, and so on.

While one can criticize the components of any particular metanarrative, or the specific attributes that make up a society's perceived identity and strategic culture, it is important to remember that this is the context in which constitutive intersubjective dialogue takes place. For individual and collective agents, action takes place within a preexisting structural and narrative context. Evolution and change are clearly possible, but actors do not operate with a blank page; the language in which intersubjective dialogue occurs shapes the direction and parameters of that dialogue. Structure in turn limits what is conceivable, or seen to be possible. Our languages and our intellectual inheritances significantly shape the ways that we can think.

In contrast to the idea of a metanarrative, postmodernists argue that there is no single truth, no single ideology, no single text, no particular authority or set of values that in claiming absolute truth deserves unquestioned loyalty and obedience. Knowledge is crucially interest-driven; "every scientific distinction and categorisation is someone's motivated action" (Sorenson, 1990: 90). This critique applies to any account of human life that claims to deal with truths. It is a critique that applies as much to environmentalism or standpoint feminism as it does to fascism, Christianity, democracy, or Marxism. For this reason, postmodernists are also skeptical of modernist critical theory, since they believe that it, too, is just another metanarrative.

Emancipationist political activity of any kind depends on a particular understanding of time and progress in which the historical achievements of one generation create a forward movement of social development. "History" is seen as the record of humanity's struggle over the course of generations to improve the conditions in which human beings live, in their social, political, and economic dimensions, to achieve greater democracy, social justice, and economic well-being for the greatest number possible. This is the modernist model of history in which deliberate acts of self-assertion progress toward the realization of a distantly recognized goal. Marxism and Christianity are classic examples of long-term emancipationist goals, which for their adherents are seen as being guaranteed by the nature of history itself.

A major feature of postmodernist critiques of traditional renderings of security is an objection to the linear narrative characteristic of the modern Western understanding of historical time. The various metanarratives of the post-Enlightenment West operate with a teleological approach to history, and an understanding of historical time seen in terms of evolutionary development in a progressive direction. For postmodernists, time is conceptualized in terms of the continuous reworking of the present, so that there is no automatic assumption that change is necessarily progressive or irreversible.

The poststructuralist approach produces a number of different attitudes to aspects of security, such as geopolitics, and the nature of security itself. As David Harvey notes, the Enlightenment was a secular movement that sought to break the links between knowledge and religion, social organization and the church, in order to promote an order based on rational thought rather than superstition or religion and by doing so to release humanity "from the arbitrary use of power as well as from the dark side of our own human nature" (1990: 12).

For postmodernists, as for many modernist critical theorists, the Enlightenment eventually betrayed these noble aspirations by allowing the objective of human emancipation to justify the creation of oppressive systems in the name of progress. But whereas critical theory can be seen as an attempt to recover the emancipatory promise of modernity from the instrumental reason into which it has largely subsided, postmodernism represents a total break with the Enlightenment. For Foucault, the Enlightenment's "will to truth" camouflages the "will to power," and because of this a critical theory cannot use the language and categories of modernity if it aims to be emancipatory.

In the 1960s the doubts about Western civilization raised by these kinds of questions led many to identify a "decline of ideology" as being under way. Westerners, at least, seemed increasingly inclined to reject moral absolutes or theories and single truths and to be suspicious of great causes. Episodes such as the U.S. participation and defeat in the Vietnam War encouraged a decline in faith in previously unchallenged beliefs. By the beginning of the 1990s, the end of the Cold War seemed to herald for some the dawn of a nonideological age.

Yet this was very far from being the case. On the contrary, the end of the Cold War saw the triumph of the values of the North Atlantic states, economic capitalism and liberal democratic political ideology. Moreover, the collapse of the Soviet Union produced the "unipolar moment," with the United States triumphant as the sole remaining superpower, a position it consolidated in a series of neoimperialist projections of force designed to discipline the international community and eliminate the governments of states unwilling or unable to accede to the Pax Americana and to accept the imprimatur of the United States.

For the U.S. foreign policy elite, the "security threat" since 1945 had appeared in many guises: the Soviet Union, Communist China, Vietnam, Cuba, international terrorists, drug smugglers, and so on. However, the real danger always was anarchy and disorder. "None of these sources posed a threat in terms of a traditional calculus of (military) power, and none of them could be reduced solely to the Soviet Union. All of them, however, were (and are) understood in terms of their proclivity for anarchy and disorder" (Campbell, 1992: 32).

Postmodernity and War

A typically "modern" way of thinking about the place of war in human history is to believe that over the centuries humanity has become less "barbaric." Wars are no longer fought for spurious reasons such as loot, territorial gains, prestige, or dynastic ambition. Nor are they simply the savage sport of nomadic tribes. War has become a rational instrument of state policy, its use limited by the nature of international society and international law, its conduct governed by moral consensus and laws of war. Its occurrence is less frequent as technology has made its use more costly, and the development of international society has limited the justifications for resorting to it.

Postmodernists, in contrast, specifically link modernity with war. Modernity is seen as a worldview in which "progress" is the end toward which all effort is directed. If this is the case, it is inevitable that an unmodern people, or an unproductive political class, should be swept aside, because they stand in the way of progress and, in that sense, of history itself. If political edict does not suffice to brush aside such resistance to progress, then violence and war must be used instead.

The brutality of the twentieth century, in the form of genocide and the mass displacement of people, is seen not just as an unintended side effect of modern warfare, but also as an inevitable result of the totalitarian imperatives that characterize modernity. War is not just about capturing a few slaves or treasure or a province, as in previous centuries. It is a struggle between contending ideologies, in which each side sees itself as representing the hope of mankind, and of historical progress itself.

In such a conflict, those who refuse to be assimilated, who reject the assumptions or arguments of the ideologues, come to be seen not only as irredeemable, but also as serious obstacles to national or indeed human progress. Their fate in such an age of extremes is to be ruthlessly marginalized or physically eliminated. This was the doom handed out to Armenians, Jews, Bosnian Muslims, the Cambodian middle class, the Russian Kulaks, the Tasmanian aborigines, American Indians, and many others. Those who were objectively "hostile" to modernity, were expendable and their elimination was crucial to enable the continuing progress of humanity.

Religious believers and racial groups of various kinds have all been considered at various points in the twentieth century to be irredeemably reactionary. They were no more than an obstacle to be overcome on the road to a truly modern society. Why should people feel any guilt in herding fellow citizens into death camps, if by doing so they are working for the future? History would inevitably absolve them of blame and see them as vital instruments in humanity's passage to a better future.

Modern security politics has been predicated upon a Hobbesian assumption that it is possible to make a clear division between an internal realm of orderly government and an external anarchy of violence, lawlessness, and war. Security therefore becomes primarily concerned with the stabilization of boundaries and identities against a threat that is always essentially external. Security, in these circumstances, is comparatively easy to locate and to understand. The external reality is always seen as being qualitatively different from the internal in a fundamental way.

Some of the features of "modernity" that postmodernists criticize are really aspects of Western metaphysics that long predate the period of the Enlightenment. A great deal of Western thinking is predicated in terms of binary divisions between inside and outside, which is a central feature of nationalist and statist conceptualizations of international relations. There is also a Manichean tendency to portray major clashes of interests as confrontations between "good" and "evil."

Modernity was seen as being aggressive in another respect. It involved constant struggle toward a predetermined end. The ideal endpoint might be perceived, but the future had to be traversed first. It inevitably involved a painful transition. Every modern ideology promised "the end of history," but anticipated beforehand a long and bitter struggle.

People did not debate the big ideas; they died for them and they killed for them. They sought to annihilate those whose vision of history was not their own. In the twentieth century, war became the recourse of almost every society that interpreted history as the outcome of a particular relentless logic. Citizens found themselves tied to a ruthless death machine that, it could be argued, was no more than a reflection of industrial life.

By the early 1980s, there were clear doubts being raised by many about the nature of modern civilization and its apparently reckless rush toward disaster in the form of environmental collapse or nuclear war. Most strikingly, it was not the poorest states or those considered most "backward" in various ways that were the problem. On the contrary, it was the richest and allegedly most "enlightened" states in the world that seemed prepared to destroy themselves and the rest of the planet with nuclear weapons in order to "defend" their own particular interpretation of human values.

In the same way, the leading economies of the world seemed perfectly content to operate a global economy characterized by simultaneous overproduction in certain categories, and the tolerance or even creation of hunger and shortage in others while bringing modernization and progress to the "underdeveloped" countries. It was a system where financial entitlement, not need, determined who would have access to the food they needed to survive.

Max Weber had predicted this, arguing that the essence of Enlightenment thinking was a commitment to instrumental rationality. In the end, the development of this approach leads not to freedom for humanity, but rather to "the creation of an 'iron cage' of bureaucratic rationality from which there is no escape" (Coser, 1977: 230–231).

A key image for understanding modernity is the idea of "creative destruction," the belief that a new and better world could only be brought into being by destroying much of what had gone before (Harvey, 1990: 16). The problem with the metanarratives is that they tended to believe there was only one possible answer to any question. And modernity is driven to answer all questions and seeks to eliminate uncertainties and ambiguities. For Hans Blumenberg, "deprived of God's hiddenness of metaphysical guarantees for the world, man constructs for himself a counterworld of elementary rationality and manipulability" (1983: 173). The world is seen as unfinished, ambiguous, uncertain, and dangerous, and humanity in profound need of the answers and clarifications that modernity and rationality can provide.

This logic is as compelling in international relations as it is in other areas of social life. But the "outside" is much bigger when the international is being addressed. The world is full of uncertainties and differences needing to be resolved. Because of this, postmodernists argue, states require "discourses of danger to provide a new theology of truth about who and what 'we' are by highlighting who or what 'we' are not, and what 'we' have to fear" (Campbell, 1992: 54). There must be a threatening "outside," so that we can recognize and value the secure "inside."

During the Cold War there was a sense in which the nuclear weapons of each side were pointing at their own populations, as much as they were at those of the "enemy." The existence of a threatening "other" and the shapeless fears produced by the danger of an unwinnable nuclear war were ways for the state hierarchies to impose discipline upon their own populations. In many ways, "discourses of otherness are usually more about the regulation of the same as they are about distancing the different" (Dalby, 1992: 107).

Derrida has targeted Western philosophy's central assumption of reason, which he sees as dominated by a "metaphysics" of presence as the cause of this tragedy. Logocentrism desires a perfectly rational language that accurately represents the real world. Derrida is outraged by what he considers to be the totalitarian arrogance implicit in the claims of reason. This perspective seems to ignore the benefits brought to humanity by instrumental reason, yet his critique is understandable in light of the horrors of the twentieth century, when such rationality brought about the Nazi death camps and the nuclear destruction of Hiroshima and Nagasaki as well as the deliberate slaughter of civilians through the conventional bombing of Hamburg and Dresden. It was the almost inevitable end result of modernity's obsession with "absolute truths, and rational planning of ideal social orders under standardised conditions of knowledge and production" (Harvey, 1990: 35).

For poststructuralists, the state maintains itself through a process of regulation and normalization in which certain norms and dispositions are accepted and encouraged while others are suppressed and delegitimized. Central to this process, "and to be understood as a privileged instance of the stylised repetition of acts, is foreign policy and the articulation of danger" (Campbell, 1992: 10). To redefine security is therefore to redefine the political, because it is via security that the political is institutionalized. Redefinition of security is therefore potentially a profoundly subversive act.

Foucault and the Power-Knowledge Relationship

Postmodernism has made a significant contribution in terms of bringing out the nature of the relationship between control of knowledge and information, and power. Postmodern work on the power-knowledge relationship has been most influenced by the work of Michel Foucault (1926–1984). Foucault was opposed to the rationalist belief that knowledge is immune from the workings of power. He argued instead that power in fact produces knowledge. All power requires knowledge and all knowledge relies on and reinforces existing power relations. Thus there is no such thing as "truth" existing outside of power. To paraphrase Foucault, "How can history have a truth, if truth has a history?"

Truth is not something external to social settings, but is instead part of them. Therefore, postmodernists want to know what power relations are supported by particular "truths" and knowledge-practices. They use this insight to examine the truths of international relations theory, to see how the concepts that dominate the discipline in fact are highly contingent on specific power relations. For Foucault, "there is no power relation without the correlative constitution of a field of knowledge, nor any knowledge that does not presuppose and constitute at the same time power" (1979: 27).

Foucault's objective was to uncover how a particular era determines what counts as knowledge and truth and what doesn't. He was particularly critical of the idea that history should be interpreted as something linear—a chronology of inevitable facts that tell a story that makes sense. Instead he explored and revealed the underlayers of what is kept suppressed and unconscious, the codes and assumptions of order, the structures of exclusion that legitimate the underlying thought structures, by which societies achieve their identities.

The postmodernist approach, like critical theory generally, can be clearly distinguished from realist ontology, in which the world is composed of objectively visible structures and processes whose existence is not dependent upon the ideas or beliefs that people might have about them. This is supplemented by a narrativizing historiography in which the facts are deemed to speak for themselves and only need to be identified and then fitted into the political requirements of the time. In contrast, a poststructuralist approach argues that "there is always an ineluctable debt to interpretation such that there is nothing outside of discourse" (Campbell, 1992: 4).

The central message of the postmodernist approach is that there is no such thing as truth, only regimes of truth. What this means is that statements about the social world are only "true" within specific discourses. Society decides what it is acceptable to believe and what is unacceptable, the latter of which is to be suppressed or merely ridiculed. Therefore, postmodernism is concerned with how some discourses and therefore some truths dominate others. This, of course, is where power comes in. Power and knowledge depend on one another. Thus the reason of rationalism requires—even creates—social categories of the mad, criminal, and deviant against which to define itself. It is thus, almost inevitably, sexist, racist, and imperialist in practice.

This perspective, however, can lead to a belief that truth is an illusion constructed by consensus, "a name that gets attached to whatever sorts of truth-claim happen to prevail from time to time within one's own interpretive community" (Norris, 1992: 66). Key identities in the international realm are the result of the repetition of actions. There is no single moment of identity creation; it is the process of repetition, seen, for example, in foreign and security policy, which creates the identity, which must be in a process of continual recreation. Security policy is thus not just a set of responses designed to protect a stable identity; instead it is in a sense the practice of statecraft itself.

Because of these particular assumptions about knowledge and identity, the broadening of security is not seen as an obvious step forward by postmodernists. "Broadening" the discourse of security can be seen from a postmodernist perspective, not as a positive step to partially demilitarize a crucial part of the political agenda, but rather as an evolution in the state's traditional technique of finding external dangers with which to ground its domestic call to order. "To talk of the endangered nature of the modern world and the enemies and threats which abound in it, is thus not to offer a simple ethnographic description of our condition, it is to invoke a discourse of danger through which the incipient ambiguity of our world can be grounded in accordance with the insistences of identity" (Campbell, 1992: 55).

Moreover, in doing so, the state invariably chooses to treat external difference as dangerous "otherness." It does so deliberately in order to use the discourses of danger to reinforce the identities of the state and its citizens. Foreign policy therefore becomes not so much an effort to project influence across boundaries, but rather a way of creating and reinforcing such boundaries. Identities do not precede securitizations; they exist in an interdependent relationship with them.

A state's identity is therefore crucially produced through a process in which dissident elements within the state, those sectors of society that resist incorporation into the "national" identity, or are deemed to do so by the state apparatus, are linked to external threats to the state by the nexus of "national security." This, for example, was the fate of Catholics in Elizabethan England and communists in Western countries during the Cold War. Identity again becomes a question not just of who we are, but also of who we are not, as well as whom we fear, or whom the government encourages us to fear.

If the end of the Cold War is taken as an example, it suggests that less has changed than meets the eye. During the Cold War a series of ritualized performances constructed an identity, the "West," the "North Atlantic Alliance," which was secured from the threat posed by the "otherness" of the Soviet Union and its allies. A "geography of evil" was an exercise in which an array of external threats helped to define the United States. The end of the Cold War saw the demise of the Soviet Union, but not an end for the need of the United States to threaten "others" against which it could distinguish itself. The United States rushed to fill its identity-building vacuum with the threat posed by "rogue" states and international terrorist groups.

A second theme of postmodernism concerns the textual strategies it uses. The central claim (following Derrida) is that the way in which we construct the social world is textual. For Derrida, the world is constituted like a text in the sense that our interpretation of the world reflects the concepts and structures of language. By "deconstructing" commonly understood concepts it can be shown that they are actually artificial contrivances arranged hierarchically so that certain terms are "privileged"—for example, good/bad, powerful/powerless, right/wrong. Therefore, deconstruction is a way of showing how theories and discourses rely on artificial stabilities produced by the use of seemingly objective and natural oppositions in language. Institutions such as the law, government, and the military place clear limits on what can be said and how it can be said.

"Double reading" of a text can also be used to point to the internal tensions within it to show how there is always more than one possible interpretation. Postmodernists working in the discipline of international relations have used this technique to effectively destabilize many of the key concepts and "timeless truths" of realist security theory. Richard Ashley (1988) has done this for the concept of "anarchy" in international relations and Robert Walker (1993) has done it for the tradition of realism more generally, showing how realists have ignored the subtleties and complexities within the thoughts of the key thinkers they cite for this tradition, such as Machiavelli and Hobbes. This is important because the idea of a common set of ideas by a series of leading thinkers over the centuries is central to the realist argument that these conceptions of reality in general, and security in particular, are timeless responses to an essentially unchanging external environment. The value of deconstruction is its ability to peel away the layers of constructed meanings and reveal the underlying arbitrary assumptions.

Ashley's deconstruction and double reading of the concept of "the international anarchy," for example, reveals that the realist assumption that it is synonymous with disorder and threat is based upon a deeper set of necessary assumptions (1988). If the difference between anarchy and sovereignty is to be meaningful, then inside the sovereign state must be found a domestic realm of identity, homogeneity, order, and progress, guaranteed by legitimate force.

Outside must lie an anarchical realm of difference, heterogeneity, disorder, and threat. Sovereign states are arbitrarily deemed to have no trace of anarchy within them. Internal dissent must be repressed or denied to make the sovereignty/anarchy distinction meaningful. In particular, the distinction rests on the ability to identify within each state a hegemonic center of decisionmaking capable of reconciling internal differences, and capable of projecting a single identity externally.

Ashley raises two key questions: What happens if the states in the system do not fit this neat set of assumptions? and second, What happens if the lack of a global central rule is not overridden with additional assumptions about the necessity for states to continuously engage in power politics? (1988: 234). A similar exercise was carried out by Bradley Klein (1994) in relation to nuclear deterrence. The significant contribution of postmodernism to the study of security, therefore, is its focus on language. A fundamental weakness of the traditional approach to security is its willingness to uncritically accept the meaning and description of central concepts such as power, war, and the state, which need to be problematized and analyzed at the deepest level. This means not just asking the question of whether or not their received meanings are true or false, but also asking the question of how those meanings were created and made dogma in the first place.

Whereas for realists certain features like "identity" are largely taken for granted, for postmodernists like David Campbell there are no primary and stable identities. States themselves are "imagined political communities" and nationalism is "a construct of the state in pursuit of its legitimacy" (1992: 11). States are therefore never finished artifacts, they are always in the process of becoming and the construction of "security" is one of the most important ways in which they do this.

Paradoxically, therefore, the pursuit of "security" by a state is central to its existence and can never, and must never, be fully achieved. The state controls its citizens and stabilizes their perceived identity by contrasting the domestic realm of order with the insecurities beyond the state's borders. The state continues to have a reason to exist, precisely because it can never achieve true security in the terms with which it chooses to define it. "The constant articulation of danger through foreign policy is thus not a threat to a state's identity or existence; it is its condition of possibility" (Campbell, 1992: 12). This is a crucial difference between modernist and postmodernist approaches to security. Modernist critical security sees identity and security as social constructions. These constructions experience insecurity in different ways. Postmodernists, however, argue that security produces these entities rather than the other way around.

Geopolitics can be seen as exemplifying the weaknesses of neorealism in explaining the nature of international relations. In the critical security approach, "the devil is in the detail." A central objective is to engage with the complexities of the world, to recognize that security is multidimensional and that individual and group security are relational. Part of the complexity of the security agenda in the 1990s was the need to promote the security of particular groups in such a way that it did not deny or substantially reduce it for others, as for example in the Bosnian and Kosovo situations.

However, even a concept as quintessentially realist as geopolitics has found itself prey to a fundamentally alternative conceptualization with the advent of "postmodern" or "critical" geopolitics. Classical geopolitics was founded on an almost static conception of space and on the assumptions that the state was the fundamental unit in international relations and that the projection of force, with limited concern for normative issues, was the basic dynamic of international politics.

A number of scholars have challenged these assumptions, describing a critical geopolitics for the postmodern world. Richard Falk, for example, contrasted the classical geopolitics of the first half of the twentieth century with a geopolitics of the globalized age, one characterized by "concern with competitiveness, financial flows, capital sources, trade expansion, coordinating mechanisms and labor markets" (1995: 9). The argument is not that the basic components of classical geopolitics, territory and the state, have lost their centrality in international relations and that objects no longer have the same meaning as they once did. It is rather that the meaning and importance of these factors has changed, and that it is important to acknowledge this and recognize the new realities that shape and govern the world (Beck, 1992).

The postmodern world has characteristic features that clearly distinguish it from earlier decades, notably a shift of political and economic power away from the pattern of governance represented by the modern state, a dramatic compression of time represented by instantaneous global communications and jet-age travel, and market-driven international relations. Many of the threats that most concern the governments of major powers such as the United States are deterritorialized problems like terrorism, transnational crime, and weapons proliferation, where state-to-state traditional military responses are inappropriate.

Traditional realist geopolitics is far too simplistic to help in understanding the complexities of the postmodern world. To retain any utility, geopolitics needs to be abandoned, or refashioned in a critical manner to make it genuinely "realistic," to make it fit the realities of a postmodern world. Without such a conceptual advance, there is a dangerous tendency to continue to work with outdated concepts and try to make reality fit them rather than the other way around. This is a recipe for misdiagnosis of the complex realities of international relations and a route to policy failure. Novel dangers are misunderstood by being conceptualized in traditional ways, so that the real nature and meaning of what is actually happening is lost or ignored. Instead of a necessarily fluid response to a deterritorialized terrorist threat, policymakers thinking in traditional terms look for simplistic explanations and seek out "rogue" states or leaderships who can be blamed and against whom a conventional military response can be directed. This may produce dramatic television coverage and short-term political gains, but it does not necessarily address the long-term realities or produce a resolution of the problem.

Terminology is also important because classical geopolitical thinking has constructed a world conceptually that is thereby shaped in terms of how the powerful would like the world to be perceived. These descriptions can be powerful ordering and disciplinary devices. Many are based on the construction of a particular kind of separateness and difference. The Arabic-speaking countries that run from the Maghreb region to the Suez Canal are described as "North African" by governments of the North Atlantic Treaty Organization, though the governments in the region itself prefer their countries to be designated as "southern Mediterranean." This is because they wish to be linked to the zone of democratic peace and stability associated with the European Union countries and they are aware that in Western geopolitical thinking "Africa" has been constructed as a region marked by violence, political instability, economic underdevelopment, and interethnic confrontation. The efforts by Slovenia and Croatia to have themselves described as "central European" rather than "Balkan" states spring from a similar recognition of the power of geopolitical constructions. Conventional geopolitical thinking is essentially unsuited to comprehending, explaining, or resolving the current security problematic, because its "metaphysical construction of security as stasis and spatial exclusion fundamentally contradicts the predominant theme of modern society, which is change, interaction and acceleration" (Dalby, 1992: 98).

Postmodernism to date has made a number of significant contributions to thinking about international security. It has fundamentally problematized the idea of state sovereignty, which is essentially a critique of the sovereign state for both material and normative reasons. It has successfully questioned core realist security assumptions such as the sovereignty/anarchy opposition. It has demonstrated how states are not timeless, finished forms and theorized the historical constitution and reconstitution of sovereign states. And it has successfully problematized a range of issues relating to questions of boundaries and identity.

Even the very idea of security is problematic from a postmodernist perspective. Traditional Western understandings of security see it as a situation where a major threat has been neutralized or abolished, with a consequent gain in objective and subjective stability and assurance. For postmodernism, absolute security in this sense is never possible and perhaps not even desirable. The pursuit of "security" is seen as part of a modernist aspiration for certainty and control of the external environment in a world that is inherently incomplete. For postmodernists, the promise of the certainties of security are unrealistic in a human social world that should be recognized as composed of "incompleteness, fragmentation, incoherence, and the celebration of difference" (Klein, 1988: 313).

For many critics of the postmodernist approach, however, deconstruction ultimately leads to an intellectual dead end, because it produces the idea that "reality" is "constructed entirely in and through language" and that essentially "we inhabit a realm of unanchored free-flowing language games" (Norris, 1992: 19). And while paying attention to the significance of metatheory is clearly important, many postmodernist contributions can be criticized for remaining at that level of analysis, and showing little desire to engage in concrete political controversies and struggles. Nevertheless, by bringing these issues under a new scrutiny since the early 1980s, postmodernism has advanced the understanding of important themes in international security.

Can Postmodernism Be an Effective Alternative Approach to Security?

Postmodernism is antifoundational; it recognizes no acceptable basis for deciding between competing knowledge claims, but believes, like critical theory, that knowledge is socially constructed by intersubjective agreement. Such an approach, taken to extremes, can lead to a position that denies that there is a valid basis for moral judgment whatsoever. Foucault, for example, argues that human beings are given "their history, their economics, their social practices, the language that they speak, the mythology of their ancestry's, and that these are governed by unconscious rules" (1972: 211), and that all "modern" knowledge claims are linked in a circular relation with systems of power (1980: 133). These assumptions seem to rule out any grounding on which to base an oppositional discourse. Jean Baudrillard, for example, has been criticized for adopting the absurd position that the 1991 Gulf War did not happen, because there is no basis for distinguishing between real events and the "hyperreality" of the world portrayed by the media (Terriff et al., 1999: 106–107).

However, not all postmodernists adopt such a position. Christopher Norris argues that Derrida, for example, "sustains the impulse of enlightenment critique even while subjecting that tradition to a radical reassessment" and that "it is a gross misunderstanding to suppose that deconstruction ignores or suspends the question of interpretive responsibility" (Norris, 1992: 17). Foucault himself is often close to adopting a genuinely "critical" position in calling for the development of a postmodern knowledge that could form the basis of localized resistance to power in a contextually specific way. He argued that the task of contemporary theory was "to analyse the specificity of mechanisms of power, to locate the connections and extensions, to build little by little a strategic knowledge" (1980: 145). Bradley Klein argues that what post-modernism does is not to make political judgments impossible, but rather to force people to accept that their political judgments and values cannot be defended in terms of absolutes (1988: 312). People must act, but do so in the awareness that their values have no ultimate grounding.

Postmodernist interpretations taken to their extreme make it difficult to incorporate poststructuralism into a deeper conception of security, because by arguing that there is no foundational basis on which one might judge truth against lies or fiction, it becomes impossible to separate fact and reality from propagandistic distortion or untruth. With no way of determining what is actually happening, it then becomes impossible to make a judgment as to whether something is right or wrong, or if it appears to be wrong, what should be done about the issue. This has come to be welcomed by right-wing and conservative politicians and commentators, particularly in the United States, since it enables them to deny the reality of alternative interpretations to the one constructed by the U.S. media and armed forces.

Poststructuralism clearly has the potential to be an important perspective on security, through its opposition to metanarratives "and its close attention to other worlds and to other voices that have for too long been silenced," such as those of women, gays, and blacks. But it has also been condemned as the "commercialisation and domestication of modernism," which can be comfortably integrated with neoconservative politics (Harvey, 1990: 42).

For Foucault, all knowledge derived from injustice and there was no right to truth or a foundation for truth (1977: 163). However, taken to its extreme, this position leaves no place for engaged political action. However, since Foucault published his work, he clearly believed that his writings could have an effect, which presupposed that humans were reflective social agents and implied that they were capable of acting upon their knowledge in a politically purposive way. He himself came to argue that his work helped to make possible "an insurrection of subjugated knowledge" (1980: 81–83).

However, he was unable to follow this line of thought through to an emancipatory political position, declaring that his arguments did not "tend toward the realization of some definite political project" (1984: 375). But it can be argued that a truly critical theory helps a person to adopt positions that do contribute to emancipation of the oppressed, when to do nothing, or to take up a different political position, would contribute to their continued subjugation.

Postmodernism stands outside the modernist commitment to enlightened critique. It can be seen as representing a "collapse of moral and political nerve" (Norris, 1992: 68). Postmodernism's weakness in terms of emancipatory potential is its extreme normative skepticism, which denies it any foundational basis on which to make ethical claims. The deconstruction of other validity claims is an essential starting point for the construction of a more holistic and human-centered concept of security, but the radical denial of normative claims allows no basis for creative political action designed to redress injustice and promote emancipation. In the end this leaves postmodernism appearing as a reactionary and defeatist perspective that effectively colludes with existing unjust structures and practices by denying the possibility of an ethical basis on which to base their rejection and replacement. A genuinely critical theory of security, like all critical theories, and unlike most of postmodernism, must move beyond "deconstruction" to "also engage in a reconstructive effort by offering a sketch of an alternative conception of theory and practice that avoids the deficiencies of dominant discourse" (Leonard, 1990: 215). The inability of postmodernism to do this means that while it can be included in the expanded scope of alternative approaches to security, there are clear limits to its utility.

It should be said that like all of the approaches examined so far, poststructuralism is itself a broad church with different approaches being held by key contributors. Campbell, Ashley, and Walker, for example, have all affirmed the possibility of an ethics of responsibility underpinned by a postmodernist sensibility. Ashley and Walker argue that the very point of postmodernist theorizing about international relations is to help the oppressed and those occupying "marginal sites" in the contemporary world order (Ashley and Walker, 1990: 260). Campbell goes even further, calling for foreign and security policy to reflect an engagement with the world that seeks to "affirm life" and that might "offer the prospect of an improved quality of life for many" (1993: 94). For the most part, however, postmodernist writers are reluctant in the extreme to suggest alternatives to current policies that might enable a more life-affirming approach to security to become the norm, and this represents a major weakness in terms of poststructuralism's ability to compete effectively with more politically engaged or policy-oriented approaches.

TEN

Critical Security

C ritical theory has influenced a number of intellectual disciplines. It is as true of security studies as of other subjects that the orthodox approach in these disciplines is "usually understood as the articulation of timeless truths, objective facts, unmediated readings of texts, causal explanation and prediction, and the like—in short a commitment to simply understanding the world as it really is." This is certainly a reasonable description of realism. Critical theory, in contrast, "has usually meant showing that the notion of understanding the world as it really is, is a philosophically incoherent, theoretically deficient, and politically pernicious idea" (Leonard, 1990: xiii).

It has been argued by Simon Dalby that the term "security" has traditionally been given a very specific meaning, and this is a meaning with very negative connotations, usually associated with threats to the state. "Security is a term limited in usefulness for denoting desirable political situations, because it is formulated as protection from some threat or danger rather than as promoting a desirable situation" (1992: 97).

Dalby goes beyond this to note that the connotations of "security" in English, when they do have a degree of positive meaning, are extremely conservative. They imply the stability of the existing order, and the continuation of that stability into the foreseeable future. This is true of much of the security-related vocabulary. Words like "peace" in English, derived from the Latin *pax,* have associations of order and settled authority, rather than justice or solidarity as they do in other languages. "This usually implies stable political arrangements; social change that might upset these arrangements is then easily targeted as a threat to security" (Dalby, 1992: 98).

This aspect is particularly crucial when security is being subjected to a genuinely "critical" analysis—that is, an analysis informed by critical theory. For critical theory is built around a fundamental commitment to human emancipation, where exposing the hidden beneficiaries of particular political orders and ideological structures is a crucial part of the exercise.

■ Critical Theory

Critical theory as an approach to the understanding of international relations made only a limited impact when it was first introduced to the discipline via dependency theory in the 1960s. The initial promoters of the approach were clearly Marxist-inspired, and in the particular intellectual and political climate of the peak decades of the Cold War this made their broader assimilation within the discipline more difficult.

In addition, although dependency theory is a critical theory in its original form, the version that social scientists bequeathed to international relations was mutilated almost beyond recognition to give it a positivist methodology. The progenitors of dependency theory in Latin America saw social structures as "the product of man's collective behavior . . . that can be, and in fact are, continuously transformed by social movements" (Cardoso and Faletto, 1979: x). Because social behavior was seen as being constituted by beliefs and institutional constructions, any explanation of human behavior by social scientists had to be interpretive and historical. In this formulation the agents of emancipation were identified as the people themselves, self-reflectively engaged in social struggles. Yet imported into international relations via U.S. social science, this approach was transmuted by behavioral and structural analysis into a rationalist methodology that was the antithesis of the beliefs of the creators of the approach. Thus it was not until the 1980s, with the advent of Frankfurt school and Gramscian approaches, that critical theory began to clearly influence the analysis of international relations generally and security studies in particular.

This is particularly important when what is meant by "critical security" is an approach to the subject informed by critical social theory, since critical theory aims to produce practical emancipatory results that increase individual and collective self-determination in the face of oppression and injustice. A critical theory is "one that is both the expression of, and an ongoing critical guide for, a particular struggle against domination" (Leonard, 1990: 93).

The critical theory examined in the context of this chapter, deriving from the work of the Frankfurt school and that of Antonio Gramsci, is consciously "modernist," with a commitment to recovering the promise of the Enlightenment. The purpose of a critical theory is to provide a coherent account of how existing structures and practices contribute to the maintenance of oppression, and to provide an alternative vision that the oppressed themselves can comprehend, embrace, and implement in ways relevant to their specific circumstances. The link between theory and practice is absolutely central, and distinguishes it clearly from postmodernist critiques. It is an approach that always requires an addressee, an oppressed audience to which it is directed.

"It is important for critical security studies to engage with the real by suggesting policies, agents and sites of change, to help humankind, in whole or in part, to move away from its structural wrongs" (Booth, 1997: 114).

In the closing years of the Cold War it was increasingly clear that existing conceptions of security were inadequate and that the diversity of security threats should be recognized. For some, this seemed to demand only the extension of existing approaches into new sectors, but for the proponents of critical security, "a basic rethinking of security [was] required" (Krause and Williams, 1997: 1).

In carrying out this rethinking, critical security advocates believed that the opportunity needed to be taken to redress a major wrong notable in the Cold War era, and reorient the focus of security concern away from an absolute attention to the needs of the state, and toward those in national and international society who had been marginalized and rendered insecure by the existing approach to understanding security. This meant, in practice, adopting a radical stance that challenged many existing political practices, and pursuing the goal of supporting the emancipation of the victims of the current international system.

In the work of Richard Wyn Jones this commitment to a Frankfurt school/Gramscian understanding of what it means to have a critical approach to security is made explicit. For Wyn Jones, critical theory can also embrace postmodernism to a degree, so long as the commitment to emancipation is central (2001: 11–12). But as noted in the previous chapter, there are very real problems associated with embracing poststructuralism as a fully critical approach to security, because the radical normative skepticism characteristic of much (though not all) of postmodernism leaves no room for a foundational understanding of what emancipation might mean in specific circumstances.

Critical theory has its roots in a line of thought that is usually traced back to the European Enlightenment, but also reflects classical Greek political theory. The ancient Greeks believed that the life of the *polis* "finds its expression in individual autonomy and the establishment of justice and democracy. Politics on this understanding, is the realm concerned with realising the just life" (Devetek, 1996: 146).

In the twentieth century it is most closely associated with the Frankfurt school, which developed at the Frankfurt Institute of Social Research, founded in 1923. The most important figures in the development of these ideas were Max Horkheimer, Theodore Adorno, Herbert Marcuse, Eric Fromm, and in the current era, Jurgen Habermas. Horkheimer argued that theories that were designed to change society could not be developed in the way that natural science developed theories. Social scientists could not be like natural scientists in the sense of being independent from and disinterested in their subject matter.

Social scientists were part of the society they were studying. Horkheimer therefore argued that there was a close connection between knowledge and power, and he distinguished between what he called "traditional theory" and "critical theory." Traditional theory sees the world as a set of facts waiting to be discovered through the application of science, the positivist approach. However, Horkheimer argued that traditional theorists were wrong to argue that the "fact" waiting to be discovered could be perceived independently of the social framework in which perception occurs.

Because of their outlook, traditional theorists were unable to critique society effectively, because this would involve value judgments that could not be scientifically "proven." For Horkheimer, traditional theory was effectively about the reproduction of the status quo. It had the effect of privileging and normalizing one particular understanding of what constitutes knowledge and excluding alternative accounts. This thereby undermined the truth-claims of those who opposed the existing order. All theories of society reflected underlying and usually unstated political objectives.

Like later postmodernists, Horkheimer and Adorno believed that behind the promise of Enlightenment rationality there lurked a logic of domination and oppression. The desire to dominate nature necessarily meant the domination of human beings as well. As Habermas put it, "the laws of self-reproduction demand of an industrially advanced society that it look after its survival on the escalating scale of a continually expanded technical control over nature and a continually refined administration of human beings" (1973: 254).

In the place of traditional theory, Horkheimer proposed the adoption of "critical theory." Critical theory did not see the "facts" in the same way as traditional theory. Traditional theory was objectivist, assuming that the world, and social reality, exists independently of the thoughts or interpretations of human beings. For critical theorists, facts are the products of specific social and historical frameworks. Accepting this allows critical theorists to explore the interests served by any particular theory. This insight applies as much to critical theory itself as to other theories. A critical theory has to recognize its own historical and contextual grounding.

Critical theory does not accept the prevailing ideas, actions, and social conditions as being unchanging or unchangeable. It refuses to accept the existing rules of society, the boundaries of action and knowledge, as natural and inevitable. The world we study is the product of ideas and human action. Critical theory argues that humanity has potentialities greater than those seen in existing society. It seeks, therefore, not simply to reproduce society by description, as realism does, but to understand society and to change it, by demonstrating the contingent and transformable nature of structures of domination and oppression.

The purpose of an effective critical theory and practice is to make clear the true interests of those to whom it is addressed. For Habermas, a truly critical theory "serves primarily to enlighten those to whom it is addressed about the position they occupy in an antagonistic social system and about the interests of which they must become conscious as being objectively theirs" (1973: 32).

In international relations the first major critical theoretical contribution came in 1981 by Robert Cox, who attacked the foundations of neorealism because of its hidden normative assumptions. Far from being an "objective" theory, realism was exposed as having a series of views about what states should pursue in their foreign policies. It was also revealed as a partial theory that defined the state in a specific way and ruled out of its view other political relations.

Although many of his ideas appear as lineal descendants of those of the Frankfurt school, Cox himself appears to have been more strongly influenced by the work of Gramsci, though as Wyn Jones has noted, the differences between Gramsci's thought and Horkheimer's are not great, particularly in terms of the forms in which both have been imported into the study of international relations (Wyn Jones, 2001: 8).

Cox argues that realism typifies what Horkheimer meant by "traditional" theory. Cox called it "problem-solving theory," which takes the world as it finds it; "the general pattern of institutions and relationships is not called into question" (Devetek, 1996: 88). The effect is then to reify and legitimize the existing order. Problem-solving theory works to make the existing distribution of power seem natural. In this sense realism is clearly a classic form of such traditional or problem-solving theory.

And Cox points out, in an important phrase, that "theory is always for someone and for some purpose" (Devetek, 1996: 87). Theories see the world from specific social and political positions and are not independent. There is no such thing as a detached, objective theory. When any theory claims to be such, it becomes all the more necessary to investigate what it is actually affirming and expose its concealed assumptions and ideological purpose. Theorists should try to achieve a critical distance in their analyses, in order that they do not simply impose their own preconceptions on them, but to achieve complete objectivity is impossible and to claim to have achieved it is deliberately misleading.

Like Horkheimer before him, Cox argues instead for critical theory. This operates with a particular ontology. Echoing many of the other "reflectivist" approaches, Cox notes that social structures are "intersubjective." That is, they are socially constructed. Therefore Cox focuses on how the "givens" of traditional theory, such as "individuals" or "the state," are produced by certain historical or social forces. Thus a state is not always a state, in the sense of representing an identical entity over time. States differ enormously throughout history, and are very different things at different times. The state emerges out of particular social forces, as do other social structures.

Critical international theory therefore focuses on the existing global power structures of the contemporary world. It seeks to make clear that those structures are contingent and have a history, and that they bring costs as well as benefits. It then attempts to outline possible alternative structures and processes. For critical international theory, the prevailing order is shot through with injustices and inequalities on a global scale, and it is on this basis that it favors alternative visions of world order.

Cox's critical international theory seeks to explain the emergence and specific development trajectory of the contemporary world order and to explain how it came about in the particular form that prevailed. It submits to analysis the features that problem-solving theory tends to take as given and inevitable. It contemplates the social and political context as a totality and, unlike realism, which emphasizes continuity, it rather explores the process of change within the international system and its component units. Because of this, it conceives of history as a process of continuous change and transformation.

This approach necessarily questions the authority and legitimacy of existing social and political institutions and examines the extent to which they are undergoing processes of change. It seeks to determine what elements are universal to world order and what elements are historically contingent. It does not completely reject the utility of problem-solving theory, which retains its value in addressing specific problems. It is marked by a modernist normative commitment to an altered social and political order. It is designed to serve as a guide for strategic action, for bringing about such an alternative order. The verification of this approach, as with any critical theory, is empirical and normative. Its truth-claims are measured against its effectiveness in producing changes in actual practice, for the audience to whom it is addressed.

Critical theory invites observers to reflect upon the social construction and effects of knowledge and to consider how claims about value neutrality can conceal the role knowledge plays in reproducing unsatisfactory social arrangements. In particular, critical theory opposes claims about the social world that assume that existing structures are immutable. On the contrary, "norms, beliefs, identity and practices are intersubjectively constituted and historically and contextually contingent" (Leonard, 1990: 261).

Particular emphasis is placed upon learning and analyses of how human beings learn to include some people within and exclude others from their particular communities. It judges particular social arrangements by their emancipatory content. Realist and neorealist arguments that communities must deal with one another through the currency of military power are rejected by critical theory.

Critical Theory and Security

Critical security theorists such as Ken Booth see security as a discursive and contested concept, see politics as open-ended and based in ethics, and call for a realistic and pragmatic theory of survival to be added to the idea of the good life, to open up the possibilities for human emancipation. The hegemonic claims of realist international relations theory are rejected in favor of an approach that seeks to address the broader security needs of humanity as a whole. Booth calls this "the security studies of inclusion rather than exclusion, of possibility rather than necessity" (1997: 105).

Key elements of the critical security approach are a "Coxian" view of security theory. Thinking about security is never a neutral intellectual pursuit; theories reflect particular values and interests, and give these priority over alternative values. This perspective leads in turn to a choice about "who" or "what" should be privileged. Critical security poses basic questions (Krause, 1998: 307): What is security? Who are being secured by the prevailing order and what are they being secured against? With whose security should we be concerning ourselves and through which strategies should this security be achieved? Why do states and other groups construct and mobilize against some threats and not others?

A fundamental question in this regard concerns whether critical theory should underpin critical security theory directly. Much of the writing on critical security in the past decade has clearly defined itself in opposition to the more conventional approach associated with realism. According to Booth, it was the "inadequacies of realism rather than the attraction of any other particular alternative" that led to the emergence of critical security studies (1997: 104). For Booth, the agenda of critical security is fourfold: critiquing traditional theory, exploring the meaning and possible implications of critical theories, investigating security issues from a critical perspective, and rethinking security in specific regions of the world (1997: 108). As with all critical theory, there is an emphasis on empirical verification.

The original impulse for the critical security approach came from scholars at Aberystwyth, where international relations as a university discipline had been born in 1919. By the 1990s, certain scholars in this department had become dissatisfied not only with traditional approaches to security, but also with the limitations of the broader approach developed during the 1980s. Booth, for example, argued that what was required was not just a "broadening" of the concept of security to embrace new domains, but also a deeper understanding of the meaning of security, in which security is investigated in terms of the potential derived from imagining different forms of politics (1997: 111).

This is a rather different approach to security. Whereas in the traditional conservative approach security is given a restricted meaning and its application limited to the survival of the state, in the critical security approach it is being explicitly linked to ideas of human emancipation. Advocates of critical theory traditionally see it as having a crucial role to play in changing the world by providing the oppressed with "insights and intellectual tools they can use to empower themselves" (Leonard, 1990: xii). As Booth puts it, the question is "why should certain issues—human rights, economic justice and so on—be kept off the security agenda? They are, after all, crucial security questions for somebody, if not for those benefiting from statist power structures" (1997: 111).

The difference here can be seen as that between a "quantitative" and a "qualitative" approach to the reinterpretation of security. The move to elaborate different sectors of security is essentially quantitative, with additional sectors opened up for analysis through a mind-set that need not move far from a military interpretation. The qualitative reinterpretation, in contrast, does not allow for easy colonization by the military dimension of security.

Within the critical security approach the concept of emancipation is absolutely central. While some of its members, such as Wyn Jones, explicitly derive inspiration from the social and political theories of the Frankfurt school critical theories, and of Gramsci, others have more eclectic influences, but the focus on the commitment to emancipation is common to all. This breadth of inspiration mirrors that of the original critical theorists themselves, for whom the only thing common to all was the commitment to exploring the potential for human emancipation.

The focus on emancipation has served both to distinguish the critical security school from the broader critique of traditional security practice, and also to distinguish it from postmodern or poststructuralist critics of traditional security theory. In the latter approach the focus has been on "deconstruction," on exposing and exploring the hidden assumptions of traditional security ideas. There has been a reluctance, however, to go beyond this, to suggest alternative conceptions or practices that might represent an improvement on those being critiqued. This stems from a postmodernist reluctance to "impose" or to suggest ideas that might begin as heresy and end up becoming the new dogma. For most critics, however, and particularly for those informed by critical theory, criticism is of little if any value unless an alternative is being proposed.

A central problem with the critical approach is that the concept of emancipation is asked to bear a huge theoretical burden. Yet both traditionalist and radical security theorists have argued that, to date, it is not clear exactly what "emancipation" does or does not mean. To a large extent this is because the critical security project is a work in progress in which the meaning and relationship of emancipation to security are still being worked through.

This is important in terms of developing a critical approach to security. Emancipation is still a problematic issue. In the messy politics of the real world it is often the case that groups have conflicts of interest in which a degree of justice can be found in the claims of each side and the problem lies in reconciling these. While it can be simplistically argued that emancipation provides the criteria by which the efficacy of security outcomes can be measured, this will sometimes be clearly problematic. When there are two or more competing groups with interests at stake, it is necessary to have normative criteria that can provide a basis upon which to judge such ethical claims. This is particularly the case if improving the quality of life for one group, emancipating them in some significant way, is clearly going to result in a loss of freedom or other important values for another group. In the Kosovo problem in the late 1990s, for example, a clear issue was that once the Albanian majority acquired justice in the sense of political, economic, and social power commensurate with their proportion of the population, the minority Serbian population would be made very much less "secure" in various ways.

Critical theory and critical security theory are not abstract approaches divorced from empirical reality. A critical theory by definition is grounded in practical intention. Its purpose is not simply to critique current or past practice, but to contribute to bringing about progressive social change. Nor is there any presumption that this has to be achieved through revolutionary alterations. The possibility of change is immanent in all societies and politics, but the nature of possible change is grounded in the limitations imposed by existing realities. Gradual, evolutionary change using existing mechanisms is valuable in itself, even while working for a more profound reinterpretation and reordering of political realities.

The critical security approach is rather more than simply a criticism of realism; it represents a fundamental challenge to traditional security thinking. While there is clearly significant overlap with the broadened agenda put forward by liberal realists such as Barry Buzan, the critical security approach goes much further and is based upon a quite different epistemology and ontology. This places it on a different trajectory in terms of the development of security theory, and gives it different objectives, referents, and addressees.

Such an approach is a fundamental challenge to the prevailing status quo, and the injustices and violence that underpin and sustain it. Seen in this light, a critical approach to security, concerned to expose and redress these injustices, is itself a threat to the status quo and therefore a "security problem" in conventional terms. And the policy proposals that flow from such a critically informed perspective must themselves be a threat to the conservative status quo.

Critical security theory can be seen as involving two distinct processes, broadening and deepening. Merely broadening the concept of security by applying it to additional sectors such as the economy or the environment is inadequate, both because it does not address the full threat agenda, and because it does not release the concept from its neorealist influence. This is not to argue that military threats do not exist, or should not be studied—far from it. Military strategy is important, but it is only one part of international relations. It is an important part of critical security studies, but only one part of a much wider subject, with referents other than the state. But military threats do not exhaust the agenda of security threats to human populations worldwide. We cannot account for threats to referents other than the state unless we deepen our understanding of security as well as broaden it and also contextualize it in terms of different understandings of political possibility. Perceptions of threat and interest remain of central concern, but the questions from the critical security perspective are how these threats and interests are constructed, how the actors involved are constituted, and how these processes change over time. It is in this sense that the proponents of critical security studies call for taking the "realities" of international relations "more seriously than the abstractions of neo-realism would allow" (Krause and Williams, 1997: 25).

As previous chapters have shown, throughout the "broadened" security agenda, the new security sectors are capable of being analyzed and operationalized within a neorealist perspective. There is nothing intrinsic to the construction of these sectors that prevents this from being the case. In sectors like economic, environmental, and societal security, it is possible to operate with a critical methodology and purpose, but it is also possible to do so with a neorealist one. As long as neorealism is capable of colonizing the new sectors, then the process may mean no more than the transformation of the security concept into a governing idea capable of serving a variety of purposes, not all of them emancipatory.

Security is a matter of real or perceived threats and the ability to take action to counter or overcome them. What is perceived as a threat is dependent on what is collectively defined as an issue, and understandings of interests are embodied in an identity. The idea of identity, what it actually is and how it is constructed and reconstructed, is central to the understanding of security problems, and this has been particularly prominent in the postmodern world. In essence, identity defines the self in relation to others; it therefore does not exist prior to interaction. But James Der Derian (1995: 42) asks whether difference necessarily has to be threatening.

Critical security studies should not be seen as a utopian belief that the state or the use of military power and violence is about to disappear. The strength of the state concept in the contemporary world and the ability of states to generate powerful political loyalties are clear. What critical security does challenge is realism's "naturalization of historically created theories, its ideology of necessity and limited possibility, and its propagandist common sense about this being the best of all worlds" (Booth, 1997: 107).

The broadening of the security concept discussed so far has welcomed it as an important move beyond the constraints artificially imposed by the realist conception of security. There is a clear logic suggesting that at the heart of the idea of security must lie the concept of emancipation. Security policy is a special form of politics and responds to the same underlying logic. Politics is the structured pursuit of the good life on behalf of collectivities, and to the extent that this objective is blocked or hampered by threats of various kinds, then the achievement of greater security is a key to emancipation. For this reason, a genuinely critical approach to security, critical in the sense of being inspired by critical theory, is essential.

Critical theory is unashamedly normative. Its purpose is to cast light upon social and political oppression and to provide people with the intellectual tools to emancipate themselves. Its goal is human emancipation; it incorporates a belief that the oppressed in a deep sense cannot be liberated, they must liberate themselves; and because it is suspicious of the hidden assumptions of positivist theory, it is self-reflexive, requiring constant concern with the question of *whose* interests are being served, by critical approaches as much as by traditional ones. Although rooted in the Enlightenment project, it is fundamentally about empowering those whom modernity has silenced or marginalized.

It recognizes also that theory is not neutral. In the struggle for the emancipation of the oppressed, theory can be as much a weapon as material tools. Humans are historical and contextual beings, and critical social science "provides the foundation for the political, social and economic liberation of human beings through its 'denunciation' of the present" (Leonard, 1990: 205). It is therefore inevitably engaged in a confrontation with ideas and belief systems that underpin or legitimize existing domination. In international relations, traditional security policy has played just such a role, helping to legitimize international structures and processes that allow a privileged minority of humanity to benefit themselves at the expense of the majority.

Booth correctly argues that "security is what we make it. It is an epiphenomenon that is intersubjectively created. Different worldviews and discourses about politics deliver different views and discourses about security" (1997: 106). The starting point for a truly critical approach to security is therefore a fundamental opposition to traditional security theory. Realism is rejected because of its placement of the security of the state ahead of the security of the population, and its refusal to place normative questions at the heart of international relations.

Thus critical security theory calls for a deepening as well as a broadening of the security agenda. When threats other than the military are included in the security agenda, it becomes clear that the reference cannot be the state alone. States tend to put threats to their own existence at the top of the security agenda, while neglecting those to individuals. Moreover, it is sometimes the state itself that is the biggest threat to its own citizens, despite the fact that their protection is in theory the state's raison d'être. And in the final analysis the state is, and ought to be, the means, not the end of the collective pursuit of human happiness. The state is a vehicle, an elaborate social construction whose purpose is to allow individuals and societies to realize their aspirations. Security in this regard is both an end in itself and a necessary precondition for achieving other individually and socially desirable goals.

The emancipatory objectives of critical security theory make it highly controversial. One reason for the skepticism with which positivist international relations scholars have received critical security theory is because of its refusal to separate fact from value, an approach that is bitterly opposed by many political scientists and by a majority of U.S. international relations scholars. Opponents argue that "we are not about to cast off our badges of professional integrity by turning our research and teaching into political advocacy" and there must be "a deep rooted and unshakeable firmness in our commitment to the search for objectivity" (Almond, 1988: 828–840). This argument misses the whole point of critical theory and is grounded in the positivist and objectivist methodology that critical theory rejects as a way of validating truth-claims.

It is precisely the commitment to human emancipation that critical theory takes so seriously, that makes it so objectionable to traditional theorists. A more telling criticism is that of J. D. Moon, who argues that critical theory "is based on a particular conception of human emancipation, and unless this value can be justified, it is open to the charge of not being a 'theory' at all, but a form of propaganda or persuasion masquerading as science" (1983: 176).

Although Moon's specific statement is full of misconceptions (critical theory has no "particular conception" of emancipation, nor does it claim to imitate the scientific method), there is validity in the argument that emancipation can take many forms, which can be contested. To some extent, however, emancipation "is not so much an end-state to be achieved, as it is a demand to put an end to practices that can be shown to be unwarranted" (Leonard, 1990: 266). Or as Keith Krause puts it in relation to critical security theory, "the purpose of theory is not explanation and prediction within a framework of transhistorical and generalisable causal claims, but rather contextual understanding and practical knowledge" (1998: 317).

▨ Critical Security and the State

Critical security theorists do not dismiss the importance of the state in the contemporary world, nor do they anticipate its imminent demise as a form of social organization. The state remains absolutely central to any understanding of contemporary international politics. It is the state's moral and practical status as a privileged actor in international relations that is contested and critiqued. It is necessary, therefore, to be skeptical of claims, such as that by Richard Devetek, that "critical international theory's aim of achieving an alternative theory and practice of international relations centres on the possibility of overcoming the sovereign state and inaugurating post-sovereign world politics" (1996: 173).

Nevertheless, the state is rejected as the *sole* referent object of security for a number of reasons. First, not all states are concerned with the security of their citizens. In fact there are circumstances where the state can pose the greatest threat to individuals. During the 1990s in countries such as Algeria and Turkey, it was the policies of their own governments that threatened the lives of the populations, rather than the armed forces of their neighbors. This is particularly true of non-nation-states that house substantial national minorities.

The state centrism of realism is criticized because of the objectivist view that is taken of the state. In realist theory, the state is treated as a concrete entity that acts rationally to implement a knowable national interest. For critical theorists, however, the state is viewed in process terms, constantly re-created through its actions and outputs, including—significantly—its security policies. And one of the effects of these acts is to define inside and outside, "them" and "us." The state may be seen as a positive force in the way that it constructs loyalties within a particular territory, but the act of doing this creates boundaries and barriers against the populations who are thereby constructed as "foreigners."

In the making of the state, the construction of the hostile "other" who is threatening and dangerous is central to the making of identities and the securing of boundaries. Indeed, as noted earlier, David Campbell (1992: 78–79) argues that the legitimization of state power necessarily demands the construction of the danger "outside." The state requires this "discourse of danger" to secure its identity and for the legitimization of state power.

The idea of the state as an "ideal community" is one that has a long history in Western political thought. The Greeks, when developing the idea of the "good life," felt that it could only be achieved on the basis of the *polis,* a bounded political society (Neufeld, 1995: 9–10). They felt that a single individual could not act politically, because being political requires a pooling of resources, the organization of a collective effort. This collectivity, to be a political actor, must also be a coherent, spatially defined entity.

Realists argue that the state is the structure that communities construct around their beliefs and values, in order to define, delimit, and distinguish the social features that justify extraordinary measures in their defense. An important aspect of this argument is the assumption that the borders of the state and the community are the same, hence the terminology "nation-state," an assumption that is brought into question in the analysis of "societal" security. State building in realist theory is an effective boundary-producing act.

Richard Ashley argues that the state is a conceptual entity that relies on a dichotomy to define its boundaries, and that these boundaries of the state represent arbitrary exclusions (1997: 414–415). In traditional mainstream Western political theory, the role of the state is to mediate between an internal realm characterized by peace and order, and an external world that is anarchic and full of danger. The state becomes an intolerant and often oppressive entity, founded upon particular conceptions of order that encourage it to oppress the very individuals it is supposed to exist to protect. At the same time, it naturally exhibits hostility toward individuals of other states, whose identities and interests are seen as a threat. Thus constructed, the contradictory nature of the modern state makes it the source of much of the insecurity in the contemporary world, rather than necessarily a source of stability and security.

This is not to lose sight of the state's capacity to be an agent for good. As Booth notes, the state is a means to an end and can act, in Hedley Bull's words, as the "local agents of the common good" (Booth, 1991b: 325). The state may have a role to play in situations where the emancipatory demands of more than one group conflict with one another. This is significant for critical security because such an approach must be informed by a clear awareness of the distinction between the state and security. In the traditional "national security" approach, the state and security were virtually synonymous. Security threats were by definition threats to the state, to its continuing existence, or to the ability of its political executive to exercise sovereign authority. This mind-set generated a particular concern with domestic security issues during the Cold War period, marked by fears of espionage and subversion within the boundaries of the national security state. But this sees the state as an end in itself, indeed the "end" to which political activity is directed. From a critical theoretical perspective, however, the state is no more than the *means*.

Security and Emancipation

Critical security theory places considerable emphasis on the concept of emancipation. Booth starts from Kenneth Boulding's premise that "security means the absence of threats," and links the two by defining emancipation as "the freeing of people from those physical and human constraints which stop them from carrying out what they would freely choose to do" (Booth, 1991b: 319) This approach places individuals as the focus of security, where traditionally the state has been the main referent object, and clearly expands the definition beyond military security into an array of additional sectors.

Booth argues that emancipation of people was a motif of the twentieth century—decolonization, freedom of women, youth, workers, homosexuals, consumers, and thought. Booth's concept of emancipation is not built on the assumption that the threat needs to be existential. This raises the problem that from the perspective of "securitization" there are no specific criteria suggested for deciding that any particular issue is a security issue. The agenda suggested clearly encompasses the broader approach, but is not limited to it. Emancipation is the freeing of people (as individuals and groups) from particular physical and human constraints. War and the threat of war are two of those constraints, together with poverty, inadequate education, political oppression, and so on.

Booth therefore calls for the security of individuals to be addressed. He defines security and emancipation as "two sides of the same coin" (1991b: 319). This is because war and the threat of war, which are treated as the main concerns under the traditional approaches, are only two of many constraints that stop individuals from carrying out what they would freely choose to do.

This interpretation of emancipation, and its relationship to the critical project, is not shared by all the authors contributing to the development of the theory. Keith Krause and Michael Williams, for example, who have made a number of important contributions, including a book-length study (1997), do not explicitly focus on a requirement for human emancipation as part of a critical security approach, though it is implicit in much of their analysis. For many critical security proponents, the "emancipatory" project is clearly present in their proposals for the reconceptualization of security and the implementation of a wider policy agenda, but the term itself is avoided.

The call for a focus on the security of the individual is somewhat misleading. It is certainly appropriate to locate security in the life of the individual human being, particularly in order to contrast this logic with an unquestioning assumption that security should always be seen from the perspective of an unproblematic state. Individuals are the ultimate relevant referent objects in the security discourse. In practice, however, even individual security is normally pursued through engagement with collectivities of various types and sizes, which in turn have specific security concerns relating to their own social construction.

Martin Shaw suggests, therefore, that the problem should not be seen as an issue of individuals versus states, because "even when we talk about state security, we are already talking about an institution constructed by human beings and which involves individuals in many ways." While a purely state-security perspective is seen as absurd, Shaw advocates society as an alternative referent. Society, in the sense of the social relations between individuals and social groups, "is not merely a [reality], but *the* reality within which it alone makes sense to look at the relations of institutions like states" (1993: 168, emphasis added).

One problem opened up by this is the question of who will be responsible for security. A security concept broadened and deepened raises the question of who the security providers are. As Emma Rothschild suggests, "the political responsibility for ensuring security" must be accordingly broadened away from the state, "including upwards to international institutions, downwards to regional or local government, and sideways to non-governmental organisations, to public opinion and the press and to the abstract forces of nature or of the markets" (1995: 55). All these security practitioners are also reducible to the individual. Rothschild talks of the "dizzying complexity of political geometry in which individuals, groups, state and international organisations have responsibilities for international organisations, states, groups and individuals" (1995: 70).

Security is a normative concept. This is true even when viewed from a traditional or neorealist perspective, but it is particularly evident from a critical security perspective. The search for "security" is the pursuit of a particular kind of social and political objective, and a call for the prioritization of specific policy outputs. This raises inevitable questions about how much security is required, and what sacrifices should be made in other areas of social policy in order to achieve it. The "emancipatory" aspect of critical security is particularly challenging in this respect, because it is also in effect calling for the social concept of security to be prioritized when its implications put it in conflict with other guiding social concepts, such as the pursuit of order, in a traditional sense. Critical security as a concept is closely linked to particular understandings of other key social concepts such as justice, order, and community. These concepts themselves are as unstable, ambiguous, and "essentially contested" as is security itself, and for much the same reasons given their political importance. The problem for critical theorists in this regard, following Habermas, is to develop a discourse ethics "that recognizes the necessity of universalist principles, while not doing violence to the fact of diversity" (Rengger, 2001: 98).

The effective commitment to emancipation that is present in critical theory–inspired approaches to security is problematic, in that it might be seen as an invitation to act wherever there is a perceived threat to individuals, so that security practice would be based on the principle of intervention rather than sovereignty. In a world still powerfully influenced by realist thinking, there would be a great deal of scope for abuse of this principle by more powerful states pursuing their own vested interests even when camouflaging them behind the rhetoric of human rights and democratization. There are also difficulties in terms of the establishment of threat—that is, in terms of who decides what should or should not constitute a threat. This is a problematic issue in a world characterized by value pluralism on issues such as the definition of human rights. This pluralism should not be exaggerated, though; there is also considerable consensus on what constitutes such rights among the vast majority of states, and indeed among the vast majority of their constituent populations. Nevertheless, there is a clear potential for states to use the principle of emancipation as a vehicle for imposing their values on other societies. This problem in fact leads Booth to oppose the general principle of intervention. From a "broad" security perspective, intervention is not necessarily problematic or counterproductive, but specific actual or proposed interventions would need to be extensively analyzed and critiqued. From a critical *theoretical* perspective, however, intervention is particularly problematic, because it makes emancipation a top-down external effect, rather than an effect brought about by the actions of the oppressed themselves.

In this regard, David Baldwin (1997: 18) notes that individuals and larger social groupings have many different goals, of which the attainment of security is one. The pursuit of security is therefore always a question of measuring the relative importance of different values, whose pursuit inevitably involves policy choices necessitating deferred gain in the areas not prioritized. This may become particularly problematic when a society that seeks security also seeks to promote human emancipation. Is the security of one group more important than the emancipation of another? Foreign policy has often been constructed in terms of such questions in the past and continues to be so in practice. Western refusal to act effectively against the apartheid regime in South Africa was justified as necessary, because the racist regime was pro-Western and protected the key sea-lanes around southern Africa in the context of the global military-political confrontation with communisim. The refusal of the North Atlantic Treaty Organization to support democracy in Turkey and Algeria is predicated on a belief that doing so would make possible the election of "Islamic" governments with policies antithetical to Western interests.

Andrew Linklater has argued that critical approaches to the study of international relations "centre around understandings of the processes of 'inclusion' and 'exclusion,' which have in a sense always been the central concerns of the discipline" (cited in Stearns, 1998: 109). But these inclusions and exclusions have also worked to exclude people on the basis of race, class, and gender.

Wyn Jones adds to this the need to focus on identity as a central aspect of the understanding of security (1996: 213). This is not just because identity is central to what it means to be human and therefore needs to be protected when it is perceived to be threatened. Rather it is that security is linked in a fundamental way to the concepts of identity and community. Societies perceive particular threats the same way, and are willing to take collective action to address those threats, precisely because they see themselves as sharing a common identity. "However, the constitutive relationship between identity, community and security makes it harder to decide who the referents for security should be." This requires critical security theory to engage with different referents for each and every case (1996: 213).

Critical security theory argues that our understanding of society is incomplete if it lacks an emancipating purpose. The approach to security in the "broad" sense is very broad indeed, yet even in the much narrower, critical theory–inspired sense it is diverse. But to a significant extent this simply reflects the diversity of critical theory itself, defined by Stephen Bronner as "a cluster of themes inspired by an emancipatory intent" (1994: 3). It places great emphasis on the need to make individual human beings the ultimate referent in our understanding of security. But this is necessary both because of its relevance to policy issues in international relations, and to counter prevailing disciplinary orthodoxies. It is also important in ensuring that critical security theory retains at all times its self-conscious connection to specific historical circumstances and practical contexts.

In the final analysis, the emergence of a critical approach was crucially required, because the conception of security dominant in the West during the Cold War period denied security to vast numbers of the world population. The desperate problems of much of the human race were largely ignored by the traditional security agenda, which instead allowed the emergence of an attitude to security that left millions to suffer poverty and starvation, while the funds that could have helped them were devoted to building the capacity to threaten millions of others with nuclear annihilation.

Conclusion

The approach to security that is inspired by critical theory offers the possibility of developing a theory of security that is sensitive to the real security concerns of the world's populations. It embraces the multisectoral approach of the broader agenda, but is not constrained by the limitations of the currently identified sectors. It embraces valuable approaches such as gender, but incorporates them into a wider and deeper approach to security.

It represents the most fundamental disagreement with realism, because while much of the former is constructed so as to argue that things change very slowly if at all, and to a large extent the realities of international relations and therefore international security are timeless, critical theory and critical security theory are premised on the belief that the world need not be as it is, that greater human freedom and possibility are always immanent within existing social realities and that it is within the capacity of human beings as social actors to bring about fundamental change.

ELEVEN

Conclusions

The overt commitment to emancipation is not present in the whole of the broader security agenda in the sectoral sense, nor is it even always explicitly present in the arguments of those with a narrower critical approach. I would argue, however, that it should be, and that while a pluralism in approaches to security is welcome, there should be a terminological distinction between the broad swathe of nonrealist approaches to security and a specifically "critical" security approach, a term that should be reserved for approaches that explicitly draw upon the literature of critical theory in its modernist, emancipatory manifestations.

The approach that offers the greatest possibilities for understanding and engaging with the practical problems of insecurity in the real world is that inspired by critical theory. It is superior to traditional realist analysis, is coherent and policy-relevant in itself, and also embraces and integrates the valuable aspects of the multisectoral and other postpositivist approaches to security. It also recognizes that to speak or write about security is never an innocent act. Theory always has an ultimate referent and purpose, and critical theory does not attempt to camouflage these in its advocacy of policies aimed at increasing the security of the marginalized.

There is a sense in which critical security studies could be interpreted as anything that is critical of the traditional realist approach to security. That is, "critical" with a lowercase *c*. It could incorporate some of the insights from nontraditional security theories advanced during the Cold War period, such as peace research and dependency theory, as well as those of the broader, multisectoral security agenda advanced in the 1980s. Much of this thinking could still be incorporated within a realist or neoliberal approach, and this places clear limitations on the degree to which this approach can take the analysis of security forward. Moreover, within the discipline of international relations as a whole, the most exciting contributions to theoretical development in the past twenty years have been in postpositivist (or reflectivist) theory. This has included important contributions drawing on Frankfurt school and Gramscian critical theory. A number of scholars, such as Ken Booth, Andrew Linklater, and Richard Wyn Jones, have brought these theoretical resources to bear on the concept and practice of security.

In looking at the various approaches to security that have emerged in the past quarter of a century, it is tempting to label all those that have emerged from out of the shadow of traditional realist security perspectives as "critical security." This is because they are all, in their own ways, critical of weaknesses or gaps in the realist approach to thinking about the nature and practice of security.

However, this does create a semantic confusion with those security approaches that are critical in the sense that they are derived from critical social theory. This confusion can be addressed to an extent by using the convention of referring to the latter as uppercase "Critical Security" and using a lowercase "critical security" for approaches that are simply critical of traditional security thinking in some way. An important part of the analysis of contemporary approaches to security therefore is to examine the degree to which the new, "broader" approaches to security really do represent a decisive break with Cold War security logics. My own preference is for the title "critical security" to be reserved for approaches that clearly *do* represent a break with traditional formulations, that are not susceptible to being annexed by neorealist orthodoxy, and that clearly reflect a vision of politics that is emancipatory in intent.

There are a number of reasons why it would be preferable to maintain a genuine distinction between the various components of the broader approach to security more generally, and the specifically Critical Theory–informed, postpositivist approaches. First, to use the lowercase "critical security" umbrella fairly indiscriminately runs the risk of including so much that the crucial distinctions between it and realism and between it and Critical Theory approaches would be lost. If it meant only "not realist," this would be an unhelpfully broad category anyway, but in reality, a second crucial problem emerges, which is that the category can be allowed to include variant realist approaches as well. Keith Krause and Michael Williams, for example, allowed "subaltern realism" to be included in a collection of essays on "critical security," so that the latter begins to expand to the point where hardly any approach is excluded (1997).

Even when the "critical security" title is limited to approaches that represent some kind of definitive break with traditional approaches to security, such as the new security sectors, there are major problems, because the sectors themselves are open to colonization by realist perspectives, so that their nonrealist character may be more apparent than real. This is certainly the case if the economic and environmental sectors are examined.

Economic security, for example, is a very broad category. There are elements within it that dovetail easily with Critical Security thinking, but there are others that are clearly inspired by a neorealist agenda. The construction of "security" that dominated during the Cold War period was somewhat at odds with ordinary understandings of the phrase, which embraced the maintenance of good health, employment, adequate accommodation, access to education, and other "economic" issues, rather than concerns about grand strategy or the military dimensions of foreign policy. These understandings lend themselves to an approach that sees human emancipation as a primary goal. This is also true of concerns with the opportunity costs of defense spending.

With the economic security concept, there has always been a recognition that the economic burden represented by defense acquisition has a direct impact in terms of efforts to address other social spending priorities. As President Dwight Eisenhower put it in the late 1950s, "the cost of one modern bomber is this, a modern brick school in more than thirty cities . . . it is two fine, fully-equipped hospitals" (cited in Baylis et al., 1975: 51). On an international scale, the opportunity costs relate to funds that were not directed toward efforts to combat absolute poverty in the developing countries.

As noted earlier, the "economic security" title embraces approaches as far removed from one another as geoeconomics and human security. There is no meeting point at all between the geoeconomics school and Critical Theory, while the human security approach easily lends itself to incorporation within a Critical Theory–informed approach to security. Characterizing economic security generally as "critical security" is therefore very misleading, since it exaggerates the coherence of the various approaches under the heading, and suggests a compatibility with Critical Theory–driven approaches that does not exist.

The same caveat can be made with regard to environmental security. The definition of environmental security as relating to the problems for humanity created by the nature of its own industrial civilization is interesting, because it questions whether as a domain it can be considered as fully a "critical" perspective. Critical security is concerned with threats to human beings. This raises questions about why natural disasters should be omitted from the threat calculus.

There is also a question mark over whether defending a very high level of material well-being should be seen as a genuinely "critical" security issue. Does the latter refer only to provision of more basic requirements? In an approach influenced by Critical Theory, the emphasis would more likely be on achieving the basic needs of the many, rather than the acquisition of a luxury lifestyle by the few.

The referent object for environmental security is not the state as such, but civilization, in the sense of the level of development currently enjoyed by the advanced states of the world. It is in this sense that it is argued that from a global perspective, "mankind is living beyond the carrying capacity of the earth" (Buzan, Waever, and De Wilde, 1998: 81). If this means that what is under threat is the ability to sustain two-car households with DVDs, dishwashing machines, and microwaves, it can be seen as a threat to affluence rather than a threat to survival.

The version of environmental security characterized by the Toronto school lends itself to a neorealist interpretation of security, but not to one informed by Critical Theory. Rather than being focused on issues of human emancipation, it is a very traditional approach to international relations in which international conflict and war are explained in terms of competition for scarce resources. It is in fact a national security perspective, specifically linked to the military security domain and to the interests of the state. It is a long way from the idea of "caring for the earth and its people as the highest priority" (Porter and Brown, 1991: 111).

A cynic might also argue that the ease with which traditional security organizations such as the North Atlantic Treaty Organization and the U.S. Department of Defense appropriated the environmental security agenda at the end of the Cold War suggests that the agenda lends itself to neorealist colonization and is not a sector where the broader approach to security and Critical Security can be seen as synonymous.

It is never possible to entirely eliminate military considerations from the multisectoral approach, because of the way in which the sectors form part of a greater whole and often interact in important ways. Nevertheless, it is important to resist the temptation to assume that a sectoral title necessarily implies that there is something quite novel and nontraditional about the approach to security being applied within it.

An examination of the broad sweep of theorizing about "security" at the beginning of the twenty-first century shows that it remains a powerful term and precisely because of this it is a battleground of contested interpretations. There are many ways of looking at security and many possible referents for it. Analysts such as Barry Buzan and Ole Waever argue that it is simply not possible to understand the complexities of international security on a global scale using a single explanatory model. There is no "master key" to a definitive interpretation (2003: 26).

The interpretations are fiercely contested because the construction of the concept of security establishes a "discourse of truth," in Michel Foucault's sense, that effectively marks the boundaries of what is considered to be "true knowledge." In the West, the provision of security has come to be seen as being the primary purpose of the state, taking priority over other social objectives and government functions. The definition of security is therefore the point of struggle both for different lobbies wishing to prioritize their particular policy agendas, and for conservative and emancipatory conceptions of politics and international relations.

Realism has not lost its significance for international relations. The advent of the presidency of George W. Bush in the United States in 2001 saw the return of realist thinking on foreign and security policy, with crucial ramifications for the rest of the international community. Understanding and critiquing realist security thinking therefore remains an important task. The academic discipline of international relations failed to do this effectively during the Cold War period, allowing a highly restricted concept of security to take hold, and failed to ask sufficiently fundamental questions about the meaning of "security" as a term and the objectives of pursuing security as a policy. In terms of fully understanding the nature of contemporary international security, realism is an unsatisfactory theory. Static and inflexible, with a limited ontology and a positivist and objectivist epistemology, it lacks the subtlety and flexibility to address the broader security agenda of the contemporary world.

The broader agenda itself, reflected in the multisectoral approach to security that became the academic and governmental norm in the 1990s, represents a major advance over the state-centric, military-oriented approach to security that dominated establishment thinking during the Cold War period. Many traditionalists themselves have accepted that the understanding of security needs to move somewhat beyond Cold War obsessions, and allow for the need to look at other issues, though a concern with the military component continues to dominate (Gray, 1994).

However, where realists have looked beyond the traditional agenda, they have done so by specifically linking phenomena in the new sectors to a classical military problematic—for example, in concern with the military implications of economic performance, or the possibility of environmental disputes over resources like water escalating into military conflict.

For this reason, while broadening the meaning of security to embrace new sectors is a crucially important development, it remains inadequate unless accompanied by a simultaneous effort to deepen our understanding of security. Different understandings of security are grounded in different understandings of the political. The contributions of Buzan and the Copenhagen school, along with a number of others, were crucial in triggering a major reexamination of the meaning of security. Buzan was challenged by traditional realists with the argument that expanding the agenda threatened to emasculate security as a meaningful concept. He quite properly responded that the way to develop a coherent meaning for security was not to restrict it to the traditional military interpretation, but rather to explore the fundamental meaning of security itself, and that "leaders and peoples have considerable freedom to determine what they do and do not define as security threats" (Buzan and Waever, 2003: 26). The advantage of a broader approach to security is that it allows us to address the real security concerns of the human race and the diversity of threats to individual and group security. From this point of view, the ability to address issues in fields like the environmental and societal is clearly welcome.

Nevertheless, the broader agenda is problematic in a number of respects, and lacks a unifying approach that relates the sectors to a clear concept of security. The attempt to do this with the idea of the "existential threat" has not been entirely successful, since it is clear that threats are identified in several of the sectors that are not existential in a consistently meaningful way. It may be the case that it is not possible to have a single concept of security that is intellectually coherent and applicable to all cases, particularly when societies may be continually securitizing some features of social reality and desecuritizing others.

The attempt to move the analysis forward with postpositivist methodologies has also been valuable in terms of our understanding of security and our ability to engage with real-world problems. To a large extent the multisectoral approach has not led to profound redefinition of security, but rather to a recognition that the logic of security can apply beyond the military realm, and significantly, to an existing logic of security being applied to a wider range of issue areas, which is a development that is unhelpful rather than positive. With the postpositivist contributions, however, the broader approach has been accompanied by a fundamental challenge to the epistemological and ontological assumptions of traditional security theory.

It is an important feature within critical theory that it is seen as providing conceptual and linguistic tools by which the oppressed can be helped to emancipate themselves. Similarly, the possibilities for emancipatory change are seen as being emergent within the existing social and political order. The function of theory is to show the oppressed that they can change their situation through their own critically informed actions.

In the case of postmodernism there has been a proven ability to criticize realist security theory very effectively and to expose its camouflaged normative preferences. However, the refusal of many poststructuralists to offer a grounded basis for normative judgments of their own renders the approach of limited utility to a policy area that is fundamentally concerned with the resolution of basic moral and political questions, though many postmodernists themselves have recognized the inadequacy and promoted an ethical turn in poststructuralist security thinking, reflected in the work of David Campbell (1992) for example.

Many postmodernists explicitly see their ideas and theories as having emancipatory intent, and certainly the approach has clear emancipatory potential. However, it embodies fundamentally different assumptions to those of mainstream modernist critical theory. This not only means that its perspective on security differs in important ways from that of critical security, but it also raises questions about whether postmodernism can indeed serve an emancipatory function in relation to the theory and practice of security.

Because it has as its core the concept of emancipation, critical security thinking is ultimately modernist. It attempts to retrieve the promise of the

Enlightenment project. A commitment to emancipation has a foundational quality that means that postmodernist and poststructuralist approaches cannot be easily accommodated within it.

Critical theory offers a better basis for understanding security than do poststructuralist accounts, because it is directed at producing effective and lasting solutions to real problems, and improving the lives of ordinary people by building stable structures and processes of security based on justice, community, and mutual satisfaction.

Feminism in most of its forms is clearly a form of critical theory and therefore lends itself to a truly critical approach to security in a way that many other approaches, including poststructuralism, do not. It is critical not just in terms of its relationship to traditional security thinking, but also because feminist theory and practice are characterized by an "ongoing critical self-examination and consciousness-raising project that makes feminist theory a genuinely critical theory" (Leonard, 1990: xxii). It can therefore make a potentially substantial contribution, both to the consolidation of a broader approach to security, and to the development of a genuinely critical understanding of security. For as Stephen Leonard notes:

> Feminist theory does not seek to define and defend a conception of theory *a priori;* on the contrary, it seeks to articulate just those kinds of practices here and now that can be considered emancipating. And the difference between the attempt to define an emancipated and an emancipating practice should not be lost to us. It constitutes nothing less than the difference between the idea of a critical theory and a critical theory in practice. (1990: 240)

From a largely modernist perspective, feminism has made an important contribution. The gender-based approach is integrative of many of the non-traditional approaches discussed in this book in its openness to the development of new security sectors, its focus on a structural understanding of violence and threat, and its social-constructivist analysis of society and politics. The emphasis on the dynamics of power and the implications of the gendered aspects of societies and their beliefs is of fundamental importance in understanding the realities of national and international security. In terms of locating feminist approaches within a critical approach to security, a crucial contribution is that feminists have demonstrated "that critique cannot be grounded in an ahistorical, transcendental or abstract understanding of knowledge and self that is separated from a particular, historically contingent context" (Leonard, 1990: 212).

From the point of view of developing a critical approach to security, the feminist approach needs to be at the heart of the enterprise. Feminists have always thought in terms of a broader approach to society in the sectoral sense. Moreover, no account of security that does not take full account of the gender variable is worthy of the name. In addition, the political and social *practice* of feminism (not explored in this book) clearly fits the model of a critical theory in practice. For all these reasons, it is essential to incorporate gender analysis into critical security theory. It is not sufficient in itself, however. While fruitful, the feminist approach to security is inadequate in building a broader approach to security because it is focused on a single variable.

While poststructuralists would condemn the critical security approach as part of a dangerous modernist metanarrative, contemporary critical theory, particularly as it has been applied in the discipline of international relations, is self-consciously aware of the need to avoid making definitions purely at the theoretical level, rather than at the level of clearly situated subjects, whose problems need to be addressed in context and analyzed in their own terms.

This approach does not totally reject the claims of the state as both actor and referent of security, as is sometimes suggested by opponents, but it is skeptical toward the state's claims. Robert Walker notes that the security of states has come to dominate our understanding of the meaning of security because "other forms of political community have been rendered almost unthinkable" (1990: 6). This has happened because of the enormous emphasis Western metaphysics and political theory have placed on the idea of a binary divide between a peaceful and ordered society within the state, and a turbulent and threatening anarchy outside it. Drawing on reconceptualizations of identity from the feminist and poststructuralist approaches is therefore a valuable part of a critical conception of security that is open to new forms of political identity and allows a broader conception that cannot be solely based on the security of states.

In their original conceptualization of "politics," the ancient Greeks saw it as being about the "pursuit of the good life." Politics is about improving people's lives, attempting to find organizational structures that will more efficiently deliver the material comforts and necessities of life, while allowing for the spiritual and philosophical needs that are such a notable feature of *Homo sapiens*. There is a sense in which this classical understanding of politics was not properly captured by traditional approaches to security. Realist security thinking largely focuses on abstractions, rather than on the concrete realities of human beings, so that it could assign greater significance to the state than to the people who compose it. There is an intellectual logic and even an ethical component to this, because if the state is the instrument for the attainment of the good life, then its continued existence, in a form that reflects the values of its population, can be seen as a prerequisite for any political or social project.

However, this logic is taken too far when the state becomes an end in itself. Carl von Clausewitz, in his writings on war, emphasized the crucial point that war was a political exercise, an instrumental means to achieve political goals. It had no meaning or validity outside that logic. Traditional security theory to some extent lost sight of this kind of crucial linkage in thinking about security. Even when limited to a military security approach, the purpose of the pursuit of security is to maintain the ability of society to pursue the good life. The ultimate purpose of seeking to maximize security is therefore to allow the pursuit of human emancipation, and so there is particular worth in an approach to security that places this at the heart of its analysis and practice.

Critical security so conceived recognizes security as a process, as much or more so than as an endpoint. It pursues a stable security based on justice and, as far as possible, mutual satisfaction with political situations. It is utopian in its goals, but not in its practice or immediate expectations of what is possible. It is never possible to satisfactorily address all the possible threats to security, particularly when they are broadly conceived, but security threats can be managed in a nonviolent culture. Life can never be free from conflicts of interest and "it is neither possible nor desirable for critical theory to treat emancipation in universal terms" (Leonard, 1990: 247). But emancipation remains central to security, and in pursuing this goal, as Booth (1991b: 319) notes, what must not be lost sight of is that states should be seen as means rather than ends, and people treated as ends rather than means.

It is tempting to believe that much could be achieved from a synthesis of the various approaches to security. Since they are interested in different aspects of reality, or see reality in very different ways, by combining the best of each of the approaches a new unified security theory might be developed that is appropriate for examining any aspect of security. Efforts to do this were made at conferences of the International Studies Association (ISA) and the European Consortium for Political Research during the 1990s, with the ISA initiative leading to the publication by Krause and Williams (1997) of a book exploring the issues.

Unfortunately, this synthetic approach is simply not capable of producing a successful outcome. While some of the theoretical approaches are comparatively similar, for example feminism and critical theory, for the most part the approaches are irreconcilable. They operate on the basis of quite different epistemologies and ontologies. That is, each operates on the basis of quite different assumptions about what is legitimate knowledge about the social world, and what the key features of that world actually are.

Realism, for example, assumes that there is a clear distinction between facts and values and that facts are independent of theory. Subjects and objects are also seen as distinct. Stephen Walt, for example, insists that "security studies seeks cumulative knowledge about the role of military force. To obtain it, the field must follow the standard canons of scientific research: careful and consistent use of terms, unbiased measurement of critical concepts and public documentation of theoretical and empirical claims" (1991: 222). In reality, such "objectivity" is a myth, camouflaging the maintenance of particular vested interests. Genuine objectivity is virtually unattainable, and where injustice is being studied, is not even desirable. Social science has as its purpose the aggregation of rational knowledge by agents who are themselves part of what they are studying, and whose theories "help to articulate, shape and justify the beliefs, goals and languages of particular practices and institutions" (Leonard, 1990: 124).

Similarly for realists, the world is largely a collection of concrete realities "out there" waiting to be discovered and analyzed. Key variables such as "identity" refer to attributes that likewise have a fixed character waiting to be described. For critical security advocates, however, "reality" is intersubjectively constituted, and identity is never fixed, but is evolutionary and subject to negotiation. This does not make it any easier to deal with security in the real world, where the competing claims of referent objects may not always be capable of being neatly differentiated between good and bad, right and wrong. It is the cases where both have valid, if different, claims that are most difficult to deal with in a just manner. It is the recognition of the pathos in this situation that gives the best of the classical realist writings their cutting edge, with their emphasis on the "acceptance of responsibility for the consequences of actions (and) on the prudential adaptation of moral principles to circumstances" (Murray, 1997: 133), and is strongly reflected in the work of Hans Morgenthau, Raymond Aron, and Stanley Hoffman.

David Baldwin argues that it is the specifics of security that are changing rather than the nature of security itself. The various security sectors, economic, environmental, and so on, "are different forms of security, not fundamentally different concepts" (1997: 23). Moreover, security is a policy objective in competition with others for scarce resources. It should not be seen as preempting all other values, but as being one among many that states can choose to pursue, and to what degree.

Security is a powerful concept with tremendous social and political resonance. It is not simply a field dealing with narrow technical issues of an essentially military nature. On the contrary, because it embraces such a wide range of fundamental human experience, it is in important ways a master concept, which makes it possible to initiate and participate in fundamental debate about the kinds of societies we wish to live in, and the values and goals that we should work toward as societies (Leitenen, 1997: 17).

The question of how security is defined is a vital one, because it is a crucial factor in determining how societies choose to allocate their scarce resources, and what is deemed to be legitimate political discourse. As both Antonio Gramsci and Michel Foucault noted, dominant ideas and concepts are part of the constructed consensus that provides the superstructure for the existing distribution of power and authority in society (Cox, 1983: 168). When a set of assumptions, definitions, and beliefs achieve the status of being regarded as common sense, they become what Foucault called "discourses of truth," marking the limits of what is deemed to be "true knowledge" (Lukes, 1986: 229).

For this reason, the definition of what is and what is not "security" is likely to continue to be an intellectual and political battleground. This is only right, for it is at the heart of what politics is, or should be, all about.

Bibliography

Adler, Emanuel. 1997. "Imagined (Security) Communities: Cognitive Regions in International Relations." *Millennium: Journal of International Studies* 26, pp. 49–277.

Adler, Emanuel, and Barnett, Michael J. 1996. "Governing Anarchy: A Research Agenda for the Study of Security Communities." *Ethics and International Affairs* 10, pp. 63–98.

———, eds. 1998. *Security Communities.* Cambridge: Cambridge University Press.

Almond, Gabriel. 1988. "Separate Tables: Schools and Sects in Political Science." *PS: Political Science and Politics* 21, pp. 828–840.

Amnesty International. 1998. Press release. "Why Are We Still Waiting? The Struggle for Women's Human Rights." London (March 1).

———. 1999. Report. "Women in Afghanistan: Pawns in Men's Power Struggles." London (November 1).

Amos, Valerie, and Parmer, Prathiba. 1984. "Challenging Imperial Feminism." *Feminist Review,* no. 17, pp. 3–20.

Anderson, Benedict. 1989. *Imagined Communities: Reflections on the Origins and Spread of Nationalism.* London: Verso.

Andreski, Stanislav. 1980. "On the Peaceful Disposition of Military Dictatorships." *Journal of Strategic Studies* 3, pp. 3–10.

Archarya, Amitav. 1998. "Collective Identity and Conflict Management in South-East Asia." In A. Adler and M. Barnett, eds., *Security Communities.* Cambridge: Cambridge University Press, pp. 198–227.

Arfi, Badredine. 1998. "Ethnic Fear: The Social Construction of Insecurity." *Security Studies* 8, pp. 151–203.

Aron, Raymond. 1954. *The Century of Total War.* Garden City, N.Y.: Doubleday.

———. 1974. *Peace and War: A Theory of International Relations.* New York: Praeger.

Ashley, Richard. 1981. "Political Realism and Human Interests." *International Studies Quarterly* 25, pp. 204–236.

———. 1984. "The Poverty of Neorealism." *International Organisation* 38, pp. 225–286.

———. 1988. "Untying the Sovereign State: A Double Reading of the Anarchy Problematique." *Millennium* 17, pp. 227–262.

———. 1989. "Living on Borderlines: Man, Poststructuralism, and War." In J. Der

Derian and M. Shapiro, eds., *International/Intertextual Relations: Postmodern Readings of World Politics.* Toronto: Lexington Books, pp. 259–321.

———. 1997. "The Geopolitics of Geopolitical Space: Towards a Critical Social Theory of International Politics." *Alternatives* 12, pp. 403–434.

Ashley, Richard, and Walker, R.B.J. 1990. "Reading Dissidence/Writing the Discipline: Crisis and the Question of Sovereignty in International Studies." *International Studies Quarterly* 34, pp. 367–416.

Ayoob, Mohammed. 1995. *The Third World Security Predicament: State Making, Regional Conflict, and the International System.* Boulder: Lynne Rienner.

Babst, Dean V. 1964. "'Elective Governments: A Force for Peace." *Wisconsin Sociologist* 3, pp. 9–14.

Baldwin, David A. 1995. "Security Studies at the End of the Cold War." *World Politics* 48, pp. 117–141.

———. 1997. "The Concept of Security." *Review of International Studies* 23, pp. 5–26.

Baldwin, David A., and Milner, Helen. 1992. "Economics and National Security." In H. Bienen, ed., *Power, Economics, and Security.* Boulder: Westview.

Baylis, J., Booth, K., Garnett, J., and Williams, P. 1975. *Contemporary Strategy.* London: Croom Helm.

Baylis, John, and Smith, Steve. 1997. *The Globalisation of World Politics: An Introduction to International Relations.* Oxford: Oxford University Press.

Beck, U. 1992. *Risk Society.* London: Sage.

Beckman, Peter, and D'Amico, Francine, eds. 1994. *Women, Gender, and World Politics.* Westport, Conn.: Bergin and Garvey.

Betts, Richard K. 1991. "The Concept of Deterrence in the Postwar Era." *Security Studies* 1, pp. 25–36.

Bigo, Didier. 1994. "The European Internal Security Field: Stakes and Rivalries in a Newly Developing Area of Police Intervention." In Malcolm Anderson and Monica den Boer, eds., *Policing Across National Boundaries.* London: Pinter, pp. 161–173.

Blainey, Geoffrey. 1988. *The Causes of War.* Melbourne: Macmillan.

Blanchard, J. F., Mansfield, E. D., and Ripsman, N. M. 1999. "The Political Economy of National Security." *Security Studies* 9, pp. 1–14.

Blumberg, Rae Lesser. 1992. *Women, Development, and the Wealth of Nations: Making the Case for the Gender Variable.* Boulder: Westview.

Blumenberg, Hans. 1983. *The Legitimacy of the Modern Age.* London: Tavistock.

Bookchin, Murray. 1980. *Towards an Ecological Society.* Montreal: Black Rose.

———. 1982. *The Ecology of Freedom.* Palo Alto, Calif.: Cheshire Books.

Booth, Ken, ed. 1991a. *New Thinking About Strategy and International Security.* London: HarperCollins.

———. 1991b. "Security and Emancipation." *Review of International Studies* 17, pp. 313–327.

———. 1991c. "Security in Anarchy: Utopian Realism in Theory and Practice." *International Affairs* 67, pp. 527–545.

———. 1995. "Human Wrongs and International Relations." *International Affairs* 71, pp. 103–122.

———. 1997. "Security and Self: Reflections of a Fallen Realist." In Keith Krause and Michael Williams, eds., *Critical Security Studies.* Minneapolis: University of Minnesota Press, pp. 83–119.

Booth, Ken, and Smith, Steve, eds. 1995. *International Relations Theory Today.* Cambridge: Polity.

Bourdieu, Pierre. 1990. *The Logic of Practice.* Cambridge: Polity.

Brandt Commission. 1985. *Common Crisis: North-South Co-operation for World Recovery.* Cambridge, Mass.: MIT Press.

Brandt Report. 1980. *Report of the Independent Commission on International Development Issues, North-South: A Programme for Survival.* London: Pan Books.

Bratton, Michael. 1994. "Peasant-State Relations in Post-Colonial Africa: Patterns of Engagement and Disengagement." In Joel S. Migdal, Atul Kohli, and Vivienne Shue, eds., *State Power and Social Forces: Domination and Transformation in the Third World.* Cambridge: Cambridge University Press.

Brennan, Donald G., ed. 1961. *Arms Control, Disarmament and National Security.* New York: George Braziller.

Brock, Lothar. 1991. "Peace Through Parks: The Environment on the Peace Research Agenda." *Journal of Peace Research* 28, pp. 407–422.

Brodie, Bernard. 1957. "More About Limited War." *World Politics* 10, pp. 112–122.

———. 1959. *Strategy in the Missile Age.* Princeton: Princeton University Press.

Bronner, Stephen E. 1994. *Of Critical Theory and Its Theorists.* Oxford: Blackwell.

Brown, Neville. 1989. "Climate, Ecology, and International Security." *Survival* 31, pp. 519–532.

Bull, Hedley. 1977. *The Anarchical Society: A Study of Order in World Politics.* London: Macmillan.

Bulloch, John, and Darwish, Adel. 1993. *Water Wars: Coming Conflicts in the Middle East.* London: Victor Gollancz.

Burguieres, Mary. 1990. "Feminist Approaches to Peace." *Millennium: Journal of International Studies* 19, pp. 1–18.

Butterfield, H., and Wight, M., eds. 1966. *Diplomatic Investigations.* London: George Allen and Unwin.

Buzan, Barry. 1983. *People, States, and Fear.* Brighton: Harvester Wheatsheaf.

———. 1984. "Economic Structure and International Security: The Limits of the Liberal Case." *International Organisation* 38, pp. 597–624.

———. 1991a. *People, States, and Fear.* 2nd ed. Boulder: Lynne Rienner.

———. 1991b. "Is International Security Possible?" In Ken Booth, ed., *New Thinking About Strategy and International Security.* London: HarperCollins, pp. 31–55.

———. 1996. "International Security and International Society." In Rick Fawn and Jeremy Larkin, eds., *International Security After the Cold War: Anarchy and Order Reconsidered.* London: Macmillan, pp. 261–287.

Buzan, Barry, Jones, Charles, and Little, Richard. 1993. *The Logic of Anarchy: Neorealism to Structural Realism.* New York: Columbia University Press.

Buzan, Barry, and Segal, Gerry. 1994. "Rethinking East Asian Security." *Survival* 36, pp. 3–21.

Buzan, Barry, and Waever, Ole. 1997. "Slippery, Contradictory? Sociologically Untenable? The Copenhagen School Replies." *Review of International Studies* 23, pp. 241–250.

———. 2003. *Regions and Powers: The Structure of International Power.* Cambridge: Cambridge University Press.

Buzan, Barry, Waever, Ole, and De Wilde, Jaap. 1998. *Security: A New Framework for Analysis.* Boulder: Lynne Rienner.

Cable, Vincent. 1995. "What Is International Economic Security?" *International Affairs* 71, pp. 305–324.

Campbell, David. 1992. *Writing Security: United States Foreign Policy and the Politics of Identity.* Manchester: Manchester University Press.

———. 1993. *Politics Without Principle: Sovereignty, Ethics, and the Narratives of the Gulf War.* Boulder: Lynne Rienner.

———. 1996. "Political Prosaics, Transversal Politics, and the Anarchical World." In M. Shapiro and H. Alker, eds., *Challenging Boundaries: Global Flows, Territorial Identities.* Minneapolis: University of Minnesota Press.

Cardoso, F., and Faletto, E. 1979. *Dependency and Development in Latin America.* Berkeley: University of California Press.

Carr, E. H. 1946. *The Twenty Years Crisis, 1919–1939: An Introduction to the Study of International Relations.* 2nd ed. London: Macmillan.

Carter, F. W., French, R., and Salt, J. 1993. "International Migration Between East and West in Europe." *Ethnic and Racial Studies* 16, pp. 467–491.

Cha, Victor D. 2000. "Globalisation and the Study of International Security." *Journal of Peace Research* 37, pp. 391–403.

Chan, Steven. 1984. "Mirror, Mirror on the Wall—Are the Free Countries More Pacific?" *Journal of Conflict Resolution* 28, pp. 617–648.

Chipman, John. 1992. "The Future of Strategic Studies: Beyond Grand Strategy." *Survival* 34, pp. 109–131.

Clark, Ian. 1999. *Globalisation and International Relations Theory.* Oxford: Oxford University Press.

Clausewitz, Carl von. 1968. *On War.* Harmondsworth: Penguin.

Cohen, Raymond. 1994. "Pacific Unions: A Reappraisal of the Theory That Democracies Do Not Go to War with Each Other." *Review of International Studies* 20, pp. 207–223.

Cohen, Saul B. 1994. "Geopolitics in the New World Era: A New Perspective on an Old Discipline." In George J. Demko and William B. Woods, eds., *Reordering the World: Geopolitical Perspectives on the Twenty-First Century.* Boulder: Westview, pp. 15–48.

Cook, Robin. 1998. "Statement on the Security and Intelligence Agencies." House of Commons Hansard Debates, November 2, 1998, Part 11, column 578.

Cooley, John K. 1984. "The War over Water." *Foreign Policy* 54 (Spring), pp. 3–26.

Coser, Lewis. 1977. *Masters of Sociological Thought.* 2nd ed. New York: Harcourt Brace.

Cox, Robert. 1983. "Gramsci, Hegemony, and International Relations: A Study in Method." *Millennium: Journal of International Studies* 12, pp. 162–175.

———. 1986. "Social Forces, States, and World Orders: Beyond International Relations Theory." In Robert O. Keohane, ed., *Neorealism and Its Critics.* New York: Columbia University Press.

Crawford, Beverly. 1995. "Hawks, Doves, but No Owls: International Economic Interdependence and Construction of the New Security Dilemma." In Ronnie D. Lipschutz, ed., *On Security.* New York: Columbia University Press, pp. 149–186.

Crawford, Neta. 1991. "Once and Future Security Studies." *Security Studies* 1, pp. 283–316.

Dalby, Simon. 1992. "Security, Modernity Ecology: The Dilemmas of Post Cold War Security Discourse." *Alternatives* 17, pp. 95–134.

———. 1998. "Human Security: Environmental Dimensions of a Contested Concept." Paper presented at the 1998 Meech Lake Conference on Taking Human Security Seriously.

Der Derian, James. 1992. *Anti-Diplomacy: Spies, Terror, Speed, and War.* Oxford: Blackwell.

———. 1995. "The Value of Security: Hobbes, Marx, Nietzsche, and Baudrillard." In Ronnie D. Lipschutz, ed., *On Security.* New York: Columbia University Press, pp. 24–45.

Deudney, Daniel. 1990. "The Case Against Linking Environmental Degradation and

National Security." *Millennium: Journal of International Studies* 19, pp. 461–476.

———. 1991. "Environment and Security: Muddled Thinking." *Bulletin of the Atomic Scientists* 47, no. 3, pp. 22–28.

Deudney, Daniel, and Matthews, Richard, eds. 1999. *Contested Grounds: Security and Conflict in the New Environmental Politics.* Albany: State University of New York Press.

Deutsch, Karl. 1968. *The Analysis of International Relations.* Englewood Cliffs, N.J.: Prentice-Hall.

Deutsch, Karl, et al. 1957. *Political Community and the North Atlantic Area.* Princeton: Princeton University Press.

Devetek, Richard. 1996. "Critical Theory." In Scott Burchill and Andrew Linklater, with Richard Devetek, Matthew Paterson, and Jacqui True, *Theories of International Relations.* London: Macmillan, pp. 145–178.

Dickson, Anna K. 1997. *Development and International Relations.* Cambridge: Polity.

Dixon, William. 1993. "Democracy and the Management of International Conflict." *Journal of Conflict Resolution* 37, pp. 42–68.

———. 1994. "Democracy and the Peaceful Settlement of Conflict." *American Political Science Review* 88, pp. 14–32.

Donnelly, J. 2000. *Realism and International Relations.* Cambridge: Cambridge University Press.

Dorff, Robert, A. 1994. "A Commentary on Security Studies for the 1990's as a Model Core Curriculum." *International Studies Notes* 19, pp. 5–27.

Doyle, Michael. 1983. "Kant, Liberal Legacies, and Foreign Affairs." Pts. 1–2. *Philosophy and Public Affairs* 12, no. 3 (Summer), pp. 205–235, and no. 4 (Fall), pp. 323–353.

———. 1986. "Liberalism and World Politics." *American Political Science Review* 80, pp. 1151–1169.

Drysek, J. 1990. *Discursive Democracy. Politics, Policy, and Political Science.* Cambridge: Cambridge University Press.

Dougherty, James E., et al. 1985. *Ethics, Deterrence, and National Security.* Washington, D.C.: Pergamon Press.

el-Hinnawi, Essam, and ul-Haque, Manzur. 1982. *Global Environmental Issues: United Nations Environment Programme.* Dun Laoghaire, Ireland: Tycooly International.

Elliott, Lorraine. 1998. *The Global Politics of the Environment.* London: Macmillan.

Elstein, J. 1987. *Women and War.* Brighton: Harvester.

Enloe, Cynthia. 1989. *Bananas, Beaches, and Bases.* London: Pandora.

Falk, Richard. 1995. *On Humane Governance: Towards a New Global Politics.* University Park: Pennsylvania State University Press.

Feigenbaum, E. A. 1999. "China's Military Posture and the New Economic Geo-Politics." *Survival* 41, pp. 71–88.

Flax, Jane. 1987. "Postmodernism and Gender Relations in Feminist Theory." *Signs* 12, pp. 621–643.

Florini, Ann M., and Simmons, P. J. 1998. *The New Security Thinking: A Review of the North American Literature.* New York: Rockefeller Brothers Fund.

Freedman, Lawrence. 1993. "The Political Context of Security Studies." *Arms Control* 14, pp. 198–205.

Friedrich, C. J. 1948. *Inevitable Peace.* New York: Greenwood.

Foucault, Michel. 1972. *The Archaeology of Knowledge.* London: Tavistock.

———. 1977. *Language, Counter-Memory, Practice: Selected Essays and Interviews.* Ithaca: Cornell University Press.

————. 1979. *Discipline and Punish: The Birth of Prison.* New York: Vintage Books.

————. 1980. *Power/Knowledge: Selected Interviews and Other Writings, 1972–1977.* Brighton: Harvester.

————. 1984. *The Foucault Reader.* P. Rabinow, ed. New York: Pantheon.

————. 1986. "Disciplinary Power and Subjugation." In Steven Lukes, ed., *Power.* Oxford: Blackwell.

Galtung, Johan. 1971. "A Structural Theory of Imperialism." *Journal of Peace Research* 8, pp. 81–118.

Garnett, John. 1975. "Strategic Studies and Its Assumptions." In John Baylis, Ken Booth, John Garnett, and Phil Williams. *Contemporary Strategy: Theories and Policies.* London: Croom Helm, pp. 3–21.

Gellman, P. 1988. "Hans J. Morgenthau and the Legacy of Political Realism." *Review of International Studies* 14, pp. 247–266.

George, Jim. 1994. *Discourses of Global Politics: A Critical (Re)Introduction to International Relations.* Boulder: Lynne Rienner.

Gilligan, Carol. 1982. *In a Different Voice: Psychological Theory and Women's Development.* Cambridge, Mass.: Harvard University Press.

Gilpin, R. 1981. *War and Change in World Politics.* Cambridge: Cambridge University Press.

————. 1984. "The Richness of the Tradition of Political Realism." *International Organisation* 38, pp. 287–304.

————. 1992. "The Economic Dimension of International Security." In H. Bienen, ed., *Power, Economics, and Security.* Boulder: Westview.

Glaser, Charles L. 1994–1995. "Realists as Optimists: Cooperation as Self-Help." *International Security* 19, pp. 50–90.

Gleditsch, Nils Petter. 1992. "Democracy and Peace." *Journal of Peace Research* 29, pp. 369–376.

Gleick, Peter H. 1991. "Environment and Security: The Clear Connections." *Bulletin of the Atomic Scientists* 47, no. 3, pp. 16–22.

————. 1993. "Water and Conflict: Fresh Water Resources and International Security." *International Security* 18, pp. 79–112.

Godson, R., and Williams, P. 1998. "Strengthening Co-operation Against Transnational Crime." *Survival* 40, pp. 66–88.

Goldstein, Joshua. 1994. *International Relations.* New York: HarperCollins.

Graeger, Nina. 1996. "Environmental Security?" *Journal of Peace Research* 33, pp. 104–116.

Graham, Edward, and Krugman, Paul. 1991. *Foreign Direct Investment in the United States.* Washington, D.C.: Institute for International Economics.

Grant, Rebecca. 1991. "The Sources of Gender Bias in International Relations Theory." In Rebecca Grant and Kathleen Newland, eds., *Gender and International Relations.* Buckingham: Open University Press, pp. 8–26.

Grant, Rebecca, and Newland, Kathleen, eds. 1991. *Gender and International Relations.* Buckingham: Open University Press.

Gray, Colin S. 1994. "Global Security and Economic Wellbeing: A Strategic Perspective." *Political Studies* 42, pp. 25–39.

Grieco, Joseph, M. 1988. "Anarchy and the Limits of Cooperation: A Realist Critique of the Newest Liberal Institutionalism." *International Organisation* 42, pp. 485–507.

Griffith, Ivelaw L. 1988. "Caribbean Geopolitics and Geonarcotics: New Dynamics, Same Old Dilemma." *Naval War College Review* 51, pp. 47–67.

Gulick, E. V. 1955. *Europe's Classical Balance of Power.* Ithaca, N.Y.: Cornell University Press.

Habermas, Jurgen. 1973. *Theory and Practice.* Boston: Beacon.

Haftendorn, Helga. 1991. "The Security Puzzle: Theory-Building and Discipline-Building in International Security." *International Studies Quarterly* 35, pp. 3–17.

Haleh, Afshar, and Dennis, Caroline, eds. 1992. *Women and Structural Adjustment Policies in the Third World.* London: Macmillan.

Halliday, Fred. 1994. *Rethinking International Relations.* London: Macmillan.

Hansen, Lene. 2000. "The Little Mermaid's Silent Security Dilemma and the Absence of Gender in the Copenhagen School." *Millennium: Journal of International Studies* 29, pp. 285–306.

Harvey, David. 1990. *The Condition of Postmodernity.* Oxford: Blackwell.

Heisler, Martin, and Layton-Henry, Zig. 1993. "Migration and the Links Between Social and Societal Security." In Ole Waever, Barry Buzan, Morten Kelstrup, and Pierre Lemaitre, *Identity, Migration, and the New Security Agenda in Europe.* London: Pinter, pp. 148–166.

Held, David, and McGrew, Anthony. 2001. "The Great Globalisation Debate: An Introduction." In David Held and Anthony McGrew, eds., *The Global Transformations Reader.* Cambridge: Polity Press, pp. 1–45.

Herz, John. 1950. "Idealist Internationalism and the Security Dilemma." *World Politics* 2, pp. 157–180.

———. 1959. *International Politics in the Atomic Age.* New York: Columbia University Press.

Hitsch, Charles J. 1960. "National Security as a Field for Economics Research." *World Politics* 12, pp. 434–452.

Hobbes, Thomas. 1946. *Leviathan.* Oxford: Blackwell.

Homer-Dixon, Thomas. 1991. "On the Threshold: Environmental Changes and Acute Conflict." *International Security* 16, pp. 76–116.

———. 1994. "Environmental Scarcities and Violent Conflict: Evidence from Cases." *International Security* 19, pp. 5–40.

Homer-Dixon, Thomas, and Blitt, Jessica, eds. 1998. *Ecoviolence: Links Among Environment, Population, and Security.* Oxford: Rowan and Littlefield.

Homer-Dixon, Thomas, and Percival, Valerie. 1996. *Environmental Scarcity and Violent Conflict: Briefing Book.* Toronto: University of Toronto Project on Environment, Population, and Security.

Howes, Ruth H., and Stevenson, Michael R., eds. 1993. *Women and the Use of Military Force.* Boulder: Lynne Rienner.

Huntington, Samuel. 1993. "The Clash of Civilizations." *Foreign Affairs* 72, pp. 22–49.

Hurrell, Andrew, and Kingsbury, Benedict. 1992. *The International Politics of the Environment: Actors, Interests, and Institutions.* Oxford: Oxford University Press.

Huysmans, Jef. 1995. "Migrants as a Security Problem: Dangers of 'Securitising' Societal Issues." In Robert Miles and Dietrich Thranhardt, eds., *Migration and European Integration: The Dynamics of Inclusion and Exclusion.* London: Pinter.

———. 1998. "Security! What Do You Mean? From Concept to Thick Signifier." *European Journal of International Relations* 4, pp. 226–255.

Jervis, Robert. 1970. *The Logic of Images in International Relations.* Princeton: Princeton University Press.

———. 1976. *Perception and Misperception in International Politics.* Princeton: Princeton University Press.

———. 1982. "Security Regimes." *International Organisation* 36, pp. 357–378.

———. 1987. "Cooperation Under the Security Dilemma." *World Politics* 30, pp. 167–214.

————. 1992. "The Future of World Politics: Will It Resemble the Past?" *International Security* 16, pp. 39–73.

Job, Brian, ed. 1992. *The Insecurity Dilemma: National Security of Third World States.* Boulder: Lynne Rienner.

Johnson, Lawrie. 1993. *Thucydides, Hobbes, and the Interpretation of Realism.* DeKalb: Northern Illinois University Press.

Jones, Adam. 1996. "Does Gender Make the World Go Round? Feminist Critiques of International Relations." *Review of International Studies* 22, pp. 405–429.

Kahn, Herman. 1960. *On Thermonuclear War.* London: Oxford University Press.

Kakonen, Jyrki, ed. 1994. *Green Security or Militarised Environment.* Aldershot: Dartmouth.

Kaldor, Mary. 1999. *New and Old Wars: Organised Violence in a Global Era.* Cambridge: Polity Press.

Kalyvas, S. N. 2001. "New and Old Wars: A Valid Distinction?" *World Politics* 54, pp. 99–118.

Kamaluddin, Mohammed. 2000. "The Right to Food Security: The State of Women and Children in Bangladesh." Paper presented to the Eighteenth General Conference of the International Peace Research Association, Tampere, Finland.

Kaplan, Robert D. 1994. "The Coming Anarchy." *Atlantic Monthly* 273, no. 2, pp. 44–76.

Katzenstein, Peter J. 1996. *The Culture of National Security: Norms and Identity in World Politics.* New York: Columbia University Press.

Kelly, Kimberley, and Homer-Dixon, Thomas. 1998. "The Case of Gaza." In Thomas Homer-Dixon and Jessica Blitt, eds., *Ecoviolence: Links Among Environment, Population, and Security.* Oxford: Rowman and Littlefield, pp. 67–107.

Kelstrup, Morten. 1995. "Societal Aspects of European Security." In Birthe Hansen, ed., *European Security, 2000.* Copenhagen: Copenhagen Political Studies Press.

Kennan, George F. 1951. *American Diplomacy, 1900–1950.* New York: New American Library.

Kennedy, Maxwell Taylor. 1998. *Make Gentle the Life of This World: The Vision of Robert Kennedy.* New York: Harcourt Brace.

Keohane, Robert, ed. 1986. *Neorealism and Its Critics.* New York: Columbia University Press.

Keohane, Robert, and Nye, Joseph S. 1977. *Power and Interdependence.* Boston: Little, Brown.

————. 1987. "Power and Interdependence Revisited." *International Organisation* 42, pp. 725–753.

Kirschner, J. 1998. "Political Economy in Security Studies After the Cold War." *Review of International Political Economy* 5, pp. 64–91.

Kissinger, Henry. 1956. "Force and Diplomacy in the Nuclear Age." *Foreign Affairs* 34, pp. 349–366.

————. 1957a. *Nuclear Weapons and Foreign Policy.* New York: Harper and Row.

————. 1957b. *A World Restored: Castlereagh, Metternich, and the Problems of Peace, 1812–1822.* Boston: Houghton Mifflin.

————. 1994. *Diplomacy.* New York: Simon and Schuster.

Klein, Bradley. 1988. "After Strategy: The Search for a Postmodern Politics of Peace." *Alternatives* 13, pp. 293–318.

————. 1994. *Strategic Studies and World Order: The Global Politics of Deterrence.* Cambridge: Cambridge University Press.

Kolodziej, Edward. 1992a. "Renaissance in Security Studies? Caveat Lector!" *International Studies Quarterly* 36, pp. 421–438.

————. 1992b. "What Is Security and Security Studies?" *Arms Control* 13, pp. 1–31.

Krause, Keith. 1998. "Critical Theory and Security Studies." *Cooperation and Conflict* 33, pp. 298–333.

Krause, Keith, and Williams, Michael. 1996. "Broadening the Agenda of Security Studies: Politics and Methods." *Mershon International Studies Review* 40, supp. 2, pp. 229–254.

————. 1997. "From Strategy to Security: Foundations of Critical Security Studies." In Keith Krause and Michael Williams, eds., *Critical Security Studies*. Minneapolis: University of Minnesota Press, pp. 33–59.

Lake, David. 1992. "Powerful Pacifists; Democratic States and War." *American Political Science Review* 86, pp. 24–37.

Layne, Christopher. 1993. "The Unipolar Illusion: Why New Great Powers Will Rise." *International Security* 17, pp. 5–51.

————. 1994. "Kant or Cant: The Myth of the Democratic Peace." *International Security* 19, pp. 5–49.

Leitenen, Kari. 1997. "The Concept of Environmental Security." Unpublished paper. Tampere, Finland.

Leonard, Stephen. 1990. *Critical Theory in Political Practice*. Princeton: Princeton University Press.

Levy, Jack S. 1988. "Domestic Politics and War." *Journal of Interdisciplinary History* 18, pp. 653–673.

————. 1989. "The Causes of War: A Review of Theories and Evidence." In P. E. Tetlock et al. *Behavior, Society, and Nuclear War.* New York: Oxford University Press, pp. 209–213.

Levy, Marc A. 1995. "Is the Environment a National Security Issue?" *International Security* 20, pp. 35–62.

Lieber, Robert. 1991. *No Common Power: Understanding International Relations.* 2nd ed. New York: HarperCollins.

Linklater, Andrew. 1990. *Beyond Realism and Marxism: Critical Theory and International Relations.* London: Macmillan.

————. 1995. "Neo-Realism in Theory and Practice." In Ken Booth and Steve Smith, eds., *International Relations Theory Today.* Cambridge: Polity, pp. 241–262.

Lipschutz, Ronnie, ed. 1995. *On Security.* New York: Columbia University Press.

Liska, George. 1957. *International Equilibrium.* Cambridge, Mass.: Harvard University Press.

Loescher, Gil. 1992. *Refugee Movements and International Security.* Adelphi Paper no. 268. London: International Institute for Security Studies.

Luard, E. 1992. *The Balance of Power: The System of International Relations, 1648–1815.* New York: St. Martin's Press.

Luciani, Giacomo. 1989. "The Economic Content of Security." *Journal of Public Policy* 8, pp. 151–173.

Lukes, Steven. 1986. *Power.* Oxford: Basil Blackwell.

Lynn-Jones, Sean M., and Miller, Steven E., eds. 1995. *Global Dangers: Changing Dimensions of International Security.* London: MIT Press.

Lyotard, Jean-François. 1984. *The Postmodern Condition: A Report on Knowledge.* Manchester: Manchester University Press.

Mackinder, Halford. 1904. "The Geographical Pivot of History." *Geographical Journal* 23, no. 4.

————. 1951. *The Scope and Methods of Geography and the Geographical Pivot of History.* London: Royal Geographical Society.

Mansfield, Edward D. 1988. "The Distribution of Wars over Time." *World Politics* 41, pp. 21–51.

Matthews, Jessica Tuchman. 1989. "Redefining Security." *Foreign Affairs* 68, pp. 162–177.

McSweeney, Bill. 1996. "Identity and Security: Buzan and the Copenhagen School." *Review of International Studies* 22, pp. 81–93.

———. 1998. "Durkheim and the Copenhagen School: A Response to Buzan and Waever." *Review of International Studies* 24, pp. 137–140.

———. 1999. *Security, Identity, and Interests: A Sociology of International Relations.* Cambridge: Cambridge University Press.

Mearsheimer, John J. 1990. "Back to the Future: Instability in Europe After the Cold War." *International Security* 15, pp. 5–56.

Mingst, Karen, and Karns, Margaret. 1995. *The United Nations in the Post–Cold War Era.* Boulder: Westview.

Mintz, Alex, and Geva, Nehemia. 1993. "Why Don't Democracies Fight Each Other? An Experimental Study." *Journal of Conflict Resolution* 37, pp. 484–503.

Mische, Patricia. 1989. "Ecological Security and the Need to Reconceptualise Sovereignty." *Alternatives* 14, pp. 389–427.

Moaz, Zeev, and Abdolali, Nasrin. 1984. "Regime Type and International Conflict." *Journal of Conflict Resolution* 28, pp. 3–35.

Mohanty, Chandra, Russo, Anne, and Torres, Lourdes, eds. 1991. *Third World Women and the Politics of Feminism.* Bloomington: Indiana University Press.

Molvaer, Reidulf. 1991. "Environmentally Induced Conflicts? A Discussion Based on Studies from the Horn of Africa." *Bulletin of Peace Proposals* 22, pp. 175–188.

Moon, J. D. 1983. "Political Ethics and Critical Theory." In D. R. Sabia and J. Wallulis, eds., *Changing Social Science.* Albany: State University of New York.

Moran, D. 2002. "Strategic Theory and the History of War." In J. Baylis, J. Wirtz, E. Cohen, and C. S. Gray, *Strategy in the Contemporary World: An Introduction to Strategic Studies.* Oxford: Oxford University Press.

Moran, Theodore H. 1990–1991. "International Economics and National Security." *Foreign Affairs* 69, pp. 74–90.

———. 1993. *American Economic Policy and National Security.* New York: Council on Foreign Relations.

Morgan, Patrick M,1992. "Safeguarding Security Studies." *Arms Control* 13.

Morgenthau, Hans J. 1948. *Politics Among Nations: The Struggle for Power and Peace.* New York: Knopf.

———. 1952. *American Foreign Policy.* London: Methuen.

———. 1978. *Politics Among Nations: The Struggle for Power and Peace.* 5th ed. New York: Knopf.

Murray, Alasdair. 1997. *Reconstructing Realism.* Edinburgh: Keele University Press.

Myers, Norman. 1989. "Environment and Security." *Foreign Policy* 74, pp. 23–41.

———. 1993. *Ultimate Security.* New York: W. W. Norton.

Nester, William. 1995. *International Relations: Geopolitical or Geoeconomic Conflict and Cooperation.* New York: HarperCollins.

Neu, Richard, and Wolff, Carl. 1994. *The Economic Dimensions of National Security.* Washington, D.C.: RAND.

Neufeld, Mark. 1995. *The Restructuring of International Relations Theory.* Cambridge: Cambridge University Press.

Niebuhr, Reinhold. 1932. *Moral Man and Immoral Society: A Study in Ethics and Politics.* London: Charles Scribner.

————. 1945. *The Children of Light and the Children of Darkness: A Vindication of Democracy and a Critique of Its Traditional Defenders.* London: Nisbet.

————. 1953. *Christian Realism and Political Problems.* London: Faber and Faber.

Norris, Christopher. 1992. *Uncritical Theory: Postmodernism, Intellectuals, and the Gulf War.* London: Lawrence and Wishart.

Nye, Joseph S., and Lynn-Jones, Sean. 1988. "International Security Studies." *International Security* 12, pp. 5–27.

Onuf, Nicholas. 1989. *World of Our Making: Rules and Rule in Social Theory and International Relations.* Columbia: University of South Carolina Press.

O'Tuathail, Gearoid. 1996. *Critical Geopolitics: The Politics of Writing Global Space.* London: Routledge.

O'Tuathail, Gearoid, and Dalby, S., eds. 1998. *Rethinking Geopolitics.* London: Routledge.

Oudraat, C. D. 2000. "Making Economic Sanctions Work." *Survival* 42, pp. 105–127.

Outhwaite, William. 1994. *Habermas: A Critical Introduction.* Cambridge: Polity Press.

Owen, John. 1994. "How Liberalism Produces Democratic Peace." *International Security* 19, pp. 87–125.

Painter, Michael, and Durham, William, eds. 1995. *The Social Causes of Environmental Destruction in Latin America.* Ann Arbor: University of Michigan Press.

Palme, Olaf. 1982. *Common Security: A Programme for Disarmament.* London: Pan Books.

Parpart, Jane. 1993. "Who Is the 'Other'? A Postmodern Feminist Critique of Women and Development Theory and Practice." *Development and Change* 24, pp. 439–464.

Peterson, V. Spike. 1992. *Gendered States: Feminist Revisions of International Relations Theory.* Boulder: Lynne Rienner.

Peterson, V. Spike, and Runyan, Anne Sisson. 1993. *Global Gender Issues.* Boulder: Westview.

Pettiford, L. 1996. "Changing Concepts of Security in the Third World." *Third World Quarterly* 17, pp. 289–306.

Pettman, Jan Jindy. 1996. *Worlding Women: A Feminist International Politics.* London: Routledge.

Pirages, D. 1997. "Demographic Change and Ecological Security." *Environmental Change and Human Security Project Report,* no. 3, pp. 36–46.

Pollard, Robert A. 1985. *Economic Security and the Origins of the Cold War, 1945–1950.* New York: Columbia University Press.

Porter, Gareth, and Brown, Janet W. 1991. *Global Environmental Politics.* Boulder: Westview.

Prins, Gwyn, ed. 1993. *Threats Without Enemies: Facing Environmental Insecurity.* London: Earthscan.

Raskin, Marcus. 1979. *The Politics of National Security.* New Brunswick, N.J.: Transaction.

Ray, James L. 1993. "Wars Between Democracies: Rare or Nonexistent?" *International Interactions* 18, pp. 251–276.

Rengger, N. J. 2001. "Negative Dialectic? The Two Modes of Critical Theory in World Politics." In Richard Wyn Jones, ed., *Critical Theory and World Politics.* Boulder: Lynne Rienner, pp. 91–109.

Rochlin, James F. 1997. *Redefining Mexican "Security": Society, State, and Region Under NAFTA.* Boulder: Lynne Rienner.

Roe, Paul. 1999. "The Intrastate Security Dilemma: Ethnic Conflict as a 'Tragedy.'" *Journal of Peace Research* 36, pp. 183–202.

Rogers, K. 1997. "Ecological Security and Multinational Corporations." *Environmental Change and Human Security Project Report,* no. 3, pp. 29–36.

Romero, Federico. 1990. "Cross-Border Population Movements." In William Wallace, ed., *The Dynamics of European Integration.* London: Pinter, pp. 171–191.

Ronnfeldt, Carsten F. 1997. "Three Generations of Environment and Security Research." *Journal of Peace Research* 34, pp. 473–482.

Rose, Gideon. 1998. "Neoclassical Realism and Theories of Foreign Policy." *World Politics* 51, pp. 144–172.

Rosecrance, Richard. 2002. "International Security and the Virtual State: States and Firms in World Politics." *Review of International Studies* 28, pp. 443–455.

Rosenberg, Emily R. 1993. "The Cold War and the Discourse of National Security." *Diplomatic History* 17, pp. 277–284.

Rothschild, Emma. 1995. "What Is Security?" *Daedalus* 124, pp. 53–98.

Rothstein, Robert L. 1986. "The Security Dilemma and the Poverty Trap in the Third World." *Jerusalem Journal of International Relations* 8, pp. 1–38.

Ruggie, John G. 1993. "Territoriality and Beyond: Problematising Modernity in International Relations." *International Organisation* 47, pp. 139–175.

Russett, Bruce. 1993. *Grasping the Democratic Peace: Principles for a Post–Cold War World.* Princeton: Princeton University Press.

Russett, Bruce, and Moaz, Zeev. 1993. "Normative and Structural Causes of Democratic Peace." *American Political Science Review* 87, pp. 624–638.

Schelling, Thomas C. 1958. "The Strategy of Conflict." *Journal of Conflict Resolution* 2, pp. 203–264.

———. 1960. *The Strategy of Conflict.* Cambridge, Mass.: Harvard University Press.

Schultz, Richard, Godson, Roy, and Greenwood, Ted, eds. 1993. *Security Studies for the 1990s.* New York: Brassey's.

Schultze, Charles I. 1972–1973. "The Economic Content of National Security Policy." *Foreign Affairs* 51, pp. 522–540.

Schweller, Randall. 1992. "Domestic Structure and Preventive War: Are Democracies More Pacific?" *World Politics* 44, pp. 235–269.

Sen, Amartyn. 1981. *Poverty and Famines: An Essay on Entitlement and Deprivation.* Oxford: Clarendon Press.

Shaw, Martin. 1993. "There Is No Such Thing as Society: Beyond Individualism and Statism in International Security Studies." *Review of International Studies* 19, pp. 159–175.

———. 1994. *Global Society and International Relations: Sociological Concepts and Political Perspectives.* Cambridge: Polity Press.

Sheehan, Michael. 1996a. *Balance of Power: History and Theory.* London: Routledge.

———. 1996b. "A Regional Perspective on the Globalisation Process." *Korean Journal of Defense Analysis* 8, pp. 53–74.

———. 1998. "Central Europe, the European Security Community and the Security Complex." In J. Huru, O.-P. Jalonen, and M. Sheehan, eds., *New Dimensions of Security in Central and Northeastern Europe.* Tampere: Tampere Peace Research Institute, pp. 35–57.

———. 1999. "Findings and Recommendations" (Rapporteurs Report). In S. Grier, ed., *Tools for Security and Stability in the Mediterranean,* NATO Defence College Monograph Series (Winter), pp. 35–57.

———. 2000. "The Evolution of the Concept of Security Since 1945." In Michael Sheehan, ed., *National and International Security.* Aldershot: Ashgate, pp. 1–31.

————. 2004. "Creating an Arms Control Mechanism in North-East Asia: The Application of the European Security Cooperation Regime." *Defense and Security Analysis* 20, no. 1 (March), pp. 39–54.

Sheehan, Michael, with Fotios Moustakis. 2002. "Democratic Peace and the European Security Community: The Paradox of Greece and Turkey." *Mediterranean Quarterly* 13, no. 1 (Winter), pp. 69–85.

SIPRI Yearbook. 2002. *Armaments, Disarmaments, and International Security.* Oxford: Oxford University Press.

Sloan, G., and Gray, C. S. 1999. "Why Geopolitics?" In C. S. Gray and G. Sloan, eds., *Geopolitics.* London: Frank Cass.

Small, Melvin, and Singer, David. 1976. "The War-Proneness of Democratic Regimes, 1815–1865." *Jerusalem Journal of International Relations* 1, pp. 50–69.

Smith, Michael Joseph. 1986. *Realist Thought from Weber to Kissinger.* Baton Rouge: Louisiana State University Press.

Smith, Steve. 1991. "Mature Anarchy, Strong States, and Security." *Arms Control* 12, pp. 325–339.

Smith, Steve, Booth, Ken, and Zalewski, Marysa. 1996. *International Theory: Positivism and Beyond.* Cambridge: Cambridge University Press.

Smoke, Richard. 1975. "National Security Affairs." In Fred Greenstein and Nelson W. Polsby, eds., *Handbook of Political Science,* vol. 8, *International Politics.* Reading, Mass.: Addison-Wesley, pp. 247–362.

Snow, Donald M. 1996. *Uncivil War: International Security and the New Internal Conflicts.* Boulder: Lynne Rienner.

Sorenson, Georg. 1992. "Kant and Processes of Democratisation: Consequences for Neorealist Thought." *Journal of Peace Research* 29, pp. 397–414.

Sorenson, Theodore. 1990. "Re-Thinking National Security." *Foreign Affairs* 69, pp. 1–18.

Spiro, David. 1994. "The Insignificance of Democratic Peace." *International Security* 19, pp. 50–86.

Spykman, Nicholas. 1942. *America's Strategy in World Politics.* New York: Harcourt Brace.

Starr, Harvey. 1992. "Democracy and War: Choice, Learning, and Security Communities." *Journal of Peace Research* 29, pp. 207–213.

————. 1997. "Democracy and Integration: Why Democracies Don't Fight Each Other." *Journal of Peace Research* 34, pp. 153–162.

Starr, Joyce R. 1991. "Water Wars." *Foreign Policy* 82, pp. 17–36.

Stearns. Jill. 1998. *Gender and International Relations.* Cambridge: Polity.

Stern, Eric K. 1995. "Bringing the Environment In: The Case for Comprehensive Security." *Cooperation and Conflict* 30, pp. 211–237.

Stewart, Alasdair. 1992. *Migrants, Minorities, and Security in Europe.* Conflict Studies, no. 252. London: Research Institute for the Study of Conflict and Terrorism.

Strange, Susan. 1988. *States and Markets: An Introduction to International Political Economy.* London: Pinter.

Sylvester, Christine. 1994. *Feminist Theory and International Relations in a Postmodern Era.* Cambridge: Cambridge University Press.

Taylor, Trevor. 1978. "Power Politics." In Trevor Taylor, ed., *Approaches and Theory in International Relations.* London: Longman, pp. 122–140.

Terrif, Terry, Croft, Stuart, James, Lucy, and Morgan, Patrick. 1999. *Security Studies Today.* Cambridge: Polity Press.

Thomas, C. 1987. *In Search of Security: The Third World in International Relations.* Hemel Hempstead: Harvester Wheatsheaf.

Thompson, Kenneth W. 1980. *Masters of International Thought.* Baton Rouge: Louisiana State University Press.

———. 1996. *Schools of Thought in International Relations.* Baton Rouge: Louisiana State University Press.

Thucydides. 1972. *The Peloponnesian War.* Trans. Rex Warner. Harmondsworth: Penguin.

Tickner, J. Ann. 1991. "Hans Morgenthau's Principles of Political Realism: A Feminist Re-formulation." In Rebecca Grant and Kathleen Newland, eds., *Gender and International Relations.* Buckingham: Open University Press, pp. 27–40.

———. 1992. *Gender in International Relations: Feminist Perspectives on Achieving Global Security.* New York: Columbia University Press.

———. 1995. "Revisioning Security." In Ken Booth and Steve Smith, eds., *International Relations Theory Today.* Cambridge: Polity Press, pp. 175–197.

Tonnies, Ferdinand. 1955. *Community and Association.* London: Routledge and Kegan Paul.

Treverton, Gregory F. 1995. "The Changing Security Agenda." RAND Paper P-7918. Santa Monica, Calif.: RAND Corporation.

True, Jacqui. 1996. "Feminism." In Scott Burchill and Andrew Linklater, with Richard Devetek, Matthew Paterson, and Jacqui True, *Theories of International Relations.* London: Macmillan, pp. 210–251.

Ullman, Richard. 1983. "Redefining Security." *International Security* 8, pp. 129–153.

United Nations Development Programme. 1995. *Human Development Report 1994.* Reprinted in "Redefining Security, the Human Dimension," *Current History,* May, pp. 229–236.

Van Evera, Stephen. 1991. "Primed for Peace: Europe After the Cold War." *International Security* 15, pp. 7–57.

Vickers, Jeanne. 1993. *Women and War.* London: Zed Books.

Waever, Ole. 1989. "Conceptions of Détente and Change: Some Non-Military Aspects of Security Thinking in the FRG." In O. Waever, P. Lemaitre, and E. Tromer, eds., *European Polyphony; Perspectives Beyond East-West Confrontation.* London: Macmillan, pp. 186–224.

———. 1995a. "Identity, Integration, and Security: Solving the Security Puzzle in EU Studies." *Journal of International Affairs* 48, pp. 389–431.

———. 1995b. "Securitization and Desecuritization." In Ronnie Lipschutz, ed., *On Security.* New York: Columbia University Press, pp. 46–86.

———. 1996. "European Security Identities." *Journal of Common Market Studies* 34, pp. 103–132.

———. 1998. "Insecurity, Security, and Asecurity in the West European Non-War Community." In Emanuel Adler and Michael J. Barnett, eds., *Security Communities.* Cambridge: Cambridge University Press, pp. 69–118.

Waever, Ole, Buzan, Barry, Kelstrup, Morten, and Lemaitre, Pierre. 1993. *Identity, Migration, and the New Security Order in Europe.* London: Pinter.

Walker, Robert B. J. 1988. *One World, Many Worlds: Struggles for a Just World Peace.* Boulder: Lynne Rienner.

———. 1990. "Security, Sovereignty, and the Challenge of World Politics." *Alternatives* 15, pp. 3–27.

———. 1993. *Inside/Outside: International Relations as Political Theory.* Cambridge: Cambridge University Press.

———. 1997. "The Subject of Security." In Keith Krause and Michael Williams, eds., *Critical Security Studies.* Minneapolis: University of Minnesota Press, pp. 61–81.

Wallerstein, Immanuel. 1993. "The World System After the Cold War." *Journal of Peace Research* 30, pp. 1–6.

Walt, Stephen. 1987. *The Origins of Alliances.* Ithaca: Cornell University Press.

———. 1991. "The Renaissance of Security Studies." *International Studies Quarterly* 35, pp. 211–239.

Waltz, Kenneth. 1959. *Man, the State, and War.* New York: Columbia University Press.

———. 1979. *Theory of International Politics.* Reading, Mass.: Addison-Wesley.

———. 1993. "The Emerging Structure of International Politics." *International Security* 18, pp. 44–79.

Weber, Steve. 1990. "Realism, Détente, and Nuclear Weapons." *International Organisation* 44, no. 1.

Weede, Erich. 1984. "Democracy and War Involvement." *Journal of Conflict Resolution* 28, pp. 649–664.

———. 1992. "Some Simple Calculations on Democracy and War." *Journal of Peace Research* 29, pp. 377–383.

Weiner, Myron. 1992–1993. "Security, Stability, and International Migration." *International Security* 17, pp. 91–126.

———. 1995. *The Global Migration Crisis: Challenges to States and Human Rights.* New York: HarperCollins.

Wendt, Alexander. 1992. "Anarchy Is What States Make of It: The Social Construction of Power Politics." *International Organisation* 46, pp. 391–425.

———. 1994. "Collective Identity Formation and the International State." *American Political Science Review* 88, pp. 384–396.

———. 1995. "Constructing International Politics." *International Security* 20, pp. 71–81.

Westing, Arthur H., ed. 1986. *Global Resources and International Conflict: Environmental Factors in Strategic Policy and Action.* Oxford: Oxford University Press.

———, ed. 1988. *Cultural Norms, War, and the Environment.* Oxford: Oxford University Press.

———. 1989. "The Environmental Component of Comprehensive Security." *Bulletin of Peace Proposals* 20, pp. 129–134.

Wheeler, Nicholas J., and Booth, Ken. 1996. "Logics of Security." Paper presented to the British International Studies Association Conference.

Wiberg, Hakan. 1993. "Societal Security and the Explosion of Yugoslavia." In Ole Waever, Barry Buzan, Morten Kelstrup, and Pierre Lemaitre, *Identity, Migration, and the New Security Agenda in Europe.* London: Pinter, pp. 93–109.

Widgren, Jonas. 1990. "International Migration and Regional Stability." *International Affairs* 66, pp. 749–766.

Wight, Martin. 1979. *Power Politics.* Harmondsworth: Pelican.

Williams, Howard. 1992. *International Relations in Political Theory.* Milton Keynes: Open University Press.

Williams, Michael C. 1996. "Hobbes and International Relations: A Reconsideration." *International Organisation* 50, pp. 213–236.

———. 1998. "Identity and the Politics of Security." *European Journal of International Relations* 4, pp. 204–225.

Wohlforth, W. 1993. *The Elusive Balance: Power and Perceptions During the Cold War.* Ithaca: Cornell University Press.

Wohlstetter, Albert. 1959. "The Delicate Balance of Terror." *Foreign Affairs* 37, pp. 211–234.

Wolfers, Arnold. 1952. "National Security as an Ambiguous Symbol." *Political Science Quarterly* 67, pp. 481–502.

————. 1962. *Discord and Collaboration: Essays on International Politics.* Baltimore: Johns Hopkins Press.

Wright, Quincy. 1965. *A Study of War.* 2nd ed. Chicago: University of Chicago Press.

Wyn Jones, Richard. 1996. "Travel Without Maps: Thinking About Security After the Cold War." In M. Jane Davis, ed., *Security Issues in the Post–Cold War World.* Cheltenham: Edward Elgar, pp. 196–218.

————. 2001. "Introduction: Locating Critical International Relations Theory." In Richard Wyn Jones, ed., *Critical Theory and World Politics.* Boulder: Lynne Rienner, pp. 1–19.

————, ed. 2001. *Critical Theory and World Politics.* Boulder: Lynne Rienner.

Yosef, Lapid. 1989. "The Third Debate: On the Prospect for International Theory in a Post-Positivist Era." *International Studies Quarterly* 33, pp. 235–254.

Young, Oran R. 1968. *The Politics of Force: Bargaining During Superpower Crises.* Princeton: Princeton University Press.

————. 1989. *International Cooperation: Building Regimes for Natural Resources and the Environment.* Ithaca: Cornell University Press.

Zakaria, Fareed. 1998. *From Wealth to Power.* Princeton: Princeton University Press.

Zielonka, Jan. 1991. "Europe's Security: A Great Confusion." *International Affairs* 67, pp. 127–137.

Zoellick, R. B. 1997. "Economics and Security in the Changing Asia-Pacific." *Survival* 39, pp. 29–51.

Zolberg, A. R., Suhrke, A., and Aguayo, S. 1989. *Escape from Violence: Conflict and the Refugee Crisis in the Developing World.* New York: Oxford University Press.

Index

About the Book

M ichael Sheehan provides a masterly survey of the varied positions that
scholars have adopted in interpreting "security"—one of the most contested terms in international relations—and asks whether a synthesis is possible that both widens and deepens our understanding of the concept.

Sheehan begins by outlining the classical realist approach of Hans Morgenthau and E. H. Carr and the ideas of their neorealist heirs. He then explores
how the economic security approach embraces both defense economics and
human security from poverty and hunger; and how environmental security
links environment and security in a fundamental challenge to the international
political hierarchy.

Next, tackling the various postpositivist perspectives on security—all of
which stem from worldviews fundamentally different from that of realism—
he explains the range of feminist thought on security, the ideas of the critical
security school, and the main concerns of postmodern security theory. In conclusion, revealing his own interpretation of security, he makes the case for a
postpositivist conception that links human emancipation, justice, and peace.

Michael Sheehan is professor of international relations at Swansea University. His recent publications include *The Balance of Power: History and
Theory* and *National and International Security.*